On the Border

Liberté • Égalité • Fraternité

RÉPUBLIQUE FRANÇAISE

This book is supported by the French Ministry for Foreign Affairs, as part of the Burgess programme headed for the French Embassy in London by the Institut Français du Royaume-Uni

On the Border

Michel Warschawski

Translated by Levi Laub

First published as *Sur la frontière* by Editions Stock, 2002

English translation first published by Pluto Press
345 Archway Road, London N6 5AA

www.plutobooks.com

British Library Cataloguing in Publication Data
A catalogue record for this book is available from the British Library

ISBN 0 7453 2326 X hardback
ISBN 0 7453 2325 1 paperback

10 9 8 7 6 5 4 3 2 1

Designed and produced for Pluto Press by
Chase Publishing Services, Fortescue, Sidmouth, EX10 9QG, England
Typeset from disk by Stanford DTP Services, Northampton, England
Printed and bound in Canada by Transcontinental Printing

To Léa,
Irreplaceable companion of voyage and struggle

Contents

Preface

This book is not a work by an historian or a study of the Israeli–Arab conflict. Nor is it an autobiography. It is the story of a fascinating and impassioned experience on the border separating states, communities and realities that make up the grid called the "Palestinian problem." This is not the story of a detached, 'objective' observer, but of an actor, a committed citizen, a militant of the border. While it seeks to be faithful to the facts, it is solely an expression of a personal and subjective view, my views and my account.

Nonetheless, I doubt that the new venture of telling rather than simply living an experience would have come to any good without the benefit of the invaluable help that I was privileged to receive: from Nicole Lapierre, who never ceased encouraging me to undertake this adventure, but also to Edwy Plenel, her companion, who persuaded me some dozen years ago to begin. From my friends Michèle Sibony and Simone Bitton, who, throughout my work, would reread and often correct the manuscript, were unstinting in their advice and criticism, and were able to help me avoid numerous pitfalls of both content and form. But it is above all to my son Dror that I must express my affectionate gratitude: his careful, detailed reading of the manuscript occasioned a rich exchange, some impassioned discussions and many clarifications and corrections. The intergenerational dialogue with Dror, notably on religion and secularism, on multiculturalism, modernity and progress, could well be the subject of another work. If, often, I did not accept his point of view, every one of his critical remarks left its stamp upon the book.

Finally, this work would never have seen the light of day without the woman who, for the last three decades, has accompanied me in the exhilarating but at times difficult voyage along the border, and with whom I continue to share the defeats and successes, the pains and joys, the disappointments and hopes. It is to her of course that I dedicate this book.

Introduction to the English edition

Three years ago, when I finished the last chapter of "On the Border," the border between Israelis and Palestinians was, once again, torn apart by fighting. It was still, nonetheless, a border. Subsequently it became the Wall. The "Wall of Separation" or "Wall of Shame," was intended to create an insurmountable barrier between Israelis and Palestinians. But no wall, no matter how high (and this one is over 25 feet high near Qalqiliya and Tulkarm), no electronic fence, no trench, even filled with crocodiles (an option that had been discussed), is capable of stopping a suicide bomber armed with the despair and the scars left by the humiliation of his father or the murder of his best friend. If that was the intent of Israeli strategy, then it has failed once more.

In fact, the wall intended to enclose the Palestinians in a ghetto (or perhaps several ghettoes) is today a looming threat not only to the people of the West Bank and Gaza, but for the Israeli people as well. In building this wall, Israel has chosen to enclose itself, creating an immense bunker, hyper-armed and paranoid in the extreme.

One need not explain yet again how the wall is an assault on the liberty of Palestinians, or how it buttresses the process of evictions and settlements, and tramples underfoot the right to self-determination of an entire people. But one does need to point out its depraved and destructive impact on the future of the Israeli community. Clearly, any wall is incapable of stopping bomb attacks and, undoubtedly, it risks provoking a new upsurge of aggression against civilians, now transformed in spite of themselves into garrison-dwellers. It slams shut the "window of opportunity," to use the phrase cherished by the American administration to describe the negotiating process launched by Yitzhak Rabin and Yasser Arafat. In fact it means that Israeli leaders have chosen to reject the hand held out by the Palestinians and the Arab world, preferring enclosure and the historically fragile military support of the United States. As the researcher, Menachem Klein, member of the Israeli delegation to the Camp David summit, wrote:

> ...the enthusiasm for a unilateral separation is not only an expression of a crisis of policy but of conscience as well. This plan, based on an

> outlook derived from both Zionist voluntarism and unilateral action, espouses enclosure behind what Jabotinsky [ideologue of the Zionist extreme right during the 1920s and 1930s–MW] called an "Iron Wall," and the use of force outside its perimeters. "A mutually agreed upon accord is impossible," wrote Jabotinsky in 1923, "because settlement must be pursued from behind an Iron Wall which the native population does not have the strength to break." What can such an outlook mean for the left, whose conscience embraces politics rather than brute force, a left that would consider the Palestinians as equals and seek a partnership with them as opposed to their submission?

It is a great historical irony that Zionism, which wanted to tear down the walls of the ghettoes, has created the biggest ghetto in Jewish history, a super-armed ghetto, capable of continually expanding its confines, but a ghetto nonetheless, turned inward upon itself and convinced that outside its walls lies a jungle, a fundamentally and incurably anti-Semitic world whose sole objective is the destruction of Jewish life in the Middle East and elsewhere.

The building of the wall makes Israeli–Palestinian cooperation doubly difficult, almost impossible. First of all, on a practical level, the border crossings, which this book chronicles, are more and more difficult: between walls, electronic fences, various barriers and roadblocks, there are few Israeli activists who still try to cross. As for the Palestinians, they no longer do so; the risks are too great. But the most important barrier is psychological. "We are a villa in the heart of the jungle," Ehud Barak, the man principally responsible for the failure of the Oslo peace process, dared to say. This description of Israel and its surrounds is a summary of a political philosophy that sees the Arab world and the Palestinians, not as enemies to be fought with everything in one's power, until, sooner or later, one can negotiate with them, make peace and reconcile, but rather, as an existential threat: ferocious beasts, barbarians. In the face of such a threat, the very idea of negotiations becomes absurd, for only permanent, preventive, and total war can try to subdue the threat of the jungle. If history can still teach us anything at all, then indeed this outlook has little chance of success.

The demented person who builds his villa in the heart of the jungle is opting for a bunker and permanent war. He leaves no room for coexistence. That explains how a conflict, namely a fight about territory, sovereignty, natural resources and borders, has become an existential war where the survival of one depends upon the eradication of the other.

As I point out elsewhere in this book, the Hebrew word for "border" also means limit. During the course of the last three years, the self-imposed limits of a civilized society or a state of laws and rights that serve as a benchmark if not for Israeli policy then for its dominant ideology and for the self-image of the Hebrew State – those limits are disappearing, one after the other. The violence against Palestinians is increasingly without limits, neither the limits of international law and conventions, nor those that would support Israel's claim to be a state of laws and rights. Even the Supreme Court, which had succeeded in imposing certain rules and restrictions, including a ban on all forms of torture, upon a no-holds-barred security-above-all-else military, has ceased contesting army orders under the pretext of the fight against terrorism.

I have described in detail in another work, the overall process of the dehumanization of the Palestinians and the systematic destruction of their society. As the Israeli sociologist Baruch Kimmerling wrote:

> I accuse Ariel Sharon of setting in motion a process which will not only intensify the blood bath on both sides but is likely to set off a regional war and a partial or total ethnic cleansing of the Arabs in the land of Israel. I accuse the army command, spurred on by nationalist leaders, of inflaming public opinion against the Palestinians, under the cover of military professionalism. Never before in Israel have so many generals in uniform, so many former generals, so many veterans of the security services, sometimes disguised as "academics," taken part in the brain-washing of public opinion. If a judicial commission of inquiry is impaneled to investigate the catastrophe of 2002, the generals must be indicted alongside the civilian criminals. I accuse the managers of the Israeli electronic media of giving the various military spokesmen the access they needed for an aggressive, belligerent and almost total seizure of control of public discourse. The generals not only control Jenin and Ramallah, but Israeli radio and television as well . . . I accuse whomsoever sees and is aware of these things, of doing nothing to prevent the looming catastrophe. The events of Sabra and Shatila were nothing compared to what is happening and to what is about to happen...

This heartfelt cry by one of Israel's most prestigious sociologists is echoed by Avraham Burg, a Labor leader and former speaker of the Knesset, the Israeli parliament, in a forum published by *Yediot Aharanot* and reprinted by *Le Monde*. The headline says it all: "The Zionist revolution is dead." Burg writes:

> Zionism is dead and its killers have occupied the corridors of government in Jerusalem. They don't miss an opportunity to put an end to whatever was really good about the national renaissance. The Zionist revolution was supported by two pillars: the hunger for justice and a leadership with a sense of civic morality. Both have disappeared. Today the Israeli nation is nothing but a pile of corruption, oppression and injustice. It is quite likely that ours will be the last Zionist generation. What will remain afterwards is an unrecognizable and hateful Jewish state... after two thousand years of struggle for survival, we now have a state that builds settlements under the leadership of a corrupt clique that laughs at civic morality and law. A state run with contempt for justice loses its power to survive. Ask your children which of them is sure to be here for the next twenty-five years. The most clear-sighted answers will shock you because the countdown for Israeli society has already begun...

By linking, in his analysis, the denial of the rule of law within the territories, on the one hand, with the endemic corruption of the political class, on the other, Avraham Burg confirms the predictions of the greatest Israeli intellectual, the late Yeshayahou Leibowitz, who maintained, since the end of the 1960s, that the occupation would destroy the democratic infrastructure and moral values upon which the vision of the State of Israel had been based.

Very recently, Moshe Negbi, legal commentator for national radio and the daily *Maariv,* published a book with the eloquent title: "*We have become like Sodom.*" In the book, Negbi states: Israel is no longer a democracy, but a banana republic, in which the police and the public prosecutor are afraid of political and financial interest groups, often Mafia, and are no longer capable of carrying out the law or protecting the rule of law. Three successive prime ministers have been suspected of corruption or embezzlement and the attorney-general closed the file in all three cases despite the recommendations of the police.

A substantial part of "*On the Border*" is devoted to the internal borders, those that divide Israeli society along social, economic, ethnic and cultural lines.

Ehud Barak's goal, when he was elected in 1999, was to rebuild a national consensus and reduce the internal fractures of Israeli society. Did he succeed? The answer is not simple, far from it.

First of all, Israeli society is united once again, behind a real obsession with security and fortified by the certain belief that its very existence is at stake. Upon returning from the Camp David II fiasco in July of 2000, Barak was not content with merely denouncing Yasser Arafat for having rejected his "extremely generous offers." He went further – and this was the most important aspect of the propaganda campaign launched by the former prime minister – stating that the rejection of the generous offers was proof of the absence of good faith on the part of the Palestinian president, who, hiding behind his so-called moderation, was planning the destruction of Israel. The whole Oslo process was nothing but a trap that he, Barak, had unmasked at the very last minute; a deadly trap that would bring the Jewish state to ruin.

This great lie, repeated *ad nauseum* for months on end by media the world over, resulted in the collapse of the Israeli peace movement and the rehabilitation of national unity in the face of the Palestinian danger. A national unity discourse that was widely accepted from the 1950s through the 1960s but then lost after the invasion of Lebanon in 1982 is back in fashion. Today it is the hyper security-conscious and racist discourse of a society turned in on itself behind a 25-foot-high wall. A society that sees anti-Semitism everywhere but chooses to ally itself with Protestant fundamentalism of the extreme right, whose theological anti-Semitism is notorious.

National unity has set aside dissensions between the religious and non-religious, between Jews of Arab and Jews of Western culture, between militants of the peace camp and partisans of Greater Israel. It has not abolished these divides but merely plastered them over with the psychosis of security.

Although the Zionist left has somewhat toned down its compromise-oriented discourse, as Avraham Burg's words show, it is still profoundly hostile to the idea of a state of Mafiosi and Messianic fundamentalists that tears to shreds its dream of a modern, secular state of laws, open to the Western world. In fact, many are leaving or dreaming of leaving, and the Jerusalem and Tel Aviv consulates of European countries report tens of thousands of requests for foreign visas. Nonetheless, emigration remains, of course, the choice of a minority.

Sooner or later the battles about what kind of state and what kind of Israeli society, about the role and place of religion, about the contradiction between a Jewish and a democratic state, about ties with the West and with the Arab East, will start up again, because the differences reflect not only contradictory ideologies but divergent interests. Any level headed examination of the balance of forces reveals the mystifying character of the existential threat propounded by Barak and Sharon. But can level heads prevail when bombs are exploding in the cafés of Tel Aviv and the buses of Jerusalem?

I have been criticized for not being sufficiently clear in this book, about the issue posed by terrorism – that is, the attacks against civilians by some Palestinian organizations. I explain my position in one of the chapters, but I affirm my choice, as an Israeli, to remain discreet as regards this issue. That said, it is clear that not only are attacks on civilians, be they bombs launched from a fighter plane or a bomb placed on a bus, morally unacceptable, but they also serve to reinforce within Israeli society the perceived existential threat that justifies not only total war against the Palestinians but all the sacrifices including numerous Israeli deaths.

Sharon is perfectly aware of this and his generals do precisely what it takes to provoke attacks, particularly by targeted assassinations of popular political leaders every time the Palestinian side declares a truce. Sharon needs terrorism to keep the spirit of a war for survival and national unity coursing in the veins.

As evidenced by the account of this book, borders express two contradictory movements: one being the separation between human beings according to their nationality, their ethnicity, religion or social class, the other providing protection and a means of asserting sovereignty and maintaining independence in the face of an imposed foreign power.

That is why those who work for a rapprochement between men and between nations often have to change hats, at times a border runner, at others a border guard; a border runner hoping to contribute to the emergence of a pluralist, transnational and multi-ethnic humanity and a world based on the values of solidarity and cooperation; a border guard charged with defending the sovereignty, self-determination and independence of a people threatened by foreign aggression. Likewise they must also guard the internal Israeli borders against any rapprochement in the name of a spurious national unity between democrats on the one hand and, on the other, racist, fascist and Nazi currents or movements that hold to antithetical ideas.

This dual task, contradictory only in appearance, has been performed daily by Israeli anti-settlement activists since July 2000, when Israeli leaders chose to turn their backs on the hopes raised by the Oslo Declaration of Principles of 1993. On the one hand they call on Israeli soldiers to refuse to participate in the colonial war in the West Bank and the Gaza Strip while conducting a political campaign for withdrawal from the occupied Palestinian territories. On the other, through actions based on political and humanitarian solidarity and through common initiatives embracing the prospect of coexistence anchored in solidarity and equality, they fight to keep open the few breaches that remain in the wall of hate and blood, which today, almost hermetically separates Israelis and Palestinians.

This book ends with a bet, a bet based on common sense, namely a bet that common sense will dictate life over death and openness rather than enclosure. Is it a realistic bet, two years later, after thousands of deaths, tens of thousands mutilated for life, systematic destruction and permanent humiliation? Has the colonial imperative and the hatred it engenders won out over common sense? Perhaps. Nonetheless we have no choice but to keep the bet open because it is the only alternative to barbarism.

It was on the border between Petain France and Franco Spain that Walter Benjamin ended his own life because on both sides of the Pyrenees barbarism had won the bet against progress and common sense. Today, on both sides of the "Wall of Shame," between Salem and Qalqiliya, around Jerusalem, and encircling the residents of Gaza, there are fighters for liberty and brotherhood. There are tens of thousands of them in Palestine and some thousands in Israel. More than enough to keep the bet alive.

Introduction

My trial ended in October 1989. It had lasted almost three years and I was finally sentenced to 30 months in prison for "aiding illegal Palestinian organizations." During the course of those three long years, a concept emerged both in the accusations of the prosecution and the arguments of the defense, a concept that would little by little become the central pillar of this judicial affair: the border.

With the charge of supporting terrorism having fallen apart, the parties confronted each other on the issue of the border, in what the public prosecutor called the *no man's land* between Israelis and Palestinians, and between legality and illegality. Indeed, I was the first to use the term, but it was only gradually that I became aware that at some point my entire life, as private person and as a militant, had been the result of a deliberate choice to live and fight on the border. My judges understood it perfectly and devoted lengthy paragraphs of their verdict to the danger the border poses for those who decide to live their lives and carry on their struggles there.

The last 35 years of my life have been in fact a long march on the border, or rather along the different borders that divide the State of Israel and the Arab–Muslim world, Israelis and Palestinians, as well as Jews and Israelis, the religious and the secular, and Jews of Europe and Jews of the Orient. Some borders intersect and sometimes overlap, are more or less open, but never impassable.

Borders not to be crossed, but also borders to break through; borders of a Jewish identity that was important for me to preserve, but also a socialism without borders; impenetrable borders between antithetical values, yet a rejection of borders that would ban exchanges and coexistence.

The border denotes a beyond that both frightens and fascinates. It is first of all a place of separation, between states, between communities, a line between us and them, and as such an element in the makeup of identities and groups. "The border is not a spatial fact with sociological effects, but a sociological fact which takes a spatial form," wrote Georg Simmel,[1] implying that borders tend to multiply as the mind

1. Georg Simmel, *Sociologie. Ètudes sur les formes de la socialization,* trans. from the German by Lilyane Deroche-Gurcel and Sibylle Muller, Paris, Presses Universitaires de France, 1999, p. 607.

becomes conscious of them. It implies a permanent questioning of what is meant by "us" as well as the "other," those on the other side of the border. In our pluralistic sociological reality, we are all surrounded by multiple borders. One needs to be aware of them and, to do so, must fight the ever-present temptation to reduce one's identity to a one-dimensional reality. There are many who would pressure us at any cost to define ourselves solely in relation to a flag, as belonging to a unique identity, and thus divide the world between an ethnic or national "us" and all the others. Conversely, when sub-commandante Marcos describes himself as an Indian cast aside by colonization, as a black confronting racial segregation, as a woman oppressed by sexual discrimination, as a Jew persecuted by the anti-Semite, as a homosexual victimized for his sexuality, as a worker crushed by exploitation, he is tracing the borders of a pluralistic identity, a choice that consciously refuses to rally behind a single flag.

The border is a place of confrontation, "a sinister zone of domination and of terror."[2] Border conflicts are often intended to protect identities and defend the right to autonomy. But they can be the expression of a desire for expansion and the negation of the identity of those on the other side. The deceptive English cognate *frontier* does not describe a boundary, but on the contrary, an open space, a place to be conquered. Israel and its inhabitants have lived this double aspect of the border, a wall that separates and protects, and a call to new conquests, for more than half a century. Shut in within its borders, in the heart of an Arab world that accorded it no legitimacy at all, the State of Israel has always refused to fix its exact borders and has in fact never stopped modifying and expanding them. The duality of the border has always conferred different, even contradictory tasks on those who chose to put themselves there: border guard or border runner, or both simultaneously. When the Israeli army invaded Lebanon it was imperative to play border guard and to call on the soldiers to go back home; likewise with the settlers who recognized no limits – one had to trace a border for them behind which the Palestinians could express and protect their national sovereignty.

If it does define territories, the border sometimes also separates human beings by national, ethnic and religious demarcations. Those borders can then be places of conflict, places of indifference, or contrarily, places of solidarity, exchange and cooperation. The

2. Ulf Hannes, "Frontières," *Revue internationale des sciences socials*, Spring 2001, p. 60.

borders between Israel and the Arab world that surrounds it have been, for fifty years, borders of hatred and of war. There the border acts "like a physical force repelling both sides."[3] At the beginning of the 1990s, when peace plans were being drawn up to erect walls of separation rather than spaces for cooperation, I chose to be a runner across the line between the two sides of the conflict. I felt strongly attached to the clan of Hebrews, or, in our language, *Ivri,* from the verb *Avar,* which means to pass, to go over there, sometimes even to transgress.[4] As a good Hebrew I wanted to be a border runner in three ways: a messenger of the values of fraternity, solidarity and the prospects of coexistence, a coexistence based on respect, equality and cooperation; a border smuggler; and a transgressor of the taboos that pressure us to shrivel up in a jingoist identity.

The border is not merely a place of separation where differences are asserted; it can also be a place of exchange and enrichment where pluralist identities can flourish. One can have encounters there that cannot take place elsewhere, certainly not in one's village nor in the bosom of one's clan: there you will most likely find replicas of yourself, hear yourself speaking through the mouths of others and be comforted by your own convictions.

The dual aspect of the border can push us to be simultaneously a border guard, respectful of the sovereignty of the other, of his freedom and independence, and a border runner who plies the exchange and crossovers of the human realities that the border separates. But it would be a mistake to believe that the border exists only between states or national communities. It also extends through our societies, between ethnic groups and cultural communities, between the dominant center and the periphery of the excluded. Its effects are no less perverse, the hatreds it arouses no less persistent than those created by external borders.

The internal border also requires a dual effort: to make openings to facilitate exchanges and solidarity, but also to build dams against the will to forge, at any cost, a national unity based on hatred of others and fear of the Other. National conciliation and reconciliation with the enemy never go hand in hand, and fraternization with the enemy often requires a break, even a fratricidal conflict within the bosom of one's own tribe. That prospect does not frighten me; on

3. Simmel, *Sociologie*, p. 608.
4. In Hebrew *avera* means the misdeed, the crime.

the contrary, I detest tribes and have always refused to shut myself within the clan's confines.

It is why I take a certain pleasure in feeling, even in the bosom of a society that I claim to be my own, as a "foreigner in my own home," like that foreigner portrayed by Georg Simmel as "not like a voyager in transit, but like the man who came from somewhere else and has settled in permanently, or at least for a long time, so that he's at the same time an insider and an outsider..."[5] Certainly, I am an Israeli, but I jealously guard my identity as Diaspora Jew, which enables me to view my own society with a certain detachment.[6]

Over the course of the years I have made many round trips between the internal and external borders. During that long march along the border, I learned that despite the discomfort, despite being marginalized, and sometimes despite the dangers, nothing in the world could make me give up my place at the border and at the periphery in exchange for a comfortable and warm seat in the bosom of my own tribe.

5. Georg Simmel, "Digressions sur l'étranger," in Yves Crafmeyer and Isaac Joseph (eds), *L'École de Chicago, Naissance de l'écologie urbaine*, Paris, Aubier, 1990.
6. *Ibid.*

PART ONE

The desert

Interlude: The speech about the border

"The border is a pivotal concept in the life of every Israeli: it is a formative element in our collective life, it defines our horizons, serves as the boundary line between threat and the feeling of safety and between enemies and brothers. In a country which is simultaneously a ghetto and a besieged bunker, the border is omnipresent, we run into it with every step. Yes, the border is not only in the heart of each soldier, as the song says, but in that of each citizen of Israel, an essential part of his very makeup.

"The border is also where the majority of the men of our society spend a few weeks a year doing their military reserve service, and it is from the border that they can glance over at the other side, regard the Other, the other world. I personally have served on the Jordanian border longer than any other reservist because it is not only the place regularly assigned to my reserve unit but it's where I have been sent every time I refuse to rejoin my unit when it has been called to serve in the heart of the Arab population in the West Bank or the Gaza Strip. From the observation post where I often find myself, one hundred meters from the banks of the Jordan, I like to look over to the other side, towards Jordan, and dream about what this region might look like if there were no wars or conflicts.

"There are also other borders, which, along with my comrades from Yesh Gvoul, I am not willing to cross: the border with Lebanon, for example, which I refused to step across on three occasions; or participate in the repression inside the occupied territories. Three times, I paid for those refusals to obey with military prison sentences. It is a refusal that one must proclaim publicly rather than shirking quietly. It is a choice that declares that one is prepared to pay the price for the refusal to participate in an unjust and deceitful war or the refusal to participate in repression. These are political statements and as such must be made in public with your head held high.

"The law is also a border that separates the permitted from the forbidden. Along with my companions in the struggle I chose to respect this border. I am not a resister like my father was; he fought against the Nazis, arms-in-hand; I am not a *porteur de valises*[1] like some of my French friends who

1. Name given during the Algerian war to the French supporters of the FLN, who put themselves at the service of the Algerian nationalists, whether to carry funds and propaganda material, or to lend a hand in the armed struggle.

risked their freedom in actively helping the Algerian fighters. Some of them paid a very high price for their solidarity. They chose to defy authority in carrying out an illegal action. We did not make that choice. We respect the law, imperfect though it may be, because we live in a political system which guarantees us Israeli Jews a freedom of action, democratic rights, and the means – although often limited – to win support for our political cause by arguing that it is necessary to radically change the existing system. There is a sort of contract between the state and myself, according to which, so long as it respects its commitments towards the citizens, that is to say their human rights and freedoms, then I will respect the rules of the game, and I will not cross the boundaries of the law. This is not just a pragmatic consideration: it safeguards the democratic framework, even when it is imperfect, with a view towards expanding it rather than provoking its replacement by a regime that would deny all forms of freedom.

"We have pushed back the boundaries, each time a little further; we were ready to be arrested, we were convicted by the courts, we appealed to the Supreme Court. But we did not agree to give up our most fundamental rights, and in so doing we have sustained rights that many democratic countries would envy. By stretching the boundary to the breaking point, one broadens one's own freedoms; by slacking off and pulling back, one loses them. It is precisely why I refuse to distance myself from the border and stay within the confines of comfortable legality; I have contempt for those who prefer to desist because they are not quite sure what is permissible. My judges reproached me for getting too close to the border. I'm sorry but that is where I decided to defend and expand our freedoms.

"There is yet another border, perhaps the most important one, which separates the two peoples who live on this land: the border between Israel and Palestine. It is a border of disputes, of wars and bloodshed. It is at that border where the conflict unfolds, where hatred and fear are unleashed. But it is also the place where our two peoples meet, and it is there one must be to extend a hand and respond to the hand held out. I have never believed in a peace that would be no more than an of absence of war, meaning: 'You stay in your place, we'll stay here, and leave us alone.' Israeli–Palestinian peace will be a peace of cooperation, of coexistence or it simply won't exist. That coexistence has to be built starting now, with dialogue, cooperation and solidarity. One cannot achieve these objectives within the constraints of the consensus, or in the comfortable security of the bosom of our society or even of the well-meaning left. Israeli–Palestinian cooperation can be built at the border and only at the border. Since 1968, that is where I decided to be, on this side, in my own society, but as close as possible to the other society. If we have contributed at all to the prospects of an Israeli–Palestinian peace, it has been by stationing ourselves at the border to facilitate Israeli–Palestinian dialogue and cooperation. I refuse to be a border guard. I want to continue being a runner across the walls of hatred and the barriers of segregation...

"This verdict is in fact directed at all of you (peace activists). It is no accident that Judge Tal explained at length that the court had decided to take into consideration the arguments of the defense, that it had been favorably impressed by my closing statement and that in the end they were generously sentencing me only to ... 30 months, with 20 months to serve. Twenty months in prison for having, according to them, shut my eyes! I do not agree with those who interpret Judge Tal's remarks as cynical. He really believes what he says, and the message of clemency is directed at you, my dear friends, even though you do not for the most part share my views about the border. You who are getting closer step by step to the border and helping to weave new links between Israelis and Palestinians. He is telling you: 'Watch out, the border is right in front of you!' And the border is a dangerous zone. Get back. There's a price to pay: 20 months for shutting your eyes. It's a good deal. Next time it will be a lot more. Stay away from the border."

Michel Warschawski
Speech made at a public meeting in October 1989,
a few days after having been sentenced to 30 months
for providing assistance to illegal organizations

I
Border cities

I was born in Strasbourg, on the border. My paternal grandfather's decision to settle there was not merely fortuitous; it had to do with the nature of border cities. To evade his military service obligations he had to emigrate from his little shtetl*[1] near Lodz, so he chose to go to Frankfurt on Main, the spiritual center for Western Orthodox Judaism,[2] where he enrolled in a Talmudic academy*. At the beginning of the twentieth century, Germany was the favored destination for a young religious Jew seeking to rebuild his life in the West. Its language was not very different from Yiddish; the Orthodox Jewish community there was strong and had numerous Talmudic schools and other religious institutions. France, which attracted Jews from the East in search of modernity and assimilation, was not a natural choice for those who remained attached to their religious way of life.

Nonetheless, lacking proper papers, my grandfather was forced to leave Frankfurt and continue his journey to the West, to France. He stopped in Strasbourg precisely because that city was on the border between two worlds. Located in the country of Rousseau and Voltaire, it was the least Latin of the French cities. Its culture and language were partly Germanic.

On the periphery of France, Strasbourg changed nationality five times in three generations, but was never truly French or truly German. A mixed city with a population of dual identity, it was a crossing point for refugees fleeing oppression or poverty as well as for conquering armies that came through to cries of: "*À* Berlin!" or "*Nach* Paris!"

The inhabitants of the Alsace region keep a certain distance from those whom they call "the people from the interior." Even when patriotic feelings are stirred up they do not evoke the typical French nationalism but rather a patriotism that smacks of the recently naturalized immigrant. The Strasbourgeois also has an ear permanently tuned towards the outside, to the other side of the

1. An asterisk indicates that a word is explained in the glossary at the back of the book.
2. Orthodox Judaism: Orthodox Jews practice the precepts of the Jewish religion in all its details, according to the mandates of rabbinical literature.

Rhine. Like it or not, the native Alsatian has more affinities with the residents of Stuttgart than with those of Montpellier. His education is French but his lifestyle is often Germanic.

The periphery is always a suitable place for immigrants, for wandering Jews in particular. As a Jew, that kind of equivocal identity, that non-identification with a common national type, suited me fine. It allowed me to feel French while always keeping a certain air of detachment, even irony, towards the native French, the French of the interior. But to live on the border does not necessarily mean to cross it: it was only long after leaving Strasbourg that I went to Germany for the first time – even though all one had to do was cross over the Kehl bridge.

The Rhine was not the only border defining the environment I grew up in. I quickly learned to distinguish others. First of all, the one that separated Jews from non-Jews. The *Concordat,* that Alsatian peculiarity that makes religion a component element of the Republic, required everyone to declare his or her particular denomination: one was Catholic, Lutheran, Calvinist or Jew (in the 1950s and 1960s, the Muslims did not exist, or rather, were simply not acknowledged). In public school, the few students who did not want to participate in any of the religious education courses had to apply for a special exemption, which was generally frowned upon. Thus, our Jewish identity was not a private matter: it belonged to the public domain. It made the community a subgroup defined by precise boundaries and represented by official institutions. It was in fact a ghetto, without walls and without police, but a ghetto nonetheless. Our culture was French and we participated passionately in national political life, but we rarely ventured outside the invisible walls of that ghetto.

For fifteen years I never had the occasion to meet non-Jews. My entire life, as well as that of most of my friends, took place inside the community: from Jewish school to the synagogue, from the Jewish youth movement to the kosher* grocery store: a voluntary ghetto from which one had neither the opportunity nor the need to leave. We encountered non-Jews in the street, at the big department stores or at the Meinau Stadium. Of course, at the high school, some of the teachers were not Jewish, but we had no relationship with them outside the classroom, unlike the Jewish teachers whom we regularly encountered at different community activities or family celebrations. It was a strange kind of school, that *high school* Akiba: there was a strong family spirit mixed with reactionary pedagogical and disciplinary methods, which had not yet been done away with by May '68. The notables of the local Jewish bourgeoisie set the tone, even if the professors were often discreetly rebellious against the narrow and bourgeois ideas that dominated.

Thanks to the *Concordat,* the Jewish community of Strasbourg was powerful, organized and above all visible. With my father, the chief rabbi of the city, I attended a number of the military marches of 14 July and 11 November, up on the podium, right next to the military governor-general of the city, the archbishop and the prefect. The Republican education delivered at school and at the Friday night table added to the fact that, in Alsace, Judaism was a state religion, allowed us to believe wholeheartedly that we were both Jews and French. There were no walls to stop us from leaving the ghetto, from crossing the border, but we never felt the need to do so. Our belonging to a national community was formal and cultural; belonging to the religious community, real and social.

In addition to the national and community borders there were even more striking intra-community barriers. Unlike the others, these were not explicit and could not lay claim to any formal legitimacy. They were, however, even more perverse. There were social, cultural and ethnic barriers between native Alsatian Jews and Ost-Juden[3] on the one hand and foreigners from other parts on the other. Before the war one did not mix with them and there was nothing but contempt for the immigrants from the East. "Better a non-Jew than a Polack!," cried out the bourgeois mother upon learning that her son the doctor intended to marry a student of Polish origin. Of course, the expulsion of the Jews from Strasbourg (at the beginning of World War II), no matter what their origin, and the terrible fate they subsequently shared, opened up the postwar relations between these communities; but only to a certain point: the boundaries did not disappear, nor did the natives' feelings of superiority. Thus the marriage of my parents – he the son of immigrants who spoke only Yiddish, she the daughter of an old Jewish–Alsatian rural family – was quite out of the ordinary, just as was being named Warschawski and becoming the rabbi of a community whose native core was extremely protective of its own identity, its particular rites and its folklore.

With my roots in both communities, I got the best and learned the worst of both sides. The sense of superiority felt by some only

3. The term designating Jews of Eastern European origin.

reinforced the scorn felt by the others, proud of their rich Talmudic tradition in the face of a prosperous and devout Judaism, but rustic and often uneducated. It is a recurring Jewish story, in which the values of education and supposed culture substitute for those of wealth and ties to landed property. The ultimate revenge of my grandfather was undoubtedly the fact that his son would become the spiritual guide of the local community. To become the chief rabbi of the Jews of Strasbourg, my father had to cross the border, and like many second-generation immigrants, he tried to be as Alsatian as the Alsatians themselves. The ultimate guardian of rituals, of Judeo-Alsatian language and folklore, expert in the history of local Judaism, he had nothing left but his name to suggest that he was but a "foreigner." We, his children, were educated in Alsatian to the point of feeling a certain aversion for Yiddish culture, particularly for the whining character of its liturgical music. Nonetheless, I had an inkling that my father maintained a strong nostalgia for the rituals of his childhood and for Yiddish culture. During the course of a Sabbatical that he spent in Jerusalem I found him on several occasions praying in Polish synagogues with a look and fervor that I had never seen in him. Yes, like a number of immigrants who chose to become assimilated, I think that he experienced a permanent disability, a painful longing for what he had left on the other side of the border.

I relived this estrangement within the Jewish community with the mass immigration of Jews from North Africa; first from Morocco after the Agadir earthquake, then from Algeria on the eve of that country's independence. Confronted with the new arrivals, the Jews of Polish origin behaved like the natives. They looked at the latter with the same surprise and condescension that they themselves had been the targets of some decades earlier. Perhaps because I was the grandson of immigrants myself, or perhaps out of plain rebelliousness, I at once felt closer to these young people coming from Agadir or Oran than to the children of the bourgeois families of the Avenue des Vosges. To the astonishment of the good folks of the community, I chose to cross the sociocultural border that separated me from the working-class districts of the suburbs and the boarding schools. Some years ago, on the website of the Jewish community in Strasbourg, I described the impact that the arrival of those who were called the "Algerian repatriates" had had on me:

> My new schoolmates suddenly changed our environment. The heavy and gray atmosphere of the Akiba School had been lifted and a new warmth had gradually seeped into the classroom. The *pied noir* accent, the style of dress and haircut contributed to the new atmosphere, as well as a certain light-heartedness *vis-à-vis* life and its constraints that we were not familiar with. It was not easy for them, having just lost forever the world they had grown up in to come live in a country where everything was different. From sunny and Mediterranean Algeria to imperial and very continental Strasbourg, the change was radical.

I felt as though they had brought the sun with them as well as another way of living one's life, even as high school students. Things like the importance of leisure, for example, and the scant attention my new friends paid to the values of competitiveness and excellence in which we had grown up, or even the importance of the body. The young girls, particularly, did not hide their bodies and were not afraid to be touched. If some of us were attracted to the Sephardic* services, it was not only because of the active participation of the faithful, the new melodies and a less solemn and rigid atmosphere than that of the Ashkenazi* synagogue, but because on coming out from prayer services we greeted each other with a hearty "Shabat Shalom!" hug.

Thus I spent the first fifteen years of my life in a border city, at the edge of *la France profonde*. Living on the periphery became such a basic component of my personality that the idea of one day living in Paris never occurred to me. Is it any wonder that, later on, I chose to live in Jerusalem, a border city *par excellence*?

When at the age of 16 I decided to leave Strasbourg to devote myself more seriously to Talmudic studies, I decided to go to Jerusalem. I had stayed there briefly two years earlier to study theology and the city fascinated me.

Jerusalem, not Israel. I had already realized that there was an Israeli center and a Jewish periphery. The center was Tel Aviv: a modern city, secular and Western. So was red Haifa, with its port and its petrochemical industry. The kibbutzim* were the center of the center, their hairy men with great moustaches bleached by the sun, and their women in shorts with Uzi machine guns slung over their shoulders. Jerusalem, by contrast, was a Jewish city, an outgrowth of the Diaspora. It was no accident that Ben Gurion and the Labor leaders of the 1940s and 1950s lived and worked in Tel Aviv. Jerusalem was the official capital of the state in name only for reasons of foreign policy, but in fact they despised it. With its synagogues, ghetto-like neighborhoods and its Oriental market, its Jews in kaftans and fur hats, it reminded them too much of the Diaspora they hated. For me it was precisely what the founding fathers of Israel scorned that attracted me to that city.

Nonetheless, I did not fall in love at first sight. There was something repellent about Jerusalem of the 1960s: the great empty spaces between neighborhoods, and the main streets of the city coming to a sudden stop at reinforced concrete walls, like bandages on amputated limbs, gave it an unfinished look. It took me a while to get over the discomfort caused by these failings and transform them into a deep and perverse attachment, akin to what many of my Berliner friends experienced before the fall of the Wall. Is it the attachment of a prisoner to his cell, the feeling of complicity that unites him with his companions of misfortune? Or maybe the simple fact of not having to wonder where to go because you've reached the end of the road? Or is it just an unconscious expectation, provoked by some temporary abnormality?

Until June 1967, all of Jerusalem was outside of Israel. Not just the eastern part, which was under Jordanian rule and accessible only to employees of the United Nations, diplomats and Christian clerics, but the western half as well. Geographically, the city, perched on the hills of Judea, was at the end of a narrow corridor bordered on both sides by Jordan. It was a breach in the ceasefire lines laid down after the war of 1948. In those days, "going up to Jerusalem" – a concept both topographical and spiritual – was a real adventure: if we chose to drive, the skeletons of the armored cars of 1948 reminded us that the narrow, winding road that we climbed up at 60 kilometers an hour was the only link between the city and the rest of Israel, and the enemy was all around within rifle range. Those who had time to spare took the train, which crossed over more than a kilometer into Jordanian territory. To provide the illusion of safety to the voyagers, an escort of border guards armed with a machine gun boarded at the Bar-Giora station, 15 kilometers from West Jerusalem. The border was everywhere but it was entirely unmarked. In May 1966, while out hiking with some friends, I wound up in Jordan without knowing it, and it was an Israeli patrol that brought us back to the railway line, an extraterritorial zone, and made us get on the next train. None of us even questioned then what an Israeli patrol was doing inside Jordanian territory.

At that time, for the Israelis who lived inland, Jerusalem was at the end of the world, the end of a journey dotted with signs reading: "Caution, border."

Beyond Jerusalem, enemy territory began, hostile, frightening and fascinating. For the other side of the border is a source of fascination, behind the reinforced concrete walls, the minefields, the barbed wire and the no man's land. Living on the border meant that one was able to look over from the heights of the roof of Notre Dame de France and see the gold cupola of the Mosque of Omar. From the Abu Tor observatory one could see the Wailing Wall. Along with other young students from the Talmudic school I would go there every week to pray and dream about the Jerusalem of yesterday. Others prayed for a future without the concrete walls and for a unified Jerusalem under Israeli sovereignty.

For the Israelis, the Arab world on the other side of the border was a threatening desert, both empty and occupied by a hostile population. From the observatory that I often went to, and from which one had a sweeping view of East Jerusalem, I do not remember having noticed the passers-by, the cars and civilian life. One saw nothing but the sentry boxes of the Jordanian Legion and bucolic images of biblical Jerusalem.

Like many mountain cities, Jerusalem is closed in on itself. While Tel Aviv opens to the sea, and through it to the Mediterranean and to Europe, Jerusalem is at the edge of the desert and shares its arid and harsh feel.[4] If the heat of Tel Aviv is humid, Jerusalem's sun burns and its light blinds. Jerusalem was always a city of fanatics, nationalist and religious, mystics of all sorts, from Jesus to the current victims of the Jerusalem syndrome; it is after all that kind of extremism that hastened its downfall in the Roman era. It is unfamiliar with the *joie de vivre* of Mediterranean cities, Alexandria, Marseilles, Beirut or Tunis, and more closely resembles continental, mountain cities like Damascus, Hebron and Fez.

Outside of Israel, or at least on its periphery, Jerusalem was also an outsider in its rejection of Zionist modernity, of which Tel Aviv claims to be the proud owner. Before 1967, Jerusalem was a city where Zionism hardly succeeded in making an impact, as the city had existed long before its advent. Even today, it is more like Vilna

4. See Uri Einzensweig, *Territoires occupés de l'imaginaire juif*, Paris, Christian Bourgeois, 1980, pp. 292–320.

or Marrakech than Herzliya or Ramat Gan. Its old Ashkenazi quarters, like Mea Shearim or Geula, evoke the shtetls of Eastern Europe, with their interior courtyards, their innumerable synagogues and Talmudic schools, their soup kitchens, and their inhabitants dressed in black kaftans and fox fur hats. As in those faraway places, extreme poverty is more common than opulence. The population, originally from Poland, Lithuania or Transylvania, does not feel Israeli and certainly not Zionist. Most of these people came to the Holy Land long before Zionism, and their attitude towards the State of Israel is not very different from what it might have been towards Poland between the two wars or towards France. They retain citizenship but they have no desire to belong to the new nation that the Zionist leaders want to build. Not only do they not recognize it but they consider it a mortal threat to Judaism, as they understand it. For many of them, the Jewish state is worse than the gentile state, because it denies them the right to be what they in fact are. At the very least, it goes all out to push them towards assimilation, and if they resist, it doesn't hesitate to cast them out to the margins of the national collective.

As for the old Sephardic quarters, like Nahlaot, built at the beginning of the twentieth century by Jews coming from Kurdistan and Yemen, or even the Boukhara Jewish district, they still resemble the Moroccan Mellahs* or the Jewish quarter of Damascus.

In 1967, West Jerusalem was not so much a city as a collection of ill-assorted neighborhoods, separated by huge empty spaces and wasteland. Every neighborhood had its own distinct population: Knesset Israel was an Eastern European township; Rehavia, with its flower beds, its well-kept gardens and its non-kosher butcher where one could buy ham, was a little Hamburg where German was more often spoken than Hebrew; Givat Mordechai was a village of young religious couples who lived in modest homes with red tile roofs surrounded by orchards. In Machané Yehuda, the Pinto, Gabaï and Eliashar – those who are called "native Sephardim"[5] – were a true local aristocracy before the seizure of the community by the Zionists. They still spoke Ladino* in the cafés where they played backgammon while drinking arak to the sound of songs by Farid el-Astrashe.

What was so seductive about Jerusalem was as much its outsiders' stance towards Israel, its marginality, as the diversity of the Jewish

5. Native Sephardim (in Hebrew *Sephardi Tashor*): Jews who claim to be descendants of the Jews of Spain, identify with a Judeo-Spanish culture and speak Ladino.

communities that lived there. Before the Six Days War, Jerusalem was in a way, the negation of Israel, a microcosm of the Diaspora, a Jewish ghetto on the border between Israel and the Arab world. But unlike other border cities, it was not a crossroads, and seemed impervious to outside influences. Its richness came from the interaction of the diverse communities that met there, entirely different from each other, but united by the tacit understanding that they were also isolated from the rest and the state of siege brought on by its geographic location. More than partition itself, what West Jerusalem and West Berlin had in common was their distance from the mother country, to which they were attached by a fragile and uncertain umbilical cord.

For, in spite of its diversity, there is something powerful uniting Jerusalem and its inhabitants. Israelis from the interior can identify someone coming from the holy city by the way they pronounce certain words or the way their children play hopscotch. The capital of Israel, as it was called stubbornly by the brochures of the time in the absence of all logical reality, was really no more than a provincial town where everybody knew each other, whether they were from Kurdistan or Bessarabia, or part of the native Sephardic elite, settled in Palestine for generations.

The center of town was the gathering place for all the diverse communities that make up Jerusalem. But even there, we were far from the modernity of Tel Aviv: by law, all the houses were faced in stone and it was forbidden to build higher than three stories. The main artery of the city, Jaffa street, was no more than ten meters wide, and that is where everybody went on Friday to do their shopping in the highly specialized stores: cakes at Neuman, shoes at Comfort, sunflower seeds (which, on Saturdays, helped one get by without cigarettes) at Beeri, and papers from old Gluck, who spoke Arabic fluently with a Polish accent you could cut with a knife. The students, whom you saw everywhere – at that time the Hebrew University was the only one in the country – absorbed, almost by necessity, the ambience and slow rhythm of the city, and often became *Jerusalmites* by adoption.

If the man of the plains could not understand how one can live on the border, in a city under a perpetual state of siege, where religious symbols and the boundaries they imposed on the inhabitants were omnipresent, where everything closed up after eight o'clock at night, the *Jerusalmite* feels like a foreigner when he goes down to

Tel Aviv. It's a relief to get back to his ghetto, its perpetual tension, which he no longer pays attention to, and the peculiar odors of its old walls, an indescribable mixture of the scent of jasmine and the stench of urine.

In the end, the change from Strasbourg to Jerusalem was not that great. From one ghetto to another, always at a healthy distance from the center, where there is too much of a tendency to turn in on oneself, to the border, where existence is carved out of a rapport with the Other. That Other who is always there because the border, by definition, is two-sided.

However, on 6 June 1967, Colonel Mota Gour's paratroopers would try to put an end to that uniqueness. From border city, Jerusalem would become the heart of the country; no longer on the periphery, it would suddenly be propelled into the center. The conquest of East Jerusalem would also mean the normalization of Jerusalem, its Israeli "naturalization."

2
David becomes Goliath

Although born after the war, my childhood and adolescence were steeped in memories of the Nazi occupation. In those days the term "Shoah" was not yet in use. The word "occupation" referred to absolute evil, fear, hatred, racism and death. Everything in daily life evoked memories of the black years that my parents and their generation lived through. My mother wore the yellow star between 1942 and 1944 in occupied Paris. My father, who moved to Limoges along with the majority of the Strasbourg Jewish community, joined up in 1944 with the Marc Haguenau Company, a Maquis group in the southwest, made up of the French Jewish scouts.

Several times a year, with the family or with the scouts, we went on a pilgrimage to Struthof-Natzwiller, the only death camp on the French side of the German border, about 50 kilometers from Strasbourg. On the Saturday night before the Jewish New Year we commemorated the evening of the deportation at the synagogue, followed by a torchlight vigil to the cemetery at Kronenbourg. For many young Jews of my age it was one of the most powerful moments of the year. Anti-fascism and a deep-rooted rejection of any kind of racism were as strongly grounded in my education as the principles of religious practice, but unlike the latter, they have lasted until the present day. I recall a memorable slap in the face I received for having used the word "nigger" at the Friday night dinner table; support for Algerian independence was as reflex as the ban on turning on the lights on Saturday. Identification with the poor, the weak and the humble was part of my Jewish identity.

The religious education I had received in my youth was indifferent to Zionism and I had only a limited knowledge of the creation of the Jewish State and of the Israeli–Arab conflict. It was through the June 1967 war that I discovered Israel, not just the Holy Land, but the State of Israel as a living and political reality at war with the surrounding Arab world. In the month of May, as the diplomatic crisis with Egypt intensified and the army mobilized the reserves, I left the Talmudic school to become a volunteer, first in a school for blind children and then in a kibbutz. Like everyone in Israel, I was convinced at the time that the Arabs wanted to throw us into the sea, and that a real danger threatened the Jewish State and its population.

On the last day of the war I was at Kibbutz Shaalvim, which then was one of only two Orthodox kibbutzim in the country. Shaalvim was on the border with the West Bank, a few hundred meters from the Trappist abbey at Latroun. That evening, Rabbi Schlesinger, the director of the local Talmudic school, asked me to accompany him on his watch around the kibbutz. That was when I saw, less than one kilometer away from our vantage point, a procession that evoked images of another time, so clearly described during my childhood and adolescence: hundreds of men, women and children marching to the east, loaded down with bundles of every sort. All deportees look alike, whether they come from Poland, Palestine or Kosovo. I had just been witness, unknowing and uncomprehending, to the deportation of the inhabitants of three Palestinian villages from the Latroun area. A few weeks later, Yallu, Beit Nuba and Emmaüs would be razed to make room for "Park Canada." Today Israeli families go there for weekend picnics and school groups go to study the flora of Eretz Israel.

One recollection from July 1967 at the Hebron market. For all the inhabitants of Israel, the summer of 1967 was a time of visits to the territories just occupied by the army. It was a time to go to pray at historic sites and to see the Arabs who, until then, had for most of us been invisible. My father, who had come with a delegation from his community to visit historic biblical sites, asked me to take his place at the head of the group for a visit to the city of Hebron. Proud of being an Israeli, I walked this group of Alsatians through the streets of a foreign city, where I not only felt at home but as if I were the owner of the place. At that very moment I saw the submissive and humiliated look of the Arab merchant, with whom I was trying to bargain for a lamb's skin with the arrogance of all the colonizers of the world. As if slapped in the face, I suddenly became aware that, this time, he was the oppressed, and I was on the other side of the border, with the strong, with the ones in power. I immediately and spontaneously refused to be on that side. That reaction was neither ideological nor political; I continued to believe that the Arabs were responsible for the war and the Israeli were within their rights. But I was unwilling to make the jump from that to being an occupier: I felt a natural compassion for the occupied. I was fortunate to find, later that evening, that my father supported me. He told me: "Any kind of occupation is wrong and morally corrupts those who take part in it; pray to the heavens that this one ends as quickly as possible."

But Israeli society was far removed from such views.

The war of June 1967 had unified the Israeli people in an unprecedented consensus. In six days every form of political, ideological or cultural opposition had disappeared. For six years unanimity would triumph and triumphalism reign unanimous. The whole of society would be united in a captivating and euphoric dream until the painful awakening of Yom Kippur in 1973.

This euphoria linked the righteousness of little David, eternal victim of all the Goliaths of human history – from Amalek to Nasser, through Torquemada and Hitler – to a new sense of invincibility and omnipotence. In 1967 Western public opinion was almost unanimous in reinforcing Israel's illusions. In the West, only General de Gaulle would try to temper the arrogance of the conquering Jewish State. But far from pressurizing Israeli leaders – or at least a part of domestic public opinion – to reflect on the power struggle or to think about the history of previous occupations, the critical positions expressed by the General Assembly of the United Nations (where the countries of the Third World and the Soviet bloc make up a majority) only reinforced the Israeli feeling of being alone against the world. As a children's song of the time proclaimed: "The whole world is against us, don't worry, we'll get them."

It was during this period of virtual trance that Israel would develop its strategy – or rather its lack of strategy: Moshe Dayan, minister of defense, spoke of "a hundred years without war or peace," and a young general named Ariel Sharon said without hesitation that the Israeli army could impose law and order from Morocco to Turkey, and that even the Soviet army did not frighten him.

The Arab defeat was truly colossal and the economic prosperity that began in 1969 was real, thanks to the money flowing in – particularly from the United States – and to the spectacular development of a military-industrial complex that would gradually become the main pillar of the Israeli socioeconomic structure and of its political class. But the overdeveloped muscles of the Tsahal* and the fat that would progressively envelop the body politic would have devastating effects on the moral sensibilities of society and on the capacity for sound judgment of its political leadership, as well as its intellectuals.

The war of 1967 marked a shift to the right throughout Israeli political discourse. It would take nearly ten years for the rest of the world to become aware of this shift, for the notion that Israel had only reacted to Arab rejectionism was still credible enough to cover up political choices that became more and more deliberately expansionist and intransigent. Nonetheless, the turn to the right was already noticeable in 1967. Out of curiosity, I attended the founding congress of the Movement for Greater Israel. There, the ex-brawlers of the infamous Unit 101 (commanded by Ariel Sharon)[1] and the veterans of radical labor Zionism rubbed shoulders with the spokespersons of mystico-nationalist sects to jointly announce the advent of the Messianic era and the impending reconstruction of the Third Temple. In 1967, this was still strictly a minority perspective, but one could sense that the organizers felt transported by the winds of history. Ten years later they would be the ones promoting and defining settlement policy in the West Bank and the Gaza Strip, the policy that would become the main obstacle to Israeli–Palestinian peace.

The Talmudic school that I had just left was known for the political Messianism of its doyen, Rabbi Zvi Yehuda Kook. That religious philosophy put it on the margins of the religious world that, for the most part, considered Messianism akin to heresy. But the notion of Zionism as the secular arm of divine will would make big inroads, and my classmates, Hanan Porat, Zalman Melamed, Menahem Felix and Haim Druckman, would become prominent leaders of the Israeli right. In the Parliament first, but mostly on the hills of the West Bank where they carried out the second phase of Zionist colonization, replacing the red flag and blue shirt of labor Zionism with the writings of Rabbi Kook and the knit skullcap. Having witnessed their mysticism personally, it was clear to me that the occupation of Hebron, Nablus and Jericho would arouse them all with the spirit of a new crusade.

How pathetic, by contrast, was the contemporary founding congress of the short-lived Movement for Peace and Security, where prominent intellectuals of the left tried to organize against this fanatic expansionism, insisting that, although the territories were

1. Commando 101: a unit of the Israeli army formed in the early 1950s to carry out punitive actions and establish new and non-conventional norms of combat. For a long time Ben Gurion would deny the existence of this unit as well as its operations, including the massacre at Kibya (15 October 1953), with 69 dead, mostly women and children. See Benny Morris, *Israel's Border Wars, 1949–1956*, Tel Aviv, Am Oved Publishers, 1996, pp. 274–84. The founder and commander of Commando 101 was a young officer by the name of Ariel Sharon.

not "liberated," as proclaimed by the right, nor were they occupied. It was decided to call them "administered territories." This refusal to face up to the reality of the occupation was the essence of the new consensus.

Before the war, the left had nonetheless conducted a courageous and successful struggle to abolish the military administration that governed the lives of the Palestinian citizens of Israel since 1948. That left was still inspired by democratic principles and socialist values imported from Europe. Throughout the 1950s and early 1960s it fought to put an end to what it called the "Mapai*-State," an ethnic democracy, totally controlled by Ben Gurion's party and its *nomenklatura*, a regime that clearly resembled in many respects the countries to the east of the Iron Curtain. The hysterical nationalism of June 1967 would silence that opposition for at least ten years.

In the fall of 1967, the dissident deputy Uri Avnery voted for the annexation of East Jerusalem. His decision could not have been based on security considerations; the rationale was the historico-religious reasoning that would become an essential component of the new Israeli consensus, the very same that would justify the full-scale policy of settlements in the future. Two years later, Avnery would go on to proclaim: "The occupation by the Israeli army is a liberal occupation." Even if a rare few intellectuals like Amos Oz and Yitzhak Orpaz warned against the pipe dreams of "Greater Israel," most former liberals were in the front ranks of the new expansionist crusade. Abraham Knaani, for example, wrote in *Haaretz* on 15 September 1967:

> One must pose the question: Doesn't the statement by Yitzhak Orpaz (*Haaretz* September 8, 1967) apply to Israeli conquests in the war of independence? It would be legitimate to annex Jaffa or Nazareth but not Jenin or Nablus? Why? Is the old city of Jerusalem less Arab than the city of Ramallah in 1948? Was Nazareth in 1948 more Jewish than Nablus in 1967? Is it only the date of the conquest that counts?

Another typical example of the abdication of the left was the affair of the Manifesto Against Repression in the occupied territories, initiated in March 1968 by 88 people, for the most part supporters of Matzpen* and the Israeli Communist Party. The manifesto denounced the violations of human rights, in particular administrative detentions and house demolition. Among the signatories was Aaron Cohen, a well-known orientalist of Kibbutz Shaar Ha'amakim and former theoretician and member of the national leadership of the left Zionist party Mapam*. He was threatened with expulsion from the kibbutz or with being sent to work ten hours a day in the wheat fields, which would clearly have prevented him from continuing his scientific researches. Cohen cracked and retracted in a manner worthy of some Moscow trial. In a communiqué published by the Labor daily *Davar*, he wrote:

> I was convinced by the arguments of my comrades that the appeal which I signed should have also taken a position on the terrorist acts of the Arabs [...]. I also accept the position of my comrades [of Mapam], according to which, in the present circumstances of Israel's struggle for its security and its existence, it is important to take into consideration not only what is said, but also who is saying it. The position of Rakah*, unilateral and hostile to Israel, excludes it as well as all its members from the debate. I solemnly declare that the case of the communiqué was a big mistake on my part from which I must learn some lessons.[2]

But not everyone retracted. Ilan Shaliff, a member of Kibbutz Negba, one of the jewels of the Labor left, refused to make honorable amends and was expelled by the general assembly of the kibbutz. The secretariat explained in the youth newspaper of Mapam, *Hotam:*

> We think that no-one should be expelled from the kibbutz for his opinions and we have in our midst a very wide range of political opinion. But Ilan long ago acknowledged that he had left Mapam and that he was linked to Matzpen. He has stubbornly refused to retract his signature from the statement at issue and he does not want to commit to abstaining from promoting his ideas in the kibbutz.
>
> After the Six Day War he dares to express publicly, and especially to children and newcomers to the kibbutz, his criticisms on subjects and events related to security, in a manner that could only infuriate our young soldier or reservist comrades as well as our oldest and most levelheaded comrades. His positions on the Six Day War are an immense affront to the living and the dead, and to the army in particular.[3]

2. *Davar*, 18 March 1968.
3. *Hotam*, 6 June 1969.

Following an appeal to the courts, Ilan Shaliff's expulsion was postponed for a few months. This was too much for some "comrades," who published the following leaflet:

> Attention! Let us not forget the decision of the general assembly of the kibbutz to expel Ilan Shaliff from our ranks! For us, that decision takes precedence over any external law, and we must be able to prove that we act in accordance with the spirit that motivated the decision of the general assembly of the kibbutz. The time has come to put him in quarantine in order to clearly show him that the decision to expel him is still in effect. We ask our comrades:
>
> – not to talk to him
> – to stay away from him
> – to not sit down next to him in the dining room and to leave the table that he sits down at.
>
> To those sensitive souls amongst us, allow us to remind you that it is in the interest of us all that we are taking these disagreeable measures. So don't stand in our way!

Not satisfied with inciting hatred, these kibbutzniks resorted to action. On several occasions they beat up the dissident, who was finally expelled from Negba, in the name of socialism and friendship among the peoples, of course.

But there were some righteous people in Sodom: Yeshayahu Leibowitz, the greatest Israeli religious intellectual, who, since 1968, had denounced in the harshest and sometimes provocative terms the new Messianic national philosophy; Israel Shahak, former deportee and president of the League of the Rights of Man, for whom liberal philosophy could not be compromised; Felicia Langer, communist lawyer who, from 1967, devoted her life to the defense of Palestinian prisoners; and, especially, the activists of Matzpen, among whom I am honored to be counted. For half a decade, that little group of the far left would symbolize, in the eyes of Israeli public opinion, the struggle against the occupation and for the national rights of the Palestinians.

Rejecting the smug comfort of consensus, hanging on like a lifeline to their moral values and to a rational analysis of reality, these few dozen men and women saved the soul of the people of Israel.

3
Preaching in the wilderness

In 1962, a small group of dissidents was expelled from the Israeli Communist Party. Their offense: demanding to know more about the Sino-Soviet dispute, the victory of the Cuban revolution (in spite of the opposition of the Cuban CP), and above all, the recent and bloody defeat of the Iraqi Communist Party, which was the most powerful of the Arab communist parties and had seemed on the verge of taking power. In short, their demand was for democratization and a more critical look at the dogmas of the international communist movement.

The dissidents quickly linked up with a group of oppositionist communists who, since the 1930s, had challenged the whole of Stalinist policy, its crimes and betrayals, and advocated a return to the values of a democratic and truly internationalist socialism. The significance of this group derived from a rigorous analysis of Zionism and Arab nationalism, the fruit of experience accumulated over several decades and set out in countless worthy texts – which practically no one had ever read.

The young expellees, mostly university students, drank in the words of the old-timers, particularly those of Jabra Nicola, a well-known and respected personality among Haifa Palestinians and comrade/rival of the Arab leaders of the PCI, Émile Habibi and Émile Tuma. Nicola, a self-educated former editor of the party's literary journal, *Al-Jadid,* made a meager living translating detective stories as well as Tolstoy. His companion Aliza, a Jewish communist militant of German origin, worked as a house cleaner. Nicola's profound knowledge of the Arab reality linked up with the rigor and Marxist culture of Yankel Taut, who had fled the Nazis in 1934 and, like thousands of other German Jewish communists, found temporary refuge in Palestine. Temporary became permanent. In 1947, Taut was seriously wounded in an Arab attack[1] on the Haifa oil refineries where he worked. After months of convalescence he gave up the idea of going back to Germany, which

1. The riot, which, on 30 December 1947, had caused the death of 39 Jewish workers in the Haifa oil refineries, was in reprisal for an attack that same day, carried out by the Irgun, at the same refineries, claiming 50 Arab victims, dead or seriously wounded.

so many of his comrades had chosen to do. During the 1960s Taut was a well-known and respected leader of workers in the Haifa Bay industrial center.[2]

Together, the veteran dissidents and the new expellees organized the Israeli Socialist Organization, better known by the name of its monthly journal, *Matzpen* ("The Compass"). The organization put forward a radical critique of Zionism: breaking with the traditional line of the PCI, it analyzed the war of 1948 as a war of ethnic cleansing[3] rather than as a war of national liberation; the program of the group called for a democratization, a "de-Zionization" of Israel, and its integration into the Arab Middle East, which, following Gamal Abdel Nasser, was trying to free itself from the tutelage of the West in order to undertake a large-scale modernization and national reunification. Some of its activists, particularly Akiva Orr, who was one of the leaders of the seamen's strike in 1952, had a wealth of trade union experience, and during the 1960s were active in struggles that challenged the role of the Histadrut*. That immense Laborite *nomenklatura* was a para-state institution that managed culture and sports, served as the National Health Service, owned the biggest industrial park, employed 40 percent of the country's salaried workers, and also functioned as a confederation of trade unions.

Apart from the avant-garde trade union circles and the bohemian cafés of Tel Aviv and Jerusalem, nobody had ever heard mention of Matzpen, which had no more than a score of activists, most of them Jews. It was the war of 1967 that would give Matzpen a political reputation and renown that nobody could have anticipated.

October 1967. I enrolled at the Hebrew University in Jerusalem to study philosophy. It was not yet the ugly bunker built at the end of the 1960s on the site of the old campus on Mt Scopus, deserted after the war of 1948. In 1967, the Hebrew University was still in West Jerusalem, in modest buildings separated by pleasant lawns where the students spent the bulk of their time.

Suddenly I saw a crowd in front of me, where insults and blows were being exchanged. As I am curious by nature, I got closer. A group

2. Alain Brossat and Sylvia Klingberg, *Le Yiddishland révolutionaire*, Paris, Balland, 1983, pp. 309–19.
3. Ethnic cleansing: contrary to what one sometimes hears, the concept was used in the Israeli–Palestinian context in 1948, long before Bosnia and Kosovo. The documents of the Hagganah and the reports of the Israeli army described as cleansing (in Hebrew *Tihour*) the expulsion of the Arabs from their villages and their country.

of students were handing out a provocative pamphlet titled *Enough is enough!* On the first page, a poem by Dan Omer, a talented young translator of American protest poetry, unambiguously declared: "Blood flows under the Damia bridge." The poem described the massacre at the Jordan River of refugees attempting to return to their country, the exodus of the inhabitants of the three villages of Latroun and the destruction of those villages. Those passing by did not like what they were handed and shouted a barrage of insults: "Slanderers," "Traitors," "Go live with Nasser." I remembered then what I had been witness to a few months before, and I made the mistake of saying: "You are wrong, what they write is precisely true, I saw it with my own eyes!" I received blows and insults. The skullcap I was wearing only seemed to make matters worse. It was my first encounter with Matzpen.

Back home, I read the entire pamphlet, and I could not stop thinking about what it said, and even more, about its tone, which resonated with my own deepest feelings: a visceral rejection of oppression and a profound empathy with the victims. Otherwise I was indifferent to the underlying analysis in the rest of the pamphlet. In the following days I met up again with those students whose courage and passion I admired. What they told me – particularly comparisons to the war in Algeria and South Africa – seemed pertinent. One of them in particular, a young professor of mathematics named Moshe Machover, was determined to take on my political education. I was ready for his indoctrination.

My religious education was not offended by their Marxist and anti-Zionist ideology, but I was shocked by their appearance: long hair, jeans and miniskirts, which provoked within me a disgust that lasted for several months.

While Israel was united in a Messianic and nationalist euphoria, *Matzpen* headlined its August 1967 edition: "Old story – Revolt against a foreign occupation," with a photo of the curfew in a West Bank town. On the fourth day of the war, the London *Times* had already published, under the aegis of the Bertrand Russell Association, a joint declaration by Matzpen and the Palestinian Democratic Front, denouncing the war and stating that the conflict would continue as long as there was no just solution to the Palestinian question and until the State of Israel was de-Zionized. A second joint statement, published a month later, affirmed:

> We say it loud and clear: A peace dictated by Israel, a public or secret *pax americana* with King Hussein, for example, will not resolve the conflict between Israel and the Arab states; at best, it will put a freeze on it. The creation of a Zionist Bantustan for the Arabs of Palestine, perpetuating the policy of segregation and repression, will not resolve the Palestine question, just as the Bantustans of South Africa cannot solve the problems that are a consequence of South Africa's racist policy. A viable solution demands the transformation of Israel into a normal country, that is, a state for all its residents as well as the repatriation of the Palestinians to their country; it is up to the Palestinians to freely decide their political future. Knowing full well that the respective political leaders have no intention of moving in this direction, we have no doubt but that the conflict will continue. To all those who insist on illusions we repeat: the economic or political superiority of one human group over another has never provided the means to resolve the political problems between nations.[4]

The mere fact of publishing a joint communiqué with the Arabs was perceived as an act of treason, a reaction that the editors of the first communiqué anticipated:

> Self-righteously, you brand us as traitors. What are we accused of betraying? A supposed national interest? Your racist prejudices? How can we betray a cause that we never claimed as our own? We are expressing our human dignity by rejecting all forms of chauvinism and racism.

Against the popular tide, alone against the world – Matzpen quickly acquired a reputation that was hardly justified considering the size of the group. For more than five years, every kind of trouble that occurred in Israel would be blamed on Matzpen. From the longshoremen's strike at Ashdod in 1969 to the demonstration by high school students for the right to wear long hair, to the bomb placed at the refineries in Haifa by a Palestinian commando – Matzpen had become the internal enemy, the fifth column, an obsession. During the month of March 1969, for example, it was mentioned fifteen times in the daily *Yediot Aharonot*. Among the headlines: "Matzpen presents a list (for the Knesset elections) demanding a return to the Partition

4. *Matzpen,* no. 36, June 1967.

borders of 1947" (16 March 1969); "A terrorist chief declares: We have contacts with Rakah and Matzpen" (17 March 1969); "Israeli Jews aid Fatah*" (18 March 1969). "News" stories were supplemented with commentaries. In the same daily, the liberal journalist Yeshayahu Ben Porat wrote (15 March 1969): "It's time that the security services take an interest in this group, because there is a difference between democracy and carelessness. The time has come to draw a line that would prohibit making mistakes that might turn out to be tragic."

A few days later, the leftist writer Amos Keinan wrote: "Blood flows in the Valley of the Jordan and Matzpen cries tears of ink," adding that it was only cowardice that kept that organization from planting bombs in the markets (20 March 1969). The blood mentioned in that quote was clearly not that of refugees trying to go back to their homes, but that of soldiers who fell in ambushes set for Palestinian guerrillas who were trying to infiltrate the West Bank and were decimated by Israel's infinitely larger and better-equipped army.

It was no accident that the intellectuals of the left were the most vicious of all in their attacks against Matzpen. In Europe, progressive public opinion, which had identified with Israel in 1967, began to step back and occasionally sympathize with the Palestinian resistance. The European left had such difficulty understanding its former Israeli friends that it got to the point where it could no longer distinguish between them, the government and the right. Matzpen thus became both a reference and an invaluable source of information coming from Israelis, many of whom were soldiers during the June 1967 war. The Avnerys, Keinans, Ben Amotzes, Moshe Snehs and others, all left intellectuals who had been previously highly regarded in the salons of London and Paris, found themselves obliged to answer the questions posed by Matzpen, now taken up by the Western left. They reacted like wounded beasts. The left journalist Boaz Evron spoke of "neo-anti-Semitism"; in his weekly, Avnery compared his former friends to Nazi collaborators and called the women activists of Matzpen "Fatah girls." In *Yediot Aharonot*, he furiously accused the people of Matzpen, saying that they "started after the Six-Day War to defend a line that no longer recognized the State of Israel, and today they are lending a hand to Fatah."[5] The general secretary of Mapam, Meir Yaari, threatened: "The activists of Matzpen have good reason not to emerge from their clandestinity or to show themselves in broad daylight..."

5. *Yediot Aharonot*, 22 October 1969.

There is another reason for this anti-Matzpen obsession: Israeli culture is a tribal culture, in which any kind of opposition and dissidence is perceived as a serious anomaly, and temporary by nature. The June 1967 war had allowed yesterday's dissidents to rejoin the fold of the sacred union and to step back into the warm ambience of national consensus and the reunited clan. The attacks by left intellectuals against Matzpen were also intended to show their former adversaries that they really had come back to the fold, and as proof of their patriotism they were ready to take up front-line positions in the struggle against traitors and their foreign allies.

Living by taking casual jobs, those of us who were students viewed the campus more as a political battlefield than a place of study and research. In general, the university was still a unique place when it came to political activity. A not insignificant minority, comprising all political tendencies, debated the Israeli–Palestinian question, sold pamphlets, organized demonstrations and occasionally fought each other. Matzpen was distinguished not only by adopting positions that broke with the prevailing consensus, but also by its omnipresence: there was not a single political or cultural initiative that failed to provoke a response by the Matzpen activists in the form of a leaflet written for the occasion.

This hyper-activism also gave the organization an impact that did not correspond to its numerical size. In January 1969 Matzpen issued a call to arms to all its activists and sympathizers to demonstrate against the violent repression that had resulted in deaths at Rafah in the Gaza Strip. More than fifty people came from the four corners of the country. By coincidence, the "Student Parliament," which deliberated from time to time on current affairs, was due to meet that same evening. The topic for discussion was: what position should be taken on the new settlements in the occupied territories? It was winter and it was snowing in Jerusalem. Apart from one or two *apparatchniks* of the Students Union, only the Matzpen activists made the effort to come, and all the attempts by the student officials to cancel the meeting, including cutting off the electricity, had failed. That evening, in the dark, the Student Parliament of the Hebrew University of Jerusalem unanimously approved a motion demanding the dismantling of all the settlements, the immediate and unconditional retreat from the occupied territories, and the abolition of all laws and institutions that affirmed and guaranteed the exclusive Jewish character of the State of Israel! It was the last time that the parliament in question met ...

Of the hundreds of people who attended Matzpen discussion circles, generally to hear a non-conventional analysis, sometimes to debate, there were few who came with the intention of really opening up to the ideas expressed there by brilliant orators like the mathematician Moshe Machover, or impressive personalities such as Akiva Orr or Chaim Hanegbi, grandson of the former rabbi of the Sephardic community of Hebron and a talented but virtually unemployable journalist. The hatred surrounding those who had for so long been described as traitors was too powerful to allow a genuine confrontation of ideas. It would be at least a quarter of a century before those who had participated in the discussion groups would admit to having done so, and then often with some pride.

One group however, had, little by little, developed more serious ties with the activists of Matzpen, and agreed to collaborate with them in the struggle against the occupation: the Union of Arab Students. A marginalized minority in the universities, the Arab students lived in a real ghetto.[6] Coming from villages in Galilee and the Triangle[7] – the only region in the center of the country where the ethnic cleansing of 1948 had failed – they were a small, privileged minority who had succeeded in entering the Israeli universities, despite the low academic level of the Arab high schools and the exorbitant tuition fees an average Arab family could not dream of paying. Until the 1967 war, the general tendency was to avoid being noticed, and the Union of Arab Students found it very difficult to recruit, not to say organize a public struggle for the rights of Arab citizens who, until 1965, were still living under military government. The Union of Arab Students had a semi-clandestine existence, and its leaders were subjected to the treatment reserved for all militant Arabs, whether nationalist or communist: house arrest, a ban from traveling outside certain zones, regular arrests followed by rough interrogations, and occasionally, administrative detention.

Khalil Toamé, the secretary of the Union of Arab Students at the Hebrew University and a Matzpen militant, decided after 1967 to get the students to show solidarity to their Palestinian brothers living in the recently occupied territories. He was quickly arrested and

6. See Adnan Abed Elrazik, Riyad Amin and Uri Davis, "The Destiny of Arab Students in Institutions of Higher Education in Israel," in Amun et al., *Palestinian Arabs in Israel: Two Case Studies*, London, Ithaca Press, 1977, pp. 93–9.
7. A small area in the center of Israel from which Arabs had not been expelled in 1948. The Arab population today is in excess of 200,000.

sentenced to 12 months in prison, but his example was followed by an increasing number of students whose political consciousness had become sharper thanks to the initiatives of the Palestinian resistance organizations. Matzpen served as a school for their political and ideological education; for many of these students, it was the first opportunity to learn about their own history, since their parents had chosen to remain silent.

Many years later, when Palestinian youth were reappropriating their own history, my friend Mahmoud Hawari, in Bernard Mangiante's fine film, *Galilée des Pierres,* told about how he had learned, in a Matzpen study circle, that his native village of Tarshiha had been bombed in 1948. Only then was he able to persuade his father to tell him how a number of his close family had been killed by Israeli bombs. "When I asked him why he had not told us anything, my father answered: I didn't want you to make trouble, for you to rebel."

That silence of the survivors of the Palestinian tragedy of 1948, the Naqba*, reminded me of the silence of my paternal grandparents, who had lost most of their close family in the genocide of the European Jews, but never wanted to talk about it. Maybe they felt guilty for having survived; maybe they also hoped that the younger generations would not turn to the past to find meaning for their own rebellion, and that they would devote their energy to building a normal life and integrating themselves into the dominant society.

The impact of Matzpen on the Palestinian youth of Israel rapidly spread beyond the boundaries of the campus. The young generation of those who were then still called "Israeli Arabs" was strongly influenced by the new Palestinian resistance, and less and less satisfied with the cautious stance of the Israeli Communist Party (Rakah). It stayed in the Party only for lack of a better alternative. The Party persisted in referring to the war of 1948 as a war of national liberation, defined itself as an "Israeli patriotic party" and limited its activity to the struggle for civil rights in the context of the Jewish State. Until the mid-1970s, the Rakah press would characterize the organizations of the Palestinian resistance as terrorist organizations.

The radical anti-Zionist positions of Matzpen and its unconditional support for the struggle for Palestinian national liberation became a source of inspiration for the young Palestinian generation living in Galilee and what was left of the Arab villages in the center of the country after 1948. These young people devoured Matzpen literature and attended its study circles in their hundreds. Some joined resistance organizations; the majority, after the war of October 1973, would join various radical nationalist organizations, later known as Abna al-Balad, or the "Sons of the Land."

These groups not only helped to end the dominance of the Communist Party, but also forced it to adopt a political line that was progressively more critical of Zionism and more conspicuously Palestinian. However, years would go by before that happened. Meanwhile, at demonstrations, one would have to endure the insults and blows of the PCI's marshals every time militant nationalists and members of Matzpen would jointly shout the slogan: "From Hebron to Galilee – one people, one struggle, one future!"

Matzpen's influence, however, was not limited to Palestinian youth. Urban Israeli high school youth was more receptive to anti-conformism and less weighed down than the previous generation with a bad conscience for the crimes of 1948; no wonder that these young men and women were fascinated by those whom the media described as responsible for all the country's ills – especially since Matzpen activists showed up regularly at the doors of the most prestigious high schools of Tel Aviv, Jerusalem and Haifa to distribute its leaflets and to discuss politics. Without necessarily endorsing the entire political analysis that was being presented to them, hundreds of young high school men and women identified with the anti-militarism and the demand for justice, which clashed with the prevailing political ambience. Matzpen can legitimately claim credit for the "High School Students' Appeal" of 1970, in which several dozen students questioned Prime Minister Golda Meir who had just barred the president of the World Jewish Congress, Nahum Goldman, from meeting President Nasser, after the latter had publicly expressed his desire to find a negotiated solution with Israel. Those students, including the son of the Minister of Health, Victor Shem-Tov, were wondering if, in the face of that categorical refusal to enter into talks, they should not think twice before going off to do their military service. Schmoulik Shem-Tov and most of his friends had received part of their training in Matzpen circles.[8]

Fighting against the 'corruption of youth' by Matzpen became a priority: some high school principals called the police, others organized gangs of students to remove the agitators by force, still others resorted to witch hunts against their own students. In 1973

8. See Shimshon Wigoder and Meir Wigoder, "The Matzpen Movement,' in *Fifty to Forty-Eight: Critical Moments in the History of the State of Israel*, Jerusalem, The Van Leer Institute, 1998, pp. 199–204.

the city of Haifa went so far as to organize a compulsory seminar for all freshmen and seniors, which it simply called the "Anti-Matzpen Seminar." That initiative, which was quickly discovered to be an excellent way of introducing Matzpen to schools where the organization was not previously known, was turned into a veritable police crusade, run by the head of the youth squad, Commissioner Hémou, with the zeal of a man charged with a sacred mission.

4
Socialism without borders

The activists of Matzpen had to work hard to earn their reputation: morning, noon and night they distributed leaflets, sold their newspaper, organized demonstrations that often ended at the police station, prepared study courses for discussion groups on Zionism, the Arab revolution and the international situation, whether it was talking about Cuba or the revolutionary perspectives opened up by May '68 in Paris, Berlin or Milan.

Matzpen people thought in terms of international revolution. If its activists felt excluded – or excluded themselves – from the national collective, it was in order to integrate into a much larger framework. The internationalism of the group was a sharp break with mainstream opinion that clung to the concept of Jewish or Israeli specificity. It was committed to a desire to understand local political reality within a global perspective, particularly that of the anti-colonial struggle. These positions clearly had the immense advantage of reversing the perceptions of who formed the majority and who the minority: Matzpen was not a marginal and insignificant minority in Israel, but rather it was Israel and its people, who, defending a reactionary policy and backward ideas in the eyes of most of the world, were a small minority in the context of the decolonization of the Arab world.

The internationalist outlook of the movement was rooted in the ideological education received in the Israeli Communist Party, modified by the Trotskyism of the old activists who were expelled from its ranks for their "cosmopolitanism" and their contempt for nationalist ideals. But the ideology did not explain all. Far from it: there were countless thousands of Israeli socialists in those black years who swapped their internationalism for a certificate of patriotism, not hesitating to rewrite their own biographies to conceal youthful transgressions.

In fact, internationalism was, above all, a reaction to the provincialism and the narrow nationalism of Israeli political culture, particularly of the left. It was a response to the need to break the barriers of clan and to escape the stifling and fetid atmosphere of an inward-looking tribe whose conscience remained untroubled by its misdeeds.

This rejection of tribalism by the Jewish activists who made up the great majority of the group was accompanied by a profound commitment to the history and culture of the Jewish Diaspora, and a real empathy for the suffering of their people. This was even a bit surprising, considering that these men and women were typical products of Israeli culture and its educational system, which increasingly denied all notions of links between Israel and the Jewish Diaspora. The activists called themselves Israelis, but deep within themselves, in the younger Sabra[1] generation, they were survivors of the Diaspora, its sufferings and its values. More or less consciously, the wandering Jew, and later the revolutionary Jew of "Yiddishland" were the archetypes with which they identified – activists such as Hersh Mendel or Israel Feld, known as Sroulik-the-Red,[2] who, from the Russian Revolution to the French resistance, through the MOI* and Republican Spain, never had any fatherland other than world revolution.

Although Matzpen activists were actually expelled from the tribe and then found themselves "beyond the borders of national existence" (the phrase used some twenty years later by the president of the Supreme Court, Aharon Barak), they soon learned to feel at home beyond those borders, where events seemed to move quickly, bringing promise of good things in the near future: Vietnam, on which Michaël Löwy, then a young and brilliant lecturer at Tel Aviv University, developed a committee; in the European capitals, where students were making revolution (Akiva Orr, who was living in London, sent daily reports); even in Warsaw, where Jacek Kuron and Karol Modzelewski's "Open Letter" appeared, a socialist and

1. Sabra*:* the name given to Jews born in Palestine, then in Israel. The word refers to the prickly pear, sharp and thorny on the outside but sweet and sugary inside. The Sabra must be the antithesis of the Diaspora Jew. My friend Michèle Sibony drew my attention to the fact that the word *sabra,* the prickly pear, which is also the symbol of Palestine, in Arabic means "patience," a very Palestinian, but remotely Israeli, quality. For this, see the fine novel by Sahar Khalifa, *Chronique du figuier barbare,* Paris, Gallimard, 1978.
2. Hersh Mendel, real name Mendel Stockfish: a Jewish revolutionary who had been involved in revolutionary struggles in Europe from the Russian Revolution to the anti-Nazi resistance in France. He would spend his final years in Israel, and published his memoirs in Yiddish: *Memoirs of a Jewish Revolutionary,* Presses Universitaires de Grenoble, 1982. Sroulik-the-Red, real name Israel Feld: Belgian, Jewish communist militant, born in Poland, volunteer in the International Brigades in Spain; deported to Auschwitz for resistance activity; left the CP and militant activity after the war.

workers' self-management critique of the Stalinist regime that was published in Hebrew even before appearing in French.

While the contrite Israeli left dozed in the euphoria of post-June 1967 and applauded the supposed liberalism of an occupation that it thought would be short-lived, we pinned our hopes and unfailing optimism on the success of the guerilla war in Bolivia, the articles by Ernest Mandel on the collapse of the dollar, and the summer visits by Trotskyist and anarchist activists who were coming from Paris or Berkeley to share with us their illusions about the final crisis of the bourgeois system.

Without its ongoing and deep ties with left movements throughout the world, and especially with Arab activists in Europe and North America, it is doubtful that Matzpen would have been able to remain impervious to the lures of nationalism. The movement circles in Tel Aviv and Jerusalem stirred with news of the Tet offensive, the uprising in Prague and the Parisian barricades of May 1968. Thanks to comrades living in Europe, our ties were strengthened with the German SDS, the anti-war movement in Britain and the Revolutionary Communist Youth in France. The ideas of May '68 were discussed even in the outskirts of Haifa. We were shaken by the attempted assassination of Rudi Dutschke in Berlin, as if he had been one of us. Thus, naturally, during one of his visits to Jerusalem, Axel Springer, the German yellow press magnate, was welcomed by a few dozen demonstrators accusing him of inciting murder and neo-Nazi propaganda. Springer, surprised, asked his close friend Teddy Kollek, the mayor of Jerusalem, what they did with hoodlums like us in Israel.

When in 1970 Danny Cohn-Bendit was invited by the Student Union at the Hebrew University, he, of course, contacted Matzpen to find out if he should accept and to think about what he should say. Upon arriving in Tel Aviv, he announced that he had come to meet his comrades, whose ideas he shared. In fact, he did not get to know them until the following day, in the course of a short briefing before the meeting for which the Student Union had paid his fare and lodging! The movement used the visit to settle its score with some Israeli intellectuals of the left, whose wish to meet the famous man was granted but not before they were rebuked for their chauvinist positions and their attacks on his Matzpen friends.

It was overseas, in Europe and the United States particularly, where the movement proved to be most effective and posed a real problem to the Zionist propaganda apparatus. Against the backdrop of the anti-war movement in the US and a strong anti-colonialist trend in

Europe, the spokespersons of Israeli anti-Zionism were much sought after as speakers on the campuses. The very fact that they were Israelis gave them the credibility that racist prejudices (entrenched even among leftist intellectuals) often denied to Arabs. Matzpen seemed to be everywhere.

Invited in 1970 to speak before students at the Free University of Berlin, the Israeli ambassador, Asher Ben Nathan, was forced to share the stage with "a representative of Matzpen who will express the viewpoint of the opposition." Refusing to appear on the same platform with a Matzpen spokesperson and heroically trying to overcome the heckling, in his anger the ambassador inadvertently exaggerated the numerical significance of the group: "But what is Matzpen, twenty thousand people at the most?"

The same year, a coalition of personalities of the American left, led by the singer Pete Seeger and Rabbi Elmer Berger, organized a tour of meetings on American campuses. Professor Ehud Schprinzak, political scientist at the Hebrew University in Jerusalem and researcher specializing in extremist organizations of the right and the left, remembers:

> I was at the time president of the Union of Israeli Students in North America. One fine day Arie Bober arrived in New York. He went everywhere: to Columbia, to New York University, to many more universities, he spoke and denounced. The problem was that they had a wealth of detailed information about what was going on, they had done their military service, they knew everything, including a lot of things, for example, about the destroyed villages. When we checked, it turned out that they were right. We (the leaders of the Zionist students) spent hours discussing what to do, how to react. As there were no answers, we decided to ask him a lot of questions that had nothing to do with the subject, to gain some time. The best we could do was to try to limit the damage. When I came back to the country, we had a meeting at the Ministry of Foreign Affairs to determine how to deal with the influence of Matzpen overseas and in the Israeli high schools. I vividly recall the panic that prevailed during that meeting: the most talented students were being attracted to the outrageous ideas of Matzpen.[3]

3. Quoted in the film by Eran Turbiner, *Forbidden Encounters* (2001).

The ability to escape from the narrow confines of the Israeli ghetto and its views gave most of us the strength to go against the current. We lived History, with a capital "H", every day, with the Vietnamese, the Fiat workers in Turin, the Black Panthers in New York or the Tri-Continental Conference in Cuba. History was synonymous with revolution, unfolding now or at least in the very near future. The Palestinian resisters were the catalysts of the soon-to-come uprising of the workers of Cairo and Damascus, which would reunify the Arab nation under socialism after overthrowing the reactionary regimes of the region, including, clearly, the Zionist state.

Matzpen's socialism without borders was expressed above all in its rejection of the hodge-podge map of the Arab world drawn up by the great powers after the fall of the Ottoman Empire. We would speak of an "Arab revolution," which would include the Israeli people. That revolution would both have to unify the Arab nation and allow for real national independence, and an economic, social and cultural development that socialism would guarantee. Israel would disappear as an entity, but, faithful to the Leninist canon, we demanded the right of self-determination for the non-Arab minorities, the Kurds, the Israeli Jews, the southern Sudanese, something the West would only begin to consider some three decades later.[4] Utopian? Certainly, but not too removed from the aspirations and slogans of the Arab nationalist or socialist left, with which we maintained an ongoing, scholarly and passionate political dialogue.

The dialogue was conducted mainly through the mail but there were also meetings in Europe or in America. The debate with Arab activists and organizations was a matter of course for us, no different from discussions we might have with Belgian or Italian activists, and we never felt like traitors or history-makers. Some years later, interviewed by an Israeli journalist about the first Israeli–Arab contacts, I tried unsuccessfully to convince him that those first encounters were so much a part of our general internationalist outlook, and therefore so routine that I had trouble remembering the details, the names and places. In fact, the meeting with Miguel Enriquez of the Chilean MIR* had made a much bigger impression on me than my first encounters with some Arab activists. We never felt then that we were living through historic moments during those meetings with Arabs or Palestinians. For the activists, those meetings were not encounters between enemies or negotiations before their time. They

4. See *La Révolution arabe – état des lieux et perspectives* (in Hebrew and Arabic), Jerusalem, Pages Rouges, 1974.

were discussions between comrades of different countries. We were not simply some Israelis meeting some Arabs, but socialist activists continuing a conversation that had started more than a century before and was still going on in the four corners of the globe.

There was a high price to pay for that internationalism. It involved voluntarily giving up an identity, a step that rather quickly proved to be politically sterile and personally destabilizing. In all aspects of political and social life, we took the opposing view to the society to which we belonged. We spoke of Israelis in the third person – "their flag," "their army," "their policy"; only a few of us observed Jewish holidays, largely for family reasons and most of us made it a point of honor to pretend that they didn't exist at all. We turned our backs on anything that smacked of "Israeli," particularly popular music and walks in the countryside, making me frustrated twice over. Having chosen to be citizens of the world, or members of an international class, we willingly cut off the roots that bound us to our society and our culture. Happily, the spirit of the activists prevented the movement from degenerating into a sect. Thus that uprooting was not viable and might explain why many of us chose to live overseas for more or less prolonged periods.

Matzpen required its Palestinian activists to make similar breaks with national symbols: it wasn't until the end of the 1980s, that the Palestinian flag, for which hundreds of young Palestinians had been killed or wounded, acquired legitimacy in our eyes. Rather than emigrate, many Palestinian activists preferred to exchange that socialism without borders for a radical nationalism. They played an important role in the development of Palestinian nationalist organizations in Israel.

But in the immediate post-1967 War years, it was that internationalism that gave a sense of direction to several dozen Matzpen activists. It prevented them from washing up on the reef of nationalist socialism and "Israeli specificity" that allowed intellectuals of that era to justify anything and to believe that Israel would never have to pay the price for a policy that was more and more openly colonialist. That internationalism, which set them outside the boundaries of the tribe, conferred on them a strong sense of being outsiders, for which they fully accepted the consequences, making a virtue of necessity. That abnegation could undoubtedly be explained by the conviction that the well-being of the Israeli community depended on its ability to break with a colonialist policy that was opposed not only to the Arab national movement but to the movement of history itself. Paradoxically, it was the fate of the Israelis that motivated us: they needed to be won to the cause of revolution, failing which there would be a new Masada,[5] that collective suicide of the last Jewish fighters against the Romans.

5. Masada: the fortress near the Dead Sea, last holdout of the Jewish resistance against the Romans. According to legend those in the fortress committed suicide rather than surrender to the Romans. The story of Masada has long been taken as a foundation myth of Israel, and paratroopers take their oath at the site. Israel's nuclear program is known as "the Masada Option."

5
Against the current

The burning issue of the revolution was the source of an unbridled militancy that knew no rest, day or night, weekends or vacations: we were professional revolutionaries who did not have the right to waste our energies on trivialities like leisure time or even family. Time was all too precious. We had to win over the Israeli people to our ideas, for they alone would guarantee their security and national existence in the Middle East of tomorrow.

I am not convinced that all the activists of Matzpen were quite the fundamentalists that their ideology would seem to require. There were many among them who did not boycott the bars of Tel Aviv or the hiking tours through occupied Sinai. As for myself, a revulsion against "wasting time"[1] was in keeping with my religious education: the sense of duty to accomplish things had excluded from my daily routine not only weekend relaxation and family breaks, but also the reading of anything that was not purely political as well as all other forms of cultural activities with the exception of some occasional concerts where the music did not quite suppress my sense of guilt that I should have been writing a leaflet or correcting some proofs. I particularly remember hitchhiking to Arab villages (we were too poor to have even one car at our disposal) where we sold our newspaper, which the villagers bought mostly out of pity. Compared to our evident devotion and the fatigue written on our faces, the attraction of our literature, whose themes were somewhat distant from their everyday worries, took a distant second place.

One of my duties was to lead a small cell in the village of Tira. Once or twice a week there, I tried to organize the political work of a dozen Palestinian activists, who, although they shared our radical critiques of Zionism and Israeli policy, found it hard to adapt to the rigid rules of an organization in which Leninism was embodied in a maze of hierarchical structures (from the political bureau to branch secretaries – despite the fact that our active membership never exceeded 50!). Politely, the activists regularly voted on the resolutions submitted by the central committee, only to do exactly as they pleased once

1. "Wasting time" (*Bitoul zman* in Hebrew) is an expression that, in the Orthodox Jewish world, signifies time that is not devoted to study.

the meeting was over. It was only after the meetings that the most heated discussions began, and it was there that I learned first hand what few Israelis would come to know: not only the living history of the Arab national movement in Palestine-Israel, but above all the real-life problems and aspirations of Palestinians living under Israeli domination. What emerged was worlds apart from the ideas picked up and repeated by the media from the mouths of those who till today are still called "experts on Arab affairs" (in fact, they are no more than cops spawned by a wave of university-titled Orientalists who never foresaw the explosive revolt of a population refusing to be pacified, from the Day of the Land[2] in 1976 to the bloody revolt of October 2000). Those discussions went on late into the night when I would leave on foot for Kfar Saba, sometimes in driving rain. Occasionally, when hitchhiking proved futile, a jitney driver would let me sleep in his car, which wouldn't fill up until morning when most normal people got up to go to work.

We were also often invited to speak in some kibbutzim. Mostly, they made a spectacle of us, for there were only a few who really wanted to hear what we had to say. Those good folks, fascinated by the radical nature of our heresy, took pleasure in venting their hatred at us when we reminded them that their socialism had been built on the ruins of this or that Arab village destroyed in 1948. Then came the question that was supposed invariably to end the debate: "Where did you serve in the army?" We had chosen never to answer it, even though some of us had served with distinction.

Hardly a week went by without a police interrogation, often followed by one or two nights at the police station. It was at the Moskobiyé[3] in Jerusalem that I got to know the prison world, an experience that would serve me well a few years later when I really got to spend time in prison. In the detention centers I met men I would never have encountered otherwise. Charlie and Saadia, for instance, two juvenile delinquents of the Mousrara quarter, with whom my comrade Shimshon spent an entire night recounting the heroic tale of the Black Panthers in America. Later on, they decided to form the made-in-Israel "Black Panthers."[4] In 1971–72, during the

2. See below, p. 43.
3. Moskobiyé: the Muscovite quarter, that is, the old Russian colony. The Jerusalem police station and its infamous interrogation center are located there.
4. Black Panthers: a movement organized in 1971 by young Jews of Arab culture, mostly Moroccans from the poor districts of Jerusalem, to protest at the discrimination of Arab Jews.

large demonstrations by the Black Panthers that usually took place on Saturday evenings, I would spend many nights from Saturday to Sunday in the Moskobiyé. It got to the point that my older son Dror, then three years old, for a long time thought that in our circles we didn't celebrate the end of the Sabbath* with candles and cloves, but instead shouted slogans in front of the somber building that provided a weekly lodging for his father. In 1969, in the Moskobiyé of Nazareth (why are prisons so often located in former Imperial Russian residences?), I met the members of the editorial committee of the Israeli Communist Party's Arabic weekly, who used to be held there for the whole month preceding each election in the hopes of paralyzing the Party's election campaign. We too had the privilege to spend two nights in jail for wanting to stand in for the locked-up activists, distributing leaflets calling people to vote for a party that we otherwise considered bureaucratic and guilty of a double betrayal, both of the working class and the Palestinian national cause. Those 48 hours of common detention were probably the longest and undoubtedly the most heated political discussions that we ever had with our rivals of the PCI.

On 30 March 1976, after a demonstration following the police assassination of six Palestinians of Israel who were protesting against a new wave of land expropriations (since that day Palestinians celebrate 30 March as the Day of the Land), I found myself in the Jerusalem jail with about twenty other activists. I heard my name whispered from the neighboring cell. It was Sirhan and Ahmad, two Palestinian activists who were being secretly detained. They wanted to inform my companion, the lawyer Léa Tsemel, that they had been questioned by the security service regarding a booby-trapped car left in the center of Jerusalem.

Nine years later, after being freed as the result of a prisoner exchange, Sirhan and Ahmad and I became friends; to this day I am still involved with them in political work that had its roots back in the encounter in the Moskobiyé. After the setting up of the Palestinian Authority, Sirhan Salaimeh Sirhan became one of the heads of the Palestinian Preventive Security and Ahmad el-Batch was a Fatah deputy elected to the Palestine Legislative Council.

The work of Matzpen activists unfolded against a backdrop of ostracism and isolation that thirty years later is difficult to grasp. Being a Matzpen militant or simply being seen with activists of Matzpen meant expulsion beyond the borders of the tribe. People avoided us like the plague, and the closer they were ideologically the more distance they kept. A friend, a militant feminist from Haifa, known for her courage and non-conformism, recently told me that when she was a student she had expressed her sympathy for Matzpen on several occasions. Her father, a high-ranking official in Foreign Affairs, had told her: "If you join Matzpen, I will break off all contact with you, because you would be capable of rummaging through my things in order to provide state secrets to the Arabs." In spite of her courage and non-conformism, she did not re-establish contact with the movement until some twenty years later.

While Léa and I had the good fortune not to be cut off from our respective families, this was far from the case for many of our comrades. In choosing not to sever ties with her daughter, and even allowing certain meetings to take place in her home, my mother-in-law knew that she was estranging herself from her neighbors and closest friends.

For an activist, the chances of getting a job in administration or at the university were very slim. In 1971, the director of the political science department at the Hebrew University offered me a position as an assistant and a grant, on the condition that I resign publicly from Matzpen. In 1973, when I was hired as a teacher of philosophy at a high school in Haifa, I had no doubt that it was owing to an administrative error. Two months later, the director informed me that I was being let go "for reasons so evident as not to require any explanation." My students organized a protest strike, but I considered my dismissal to be entirely predictable.

In this regard we were in good company: any Arab lacking clearance from the security services, particularly if active in the PC, had no chance at all of finding a job as a teacher, even for inoffensive courses such as chemistry or design. Until the 1980s, an Arab did not need a diploma to teach, but it was essential that he or she be a collaborator or at least supported by collaborators. This may explain the abysmally low level of teaching in the Arab colleges and high schools of Israel.

Even in the most totalitarian societies there are righteous people who refuse to submit to the tribal spirit and are not afraid of what is said about them. Disgusted by the phenomenon of expulsion, Professor Yona Rosenfeld, of the training school for social workers of the Hebrew University, had transformed his research unit into a refuge for activists with degrees but without work. But far from expressing their acknowledgement with serious professional contributions, his protégés quickly transformed the school into a political club!

It was not always easy to endure the ostracism, but there were compensations: the brotherhood forged with the Palestinians, the hopes aroused by the struggles in the Third World, the upheavals that were shaking Europe, the conviction that our cause was just, and faith in the glorious future that inspired our struggle. The same could not be said for our children. There were not too many of us who had decided to have kids. The majority of the activists preferred to put off that aspect of normal life for better days.

To be born a child of a militant anti-Zionist in Israel in 1972 was to set off on life's journey on the wrong track. Dror left Israel with his mother, my first wife, when he was five years old. He only knew the life of a "militant's kid" during the summer months, which he regularly spent with us. But my younger son, Nissan, had to deal with that difficult reality throughout his childhood.

Léa and I shared a vision of militancy and commitment that did not leave a lot of room for parental duties. Between meetings, demonstrations, training classes and newspaper sales on the weekends, the time devoted to Nissan was quite limited. Our son quickly became the collective responsibility of the group. Other activists took care of him when our political work took up all of our time, which seemed to be permanently the case. We would have considered it unworthy and shameful to give up some political activity just to take care of our son or to squander a weekend for him or to miss a newspaper sale in order to organize a birthday celebration. While the life of his friends was structured around Jewish holidays and family gatherings, Nissan's was bound up in political events like May Day and the Day of the Land. We often dragged him along to demonstrations that broke out into fairly serious violent episodes. For a long time he retained the traumatizing memory of a young Palestinian covered with blood, being violently shoved by the police into a patrol wagon, as we fled along the roofs of the old city, dragging him with us like a shopping bag.

But for a child, the worst thing was the social isolation in which we lived and the awareness of the hostility that surrounded us. Beyond the world of the tiny group in which we were completely at ease, there was hatred, and for Nissan, fear. The patriotism of some adults was often mixed with spitefulness and stupidity, like that nursery school teacher who made him repeat in front of his little classmates that it was the Arabs who wanted to take land from the Jews and not the contrary, even though he had no idea what she was talking about. That same "educator" one day subjected him to some sharp questioning about the communist lawyer, Felicia Langer, known for her defense of Palestinians, but whom Nissan had never met or even heard of.

The two lawyers who were at the disposal of Palestinian fighters (is it an accident that only women chose to do that work back then?) were the favorite targets of the prevailing hatred: death threats, slashed tires, etc. Nissan had the misfortune to be the son of one of them; he regularly heard his mother called a traitor, a bitch, an "Arafat whore." He was witness to some minor assaults against Léa, usually insults followed by some spit, ending in a fight, because Léa was not a "*savonette*." [5] She gave blow for blow and the coarseness of her replies would have made a sailor blush.

At the age of six, Nissan decided to differentiate himself from his mother: he would often walk along the other sidewalk proclaiming loud and clear that his mother was not a lawyer but a maker of marionettes. He was trying to change places with his buddy who lived in the house across the way. The attacks against us were more verbal than physical and the numerous threatening letters were never followed up with acts, but the fact remains the atmosphere was tense and harrowing; it was not paranoia. As a teenager, feeling more Israeli than Jew, Nissan decided to be a fighter. Endowed with great physical strength, he succeeded in imposing respect for himself and his family, sending several people to hospital.[6] But the anguish that tormented him did not dissipate until much later, when, after the signing of the Oslo agreement, his parents became sought-after personalities in circles of the salon left, whose adherents wanted to rewrite their personal histories in a way that would not be out of tune with the newly fashionable melodies of the moment…

But at the time the left had built a vacuum around Matzpen, setting up a real iron curtain between itself and us. For that left, searching for legitimacy, we were always the object of a paranoiac obsession: the fear of contamination. I confess that that absence of relations with those who did not share our positions was not exclusively imposed from outside: we were also fully responsible for it, as we ourselves were haunted by the danger that the repugnant spirit of tribalism and its false consensual truths would contaminate us as

5. *savonette:* a bar of soap. See p. 153 below.
6. Nissan's youth is very well portrayed in Yitzhak Lerner's film, *Avocate sans frontières* (1998).

well. It was only among the Arab activists of the Israeli PC that we encountered a certain sympathy, indeed, even occasional envy of our forthright enthusiasm and radicalism. One evening in 1969, in a bar in Jerusalem, where we were celebrating the wedding of Ilan Halevi, a Matzpen militant who some years later would join the diplomatic service of the PLO, the parliamentary deputy and poet, Émile Habibi, who'd already had a few whiskies, took me aside, and banging his fist on the bar for punctuation, his eyes damp with alcohol and sadness, told me: "Twenty years that I've been in the Knesset, holding up my hand like an idiot! Do you think that's the life I dreamed of when I was your age? How I envy you..." Before being forced by Moscow to swear allegiance to the Jewish State and to preach Israeli patriotism, Émile Habibi had been one of the young, courageous and popular leaders of the Arab national movement in Palestine...

6
Border runners

Madame Mandouze taught literature at the Jewish high schools in Strasbourg. She was one of those teachers who left their mark on the lives of students by their force of personality, the scraps of knowledge they communicated and the values they transmitted. I am indebted to her for my love of classical literature and my hatred of all forms of injustice. Jeanne Bouissou-Mandouze and her husband had been in every struggle for justice and human dignity from the anti-Nazi resistance to Algerian independence. Profoundly Christian and uncompromisingly humanist, André Mandouze was one of the initiators of the *Appeal of the 121* against torture in Algeria, but not being as well known as Jean-Paul Sartre, he was jailed for that act of resistance. I had never met him, but the little that I did know at the time of his life and his struggles, as well as the admiration I felt for his wife, surely served unconsciously as a guide for many of my choices. More than thirty years later, I came across the first volume of his memoirs: reading them, I felt proud for having chosen to consider myself a disciple of that courageous couple.

Porteurs de valises. That's what they called the French who put themselves at the service of the Algerian nationalists, whether to carry funds and propaganda material, or to lend a hand to the armed struggle. It would be presumptuous for us to call ourselves *porteurs de valises,* because throughout the years we generally tried not to carry out actions that would put us at odds with the law. In the speech cited at the beginning of this book I tried to explain that choice.

Not to cross the border, but to place oneself at the edge of legality, between the law and the forbidden. In a democracy anything not specifically forbidden is legal. In fighting for democracy, one cannot limit oneself to that which is explicitly authorized. It is imperative to test the law, to occupy all the free space not explicitly forbidden, and sometimes to challenge the law in order to establish new freedoms. In the realm of freedoms, every abandoned space is occupied by power and its prohibitions.

So we were not *porteurs de valises*. We were at best border runners for whom solidarity was the soul of the struggle.

In 1967, the activists of Matzpen sought out contacts in the occupied territories. Ideological contacts, of course, for in the communist left, everything begins with the program. That is how the first encounter with Taissir Kubaa, president of the Student Union of the West Bank and militant of the Movement of Arab Nationalists, soon to become the "Popular Front for the Liberation of Palestine," took place. Taissir would shortly be expelled from the occupied territories and then become the spokesperson for the PFLP. The arrest of Khalil Toamé, an Arab militant of Matzpen who made the connection with Taissir, and his conviction "for contact with a foreign agent," cast a chill over the enthusiasm for making contacts, all the more so as the Palestinian activists of the left were systematically expelled.

Little by little, ties were established with intellectuals on the left, mostly at Bir Zeit University. A discussion group was formed around Ilan Halevi, including – among others – Hanan Ashrawi, professor of literature, the sociologist Salim Tamari and the economist Adel Samara (who, in contrast to the others, already had considerable experience as an activist as well as several years of prison behind him). Action was not the goal of these encounters. Focusing entirely on propaganda, it was more a matter of forging common political positions, which both the Israelis and Palestinians would undertake to disseminate in their respective communities. We wanted to demonstrate that our common goal – a bi-national and socialist political structure, freed of Zionism – would be supported by each community, and thus would no longer merely be utopian. We still believed in the power of the word and the power of logical and noble ideas to change the world.

Later on there would be other circles, comprised especially of students close to the Palestinian left, at Bir Zeit or at the University of Bethlehem. That is where I got to know Riad Abu Awad, leader of the students' union at Bir Zeit. He was an unrelenting advocate of public activity such as organizing demonstrations and volunteer work brigades in the villages and refugee camps, but also seeking out contacts with Israeli activists. Towards the end of the 1970s I often spent the night in the student dormitories at Bir Zeit, giving courses on the development of Israeli society, or discussing Palestinian strategy and revolution. *Al-Mounadel,* Matzpen's Arab monthly, as well as our theoretical review, *Umamiye* ("Internationale"), was often the basis of discussion. But at those meetings we also organized the participation of Israelis in the political initiatives of the students, as well as solidarity actions in Israel, focusing mostly on the struggles inside the prisons. Those evenings gave birth to the idea of opening an Israeli–Palestinian information center, inspired in large part by Riad Abu Awad.

We were slowly moving from the phase of political analysis to the coordination of solidarity actions. Since 1967 we had practiced solidarity with the Palestinians, but just like Molière's M. Jourdain used to practice prose, without being aware of it and mainly without reflecting upon it. Only in the 1970s did that solidarity begin to rely on political analysis and become a clear-cut choice. After several years of propaganda activity, of denouncing Zionism and the occupation, and of political education, questions arose regarding the relationship between those types of activities and our ultimate goal – a radical change in the existing regime and its replacement by a democratic, socialist, Israeli–Palestinian or Pan-Arab structure. Thus a debate opened up inside the ranks of Matzpen.

The various solutions proposed were clearly linked to the analysis that we had made of the State of Israel. For some, the capitalist character of the Israeli economy and the existence of class conflicts would, sooner or later, exacerbate the internal contradictions. That would favor the emergence of a workers' movement in conflict with the regime, would unite Jews and Arabs, and would give rise in time to a revolution that, by its very nature, would "de-Zionize" Israel. For others, by contrast, the colonial aspect of Israel was the dominant factor: the entire Jewish population enjoyed the privileges conferred on it by Zionism, and consequently had no interest in changing the situation in favor of the Palestinians. Thus, in the short or medium term, the prospect of a break with the national consensus was illusory. Change could only be provoked from outside, by the Palestinian national movement or by the Arab states.[1]

These analytical differences had direct repercussions on the definition of our role. The defenders of the second analysis were quick to draw the conclusion it implied: Those few Israelis who opposed Zionism should join the Palestinian national movement and its struggle. Their presence at the heart of the Palestinian struggle would pave the way for true coexistence in a Palestine freed of Zionism. That is what led Udi Aviv and three other Jewish activists to want to join the DFLP in 1972. Udi was a "prince": the first born of the third generation of Kibbutz Gan Shmuel, a non-commissioned

1. See A. Said and M. Machover, "The Arab Revolution and the national questions in the Arab East," *Matzpen,* no. 65, June 1972.

officer in the paratroopers, tall, blond, with a clear complexion, he had all the trappings of the elite. Nonetheless, he hated his kibbutz, the hypocritical clear conscience of the left Zionists and the fate carved out for the Palestinians of the occupied territories. He had joined Matzpen but quickly found that our positions were timid or incoherent. Udi and his comrades felt that they had to join up with the Palestinians. They were arrested before carrying out their plan along with several dozen Palestinian activists from Galilee and the Triangle. After a hateful and totally mendacious press campaign, the systematic use of torture (the Arabs were tortured in the hopes of getting the Jews to confess) and a series of show trials, they were all condemned to staggeringly severe prison terms. It became known as the "Jewish–Arab network affair," a network that in fact never existed and that the great majority of the accused had never heard of.

Udi Aviv's choice implied *crossing the border* in all senses of the term, for he was also convicted of illegally crossing the border in order to meet Palestinian activists in Syria. His judges used the expression "crossing the boundary of national life," and they were not entirely wrong: For Uri Adiv, Dan Vered, David Zuker and Yehezkel Cohen, the entire Israeli community was a society of settlers, and only through a process of "de-Israelization" and integration into the Palestinian nationality could it legitimize its existence in Palestine. In choosing to be Palestinians they were setting an example that in their eyes was the only safe path for the Jews of Israel, at least for those who wanted to stay, for, according to that analysis, the majority of them, upon seeing their privileges disappear, would return to their countries of origin.

Along with most of the other Matzpen activists, I did not share the analysis of Udi Aviv and his comrades. While Israeli society was in fact the product of a colonial process, and lived on the privileges procured for it by the Jewish State, one could not stop there. A nation had been created, and even sharper contradictions would sooner or later assert themselves: between the policy of settlements and the desire to end the condition of permanent war, between Zionism and secularism, between the Jewish State and a democratic State, between rich and poor, between the impulse towards a cultural melting pot and the persistence of diverse identities. These contradictions would give rise to future explosions and ruptures of the national consensus. That, at least, is what we were betting on. Our role was to hasten the ruptures and to deepen them as much as we could.

Two different dynamics were at work: the dynamic of Palestinian national liberation, and the dynamic of the internal contradictions of Israeli society. One could not deny the existence of a political and social struggle within Israeli society, nor reduce it to a mere reflection of the Israeli–Arab conflict, even though it was clear that the latter had an impact on the ups and downs of the internal struggle.[2] In my view, as well as that of a number of my comrades, the historical slogan of Matzpen in favor of "a common struggle of Jews and Arabs against Zionism, Imperialism and Arab reaction" was not an immediate guiding principle but a long-term, even ultimate, goal. Meanwhile, two parallel struggles, each relatively independent of the other, had to be fought, and our main task was to advance the struggles in our own society. Uri Adiv's harsh assertion: "A united struggle or nothing!" led to fantasizing about an impossible meeting ground between the two nations, and a de facto denial of the possibility of any meaningful action within the Israeli community.

For those who, on the other hand, believed in a gradually changing awareness within the Israeli community, it was necessary to remain part of that community and to stay within it until it broke down:

> Since 1968, that is where I decided to be, on this side, in my own society, but as close as possible to the other society. If we have contributed at all to the prospects of an Israeli–Palestinian peace, it has been by stationing ourselves at the border to facilitate Israeli–Palestinian dialogue and cooperation. I refuse to be a border guard. I want to continue being a runner across the walls of hatred and the barriers of segregation...[3]

A messenger, but with what message?

First of all, a better understanding of the other. This task is not as easy as it might seem: on the Palestinian side it means explaining that Israeli society, unified as it appears to be, is not a military stronghold that makes every individual a soldier who must be eliminated in order to achieve liberation; that it is a society full of contradictions and that the long-term interests of important sectors will lead them to confront the existing regime. It also means understanding that unlike other colonial situations, the majority of Israelis do not have a "mother country" to which they can "return," and therefore will fight with their backs to the wall, or better yet, to the sea. They will

2. See the introduction to *The Other Israel – The Radical Case against Zionism*, ed. Arie Bober, New York, Doubleday, 1972.
3. See "Interlude: The speech about the border."

fight with the strength of those who have nothing to lose unless they are offered a sufficiently credible and attractive alternative. In their eyes, any proposal that does not recognize them as a nation or fails to guarantee them sovereignty and the means of self-defense is not acceptable, especially after Auschwitz.

The problem with this reasoning did not lie in the absence of empirical or rational arguments or the lack of a common analytical approach. We had rationales by the dozen, and Marxism provided us with a common method of analysis. The difficulty was psychological: how not to be perceived as merely another incarnation of the many Israelis, who, for their own obvious benefit, were trying to persuade the Palestinians to change their political line, to tone down their demands? Only our political commitment and our unconditional support (unconditional but not uncritical) for their struggle for national emancipation could make them receptive to our analyses. For three decades I have been trying to explain that to many Zionist friends on the left: it is pretentious to think that your criticisms, even when pertinent, will provoke any changes among the Palestinians, precisely because they express the point of view of the enemy. If you want to convince (rather than denounce) anybody of the pitfalls of a particular tactic or the questionable morality of certain forms of struggle, then that criticism must be perceived as coming from within and from the vantage point of support for the struggle.

It is also necessary to make Palestine and the Palestinians better known to the Israelis. Here, the main obstacle is the colonialist outlook, which denies the Other, starting with its very existence, but extending to its humanity, its rights and finally its self-determination as a nation. There is a constant back and forth between knowledge and acknowledgement: to recognize the Palestinians one must know something about their reality, their history and their narrative, although political recognition of the other does not necessarily imply (one saw this throughout the Oslo process) a better knowledge of who he really is or of his own aspirations and perceptions. As brilliantly demonstrated by Albert Memmi in the introduction to his *Portrait du colonisé,*[4] the colonial mentality denies the very words of the colonized and attributes to them the perceptions and prejudices of the colonialists themselves.

Thus providing information about the other is an important job, but it alone is no guarantee of a permanent change in the relationship.

4. Albert Memmi, *Portrait du colonisé,* Paris, Gallimard, 1985.

That requires a radical change in perception based on the concept of solidarity.[5]

To begin with, there is the tribe, with its totems and taboos around which everybody is united. There is the tribe and that which is outside the tribe, the tribe and the others. In the Zionist narrative, for the last two millennia, the Jews are always the victims and the others are always hostile. Up against the others, all Jews must be united, all Jews are united – with the exception of the renegades, who are *self-hating* Jews,[6] suffering from *selsthass (*the syndrome of self-hatred).

The acknowledgement of the other, of the non-Jew as a possible victim, is an important break with the Zionist narrative; the recognition that he may be *our* victim is yet another. It is this realization that enables one to back away from the tribe and to come closer to the border that separates the tribe from the rest of humanity. This rapprochement is called solidarity when one is ready to support the other in his conflict with one's own national collective, with moral, political or material support. It also means denouncing the crimes committed by one's own state, supporting the struggle of the other materially, offering legal assistance, and finally weakening the internal cohesion of one's own society.

Solidarity, by definition, is a border phenomenon: it develops at the point where two collectives collide in conflict. It is also, by definition, external: one is in solidarity with the other, and in this sense it always starts with the expression of one's own identity, distinct from that of the victim with whom one is in solidarity.

Paradoxically, it was through solidarity with the Palestinians that my identity as an Israeli Jew was strengthened and I was able to step beyond the supranational, global identity *à la proletariat* that I had adopted in the early days of my activity as a militant. Those of my comrades who had chosen to cross the border and join the Palestinian national movement had effectively rejected their Israeli identity by adopting a future Palestinian identity. Opting for solidarity and staying on our side of the border forced us to assert our claim of belonging to the community that lived there. So it was not as

5. Michel Warschawski, "The price of a real peace," *Foi et Développement,* no. 297, October 2001.
6. The concept of "self-hatred" has recently enjoyed a revival, as some Jewish papers in France have abused the notion to the point of ridicule. *Information juive,* for example, in the same breath, cites Pierre Vidal-Naquet, Rony Brauman, Léa Tsemel, Michel Warschawski... and Zeev Sternhell, David Grossman and other Israeli Zionist intellectuals.

Palestinians that we supported the struggle of the Palestinians, nor as citizens of the world, but as Israelis, Israelis who had chosen to break with the dominant practices and ideology of their own society.

I tend to think that this was the cause of a peculiar handicap of mine: despite years spent studying the Arabic language, I was never able to speak it. It was as if in my relations with the Palestinians I always wanted to make clear who I was, and above all who I was not, and what I was not trying to be. But maybe that's just a bad excuse for an inexcusable intellectual laziness...

Solidarity also provided a sort of mediation between parallel and independent struggles that mobilized the two communities and the prospect of a joint struggle to build a common future. But in order for those parallel struggles to be able to meet and link up it was necessary for Israelis and Palestinians to work together to trace the broad policy lines leading towards that future path. One had to demonstrate that not only was another path possible but that it was the only way to avoid the catastrophe looming in the present conflict. Those broad lines showed the way to another future, one not based on false *realism* regarding the present relationship of forces and current levels of consciousness; instead, they projected a utopia that would link the aspirations of two communities to security, to national existence and the fulfillment of their fundamental rights. In other words, one had to be able to demonstrate that each side of the border favored the same solution, and that the utopia one was defending was possible precisely because it was shared by the other side. That is why the Israeli–Palestinian meetings were so important: the current situation, the immediate tasks of each side, and the future, were all discussed.

7
Encounters

Our Palestinian friends from the West Bank and Gaza quickly led us to understand that if we wanted to have an impact on the positions taken by the national movement then we needed to be in touch with the activists outside the country. In the 1960s and 1970s the Palestinian national movement was embodied in the armed struggle conducted by the fedayin* commandos who crossed over from Jordan or the Lebanese border, the hijackings of airplanes by the PFLP and by attacks on Israeli targets in Europe. The struggle inside the occupied territories was seen only as a backup, even by its participants. Liberation could only be achieved by the fighters of the refugee camps in Jordan, Lebanon and Syria. Thus, with the epicenter of the Palestinian revolution located outside the country, we had to go there to meet its real representatives.

Those meetings began very early; soon after several Matzpen members had left Israel towards the end of the 1960s. In London, Paris, Brussels and Berlin, they got to know Palestinian activists with whom they developed very close relations. They conducted joint activities, heightening public awareness and acting together in solidarity with the Palestinian cause. It was through intermediaries like Moshe Machover and Sylvia Klingberg in London, Elie Lobel in Paris, Khalil Toamé and Mario Offenburg in Germany, that, in the 1970s, I was able to meet Saïd Hamami, Mahmoud Hamshari and Naïm Khader, the respective representatives of the PLO in Great Britain, France and Belgium, as well as Omar Al Ghul, Hisham Mustafa and many others, whose real names I still don't know.

In addition to contacts with the Palestinians we also met activists of the Arab left, the nationalist or communist left. Among them, the Moroccan activists of Ilal Amam; those of the Lebanese Communist Action Organization and the small Trotskyist groups of Lebanon, Algeria, Syria and Tunisia all made important contributions to our knowledge of the Arab national movement, its struggles and its outlook. The Lebanese militant Salah Jaber was not only a true brother but a great teacher to whom I owe just about all I know about our region. But it was Abraham Serfaty whose influence was most sharply felt, more by his life and personality than by the rare writings that reached us from the Moroccan prison where he was serving a life sentence. Abraham was a leader of the Moroccan communist left, an Arabic Jew, or rather, a Jewish Arab. Although we were not always in agreement with his conclusions, his writings awakened us to the issue of Jews of Arab culture and enabled us to understand their place at the border between Jewish and Arab identity.[1] Every year, Abraham Serfaty was elected honorary chairperson of the Matzpen Congress along with Nelson Mandela and the imprisoned Palestinian leader Abu Jamal. Needless to say, they knew nothing about it, and I doubt that they would have been happy to learn that they served as figureheads of an organization that defined itself as Trotskyist and passionately anti-Stalinist. When Abraham was freed and exiled in France I immediately flew over to embrace him. After that first encounter, the high political esteem I had for him was enhanced by a heartfelt affection, which I dare to think is reciprocal.

Among those in Morocco working to obtain Serfaty's freedom and to improve the conditions of his imprisonment was a Palestinian militant named Leila. Daughter of two of the grandest families of the Palestinian aristocracy, the Alamis and the Husseinis, wife of a Moroccan writer, she played an important role in exposing the Israeli crimes in Lebanon in 1982, particularly in Sabra and Shatila. We developed a working relationship that has never ceased to grow deeper. Leila Shahid became the spearhead of Palestinian diplomacy in Europe and since she became the Palestinian ambassador in France I have never visited the country without going to see her and sharing with her the latest developments at home.

We often did not know to which organizations those with whom we were meeting belonged, and it didn't much matter to us. The main thing was that they were part of the Palestinian resistance or the Arab national movement and that they showed a willingness to exchange ideas and information. We never went to Europe as tourists but rather to satisfy a thirst to encounter the world of Arab activism, to bring about what one day would come to be known as "the common struggle of Arabs and Jews against imperialism, Zionism and Arab reaction." At the same time, for us Israelis, it was a way to learn about the Arab world and its struggles, and an opportunity to explain Israel, its society and its contradictions to our exiled comrades. We

1. Especially Abraham Serfaty, *Lutte antisioniste et révolution arabe*, Paris, Quatre Vents éditeurs, 1977.

discovered what Israeli culture was desperately trying to conceal from us: our Arab environment, its reality, its hopes, its contradictions. The Arabs we met also began to perceive a different Israel, more complicated than the one-dimensional picture they had of it, and more promising as well.

In the 1970s trips to Europe were relatively expensive and therefore infrequent: one had to make the most out of encounters that often lasted until dawn, and then started up again a few hours later. I remember vividly two days of intensive discussions with Hassan, a member of the political bureau of the PFLP, who had come to Europe specifically to meet with a representative of Matzpen. The meetings with the activists of the Palestinian (or Arab) left had a very precise agenda: analysis of the world situation, then the region and finally the Palestinian national movement. Following that, it was my turn to present a report on the political situation in the occupied territories, then Israel and finally an account of the Israeli left, its internal debates and perspectives. We finished with a discussion of tasks and what each expected of the other. One took a lot of notes to help repeat the smallest details of what one had learned to those comrades not been fortunate enough to attend the meetings.

The exchange was an important objective in itself and often led to a request for the publication of articles in our respective journals or for supplementary literature to support this or that aspect of the analysis. The Palestinian activists respected our decision to remain within the confines of legality, and I was never confronted with demands that would have led to a break with that policy.

In 1976 I participated in a different kind of meeting. Ilan Halevi, who had recently settled in France and joined the PLO (which we did not yet know at the time), informed me that the Curiel[2] group had organized a meeting between three organizations that had originated in Matzpen and an official representative of Yasser Arafat. Contrary to all of the preceding meetings, this one was organized in clandestine fashion, something that seemed quite strange. It took place in an opulent villa in a Paris suburb where Elie Lobel, Moshe Machover, Ilan Halevi and I met Doctor Issam Sartawi and his faithful assistant, Abu Feiçal. Some years later, after the assassination of Sartawi in Lisbon in 1993, an Israeli journalist asked me how I had felt during the course

2. Curiel group: an anti-imperialist network made up of veteran Egyptian communists and led by Henri Curiel, who, among his many activities, served as a mediator for some of the first Israeli–Palestinian encounters.

of that "historic encounter" (those were his words), which was to open the way for subsequent meetings between Sartawi and more moderate Israelis. I replied that the meeting had seemed as natural and ordinary as the meetings with activists of the German SDS, the Communist League of France or the American anti-war movement. But if my answer was correct with regard to the general character of our meetings with Palestinian activists, it was not entirely true about those two days spent with Issam Sartawi.

In the car taking us to that suburban villa, driven by a member of the Curiel group[3] and followed by a second vehicle carrying those responsible for our security, I was still full of the enthusiasm that had taken hold of me two days before when meeting comrade Hassan of the PFLP in a tiny room in a modest hotel in the 19th arrondissement. I quickly realized that this was not the same thing. The contrast was striking: an extremely formal meeting, with long and solemn introductory remarks about the historic importance of this encounter followed by a long exchange on the significance of Israeli–Palestinian collaboration. The tone was not that of the unreserved comradeship that I was accustomed to, nor were the meals that took up an important part of the evening and the following day. These were true banquets whose guests were well versed in comparing the qualities of the various wines served at table. At that time I was a total stranger to diplomatic language, and if my European education had provided me with the rudiments of social graces I did not have the manners that are expected in that setting, nor the easygoing conversation, unless it had to do with politics. I was certainly impressed by Sartawi's intelligence, but his history as a fighter made more of an impact on me than his renown as a cardiologist. In the end, the formality of the meeting and the fact that one spoke as "representatives" of the two communities put me ill at ease.

Of all those present, I was the only one who had come from Israel. Moshe had been living in London for quite a few years, Elie and Ilan were in Paris, and Issam and Abu Feiçal came from Lebanon. I had a lot to relate: Jerusalem was experiencing what would become known later on as the little Intifada, a revolt of young Palestinians that had already resulted in several deaths and with which we were actively cooperating. In the Galilee, the Day of the Land had shattered Jewish–Arab relations. A revolt was about to break out among political

3. Years later, I was informed by members of the Curiel group that the car had not been driven by any of its members.

prisoners and through Léa's work I was aware of serious problems regarding the clandestine organization of the resistance in the occupied territories. I would really have liked to discuss these matters with this leader of Fatah and the PLO, to get a better understanding of the situation, and even to make some modest suggestions. After the meal I tried to speak privately with Sartawi but with a good deal of condescension he told me how much he admired our work, Léa and myself, and as for the rest, there was nothing to worry about. At that point my only wish was for that meeting to end as quickly as possible.

The following day we readily agreed on a joint document, which we all signed on behalf of our respective organizations. The document was never made public but several years later it served as the basis for a common platform between the PLO/Fatah and some members of the Israel Council for an Israeli–Palestinian peace, led by the former Deputy Uri Avnery and reserve General Matti Peled. We had managed from our spot on the sidelines to build a conduit between the Palestinian national movement and Israelis who did not belong to the anti-Zionist far left. So in the end it was not all that bad, even though I would have greatly preferred encounters with activists where the passion of discussion made us skip dinners and where we carried on building the future late into the night over some Tunisian sandwiches and a glass of beer.

The meeting with Issam Sartawi had yet another positive effect: It put into proper perspective for me the importance of those meetings abroad and reinforced the fact that Israeli–Palestinian cooperation on the ground was paramount. It was in that suburban Parisian villa that I realized that the perceptions held by the Palestinians back home of the reality of the occupation and more generally of Israel, were closer to those held by ourselves as Israeli activists. It would be with them that we developed the most promising ties.

The first contacts with students at Bir Zeit University enabled us to move on from work that was primarily devoted to political discussion and strategy to joint or at least coordinated activities. That experience proved useful when new forces began to emerge from the ranks of the Israeli population, people who were ready to act against the occupation. It was through the initiatives of Daniel Amit, professor of nuclear physics at the Hebrew University, and of a former chief doctor in the paratrooper corps, the film director Jud Neeman, that Jewish university students close to the Communist Party, Matzpen and the Sheli Party – left Zionists – as well as a number of unaffiliated newcomers, came together to denounce the Jewish settlement at Hebron and the increasingly draconian repressive measures taken against the most important institution of higher learning in the West Bank, the Bir Zeit University.

Bir Zeit is not only a university but a veritable political center. Its importance might have been occasionally exaggerated, yet it played a vital role in the resistance to the occupation. As a result towards the end of the 1970s the army began intervening more and more, arresting students, suppressing demonstrations and often closing the campus entirely.

On 28 November 1981, a demonstration of more than one hundred Israelis in the center of Ramallah was broken up by the army, which for the first time used tear gas against Jews. About 30 demonstrators, including well-known intellectuals, were arrested. Unlike the activists of Matzpen or the PC, these were acknowledged Zionists. Massive arrests of Palestinians, expulsions and the systematic use of firearms against Palestinian demonstrators during the previous ten years had failed to provoke the reaction unleashed within 48 hours of the use of tear gas against a handful of Israeli intellectuals. There was considerable commotion in Jerusalem university circles and Tel Aviv's bohemia.

The event gave birth to the Committee of Solidarity with Bir Zeit University. From 1981 to 1985 the committee initiated numerous activities – all of them highly publicized – against the occupation. It combined demonstrations in the occupied territories – by definition illegal – with actions to heighten awareness in Israel: public meetings, lectures, petitions, demonstrations as well as exhibitions by Palestinian and Israeli artists, and the production of posters created by the best-known graphic designers in Israel. Because the right was in power for the first time, more and more left Zionists participated in the efforts of the committee.

For several hundred Israelis the Committee for Solidarity with Bir Zeit was their first experience of clashing with the occupation and of meeting Palestinians. For older Matzpen activists it meant the end of our fifteen-year isolation within our own society. The first obstacle had been eliminated, and the initial interaction took place between us and some Israelis who shared only some of our political positions. It wasn't that easy, for them or for us. They had to get over their fear of being identified with those who had been perceived as enemies of Israel in addition to the fear of being used by an organization whose tactical capabilities had been widely exaggerated. We had to learn how to work with a base of broader consensus and to gain some credibility, yet without resorting to flattery or compromising our own political and ethical values. But we had two advantages that made things a little easier for us: a profound knowledge of Palestinian political reality and solid contacts with political and intellectual circles in the West Bank.

Thanks to those contacts, solidarity actions were extended from Bir Zeit University to the University of Bethlehem (where I was closely acquainted with the president of the student union, Faez Damiri), then from the universities to the refugee camps, starting with the Deheisheh camp, where Hassan Abdel Jawad and Hamdi Faraj, journalists and activists of the PFLP, with whom we had cooperated for many years, were very influential. For those Israelis who did not share our ideas, the contact with the refugees was not at all a matter of course. It was a radicalizing factor for some, while for others it was a pretext to distance themselves from the struggle against the occupation. The refugees of Deheisheh or Al-Amari were not very good at hiding their feelings; unlike some professors of English or history at Bir Zeit or Bethlehem, they did not know how to deal with Israeli sensitivities. Albert Agazarian, in particular, knew how to gain the confidence of his Israeli colleagues in no time. This spokesman for Bir Zeit University had no equal when it came to charm. His Hebrew was impeccable (one of eight languages that he spoke perfectly), his profound knowledge of the Israeli mentality, and above all, his talents as a storyteller had made this Armenian of the old city of Jerusalem the privileged interlocutor for Israeli pacifists of that era. I had got to know him a few years earlier when he showed up at our door in driving rain in the middle of the night. He had come looking for Léa so that she might negotiate the release of some students who had been arrested in a night-time raid. Albert Agazarian and Hanan Ashrawi were the contacts for Léa, who was at that time the lawyer for Bir Zeit students. Both of them quickly became our close friends and remain so to this day, although Hanan's ministerial responsibilities after the establishment of the Palestinian Authority have weakened our ties a bit. In her autobiography Hanan Ashrawi recounts the friendship that linked her to Léa:

> I have seen her hazel, green-speckled eyes undergo many transformations: from sorrow over the pain of her Palestinian clients and their families to exasperation and anger at the injustice

> she witnesses every day, at her sense of helplessness before it, to the laughter of her undefeated sense of humor, to the gentleness of a mother deeply concerned at the heavy price that her children are being made to pay – both for being part of a system of occupation and conflict as well as for being the children of Léa Tsemel. One image I can never erase from my memory is that of her deep hurt and bewilderment at her son's denial of her when taunted and threatened by his classmates as the son of "the Arab-loving traitor."
>
> Our special friendship is no secret. We are a strange combination: this fierce yet gentle Israeli woman who early on took a moral and legal stand against cruelty and injustice, and her academic Palestinian counterpart who recognized in her a kindred spirit. Ours is a bond of sisterhood and instinctive recognition that defies history and national boundaries, or perhaps is the outcome of precisely these forces; in our own way, each of us is the product of the unique experience of her race. Our daughters, Zeina and Talila, are "milk sisters," for I breast-fed Talila along with my Zeina when Léa had to go to court on behalf of my students. Neither child speaks the verbal language of the other, but on family picnics they hold hands and go off merrily in search of wildflowers or muddy streams.[4]

Hanan and Léa, Zeina and Talila, were they fortunate enough to have abolished the border in their personal relations? I am not entirely sure. Many Israelis of the left like to speak of their Palestinian friends, and I have used the phrase myself several times in preceding chapters to describe the ties that bind me to some of my Palestinian comrades. But I do not think that the concept fits. Not that friendship isn't possible between men and women belonging to communities at war; but in the specific context of Israeli–Palestinian relations, an intimacy in personal relations that does away with ethnic or religious belonging, and which one calls friendship, is almost impossible to achieve.

As Albert Memmi described with great precision, a colonial relationship is all-encompassing. It is expressed not only through ideology and in political positions but above all in attitudes and behavior that are the product of a culture that requires an enormous effort to escape. Several conditions are necessary: first of all to be

4. Hanan Ashrawi, *This Side of Peace*, New York, Simon & Schuster, 1995, p. 38.

conscious of the relationship of colonial domination that ties us to the Other in order, precisely, to do the utmost to free oneself from it. To begin with that excludes the left Zionists, who refuse to recognize that basic reality. Then, one must be able to listen to the Other and, at the very least, demonstrate empathy for their suffering, their resentments and their reluctance to trust those who belong to the enemy camp. In listening to the Other, there is a very narrow margin between, on the one hand, the reproduction of a colonial and paternalistic rapport, and on the other, flattery and self-denial. While a tiny minority of Israelis give way to self-flagellation, the majority of those who think that they have Palestinian friends remain profoundly insensitive to the Other.

Not too long ago I was invited to a little party organized by a group of Israeli women pacifists. Rare enough an occurrence to be worth mentioning, some Palestinian women activists were present. Most of the Israeli women, including a feminist deputy well versed in the Israeli–Palestinian dialogue, were firmly convinced that the Palestinian women present were part of their circle of best friends. The atmosphere was pleasant and gave the impression that the women were neither Israeli nor Palestinian, but simply women (and two or three men) sharing the same values. The MP, a university scholar and specialist in multiculturalism, was relating in great detail the hard day she had just spent in the Parliament, and in particular, a long argument with the extreme right deputy Rehavam Zeevi, whom she referred to, like all Israelis, by his nickname, Gandhi.[5] She wasn't able to hide the clubbish relationship that in spite of real ideological differences, linked her to this individual who openly advocated the expulsion of the Arabs. Not for a second did this intelligent and educated woman think that her intimacy with Zeevi and her casual manner in discussing someone whom her Palestinian "friends" would consider a Nazi brute would profoundly shock the Palestinian

5. Rehavam Zeevi: young commander of Palmach units in 1948, career officer in the Israeli army, he was, after 1967, the commanding officer of the Central Region, and as such, responsible for the West Bank. In 1969 he became famous for his "safaris," real manhunts directed against the fedayin who had infiltrated the Jordan Valley, to which he liked to invite his friends. After his discharge, he was implicated by the daily *Haaretz* for links to heroin trafficking. In 1986 he founded the Transfer Party (represented in Parliament after 1988 under the name Moledet Party, "Party of the Fatherland"), which he represented as a deputy until his death. Named Minister of Tourism in 2001 in the Shimon Peres government, he was assassinated on 18 October by a PFLP commando.

women who were present. Not for a second, even after the sudden but discreet departure of the Palestinians, did she become aware of their discomfort. None of the Israelis present, except Léa, realized that for Rawda, Ghada or Amal, everything that had just happened was as if a French progressive had told his Algerian friend back in 1960 about a chummy exchange with General Bigeard, Bibi to his friends, or a German communist had, in 1933, told his Jewish friend about a friendly chat with Reinhardt (Reini to his intimates) Heydrich. More than ten years of dialogue had taught them very little about their "friends" and had hardly made a dent in their cultural armor.

In trying to forge a relationship of friendship, one has to realize that when talking to a Palestinian, it is imperative to use the original Arab place names, even if one is speaking in Hebrew, which in itself is already a problem. One has to throw out once and for all such terms as "the War of Independence" or "the Six Day War." When one speaks about experience in the military – yet another problem that makes friendship difficult – one has to make a long-term effort (years perhaps) to demonstrate that it is not at all obvious that one can support the rights of Palestinians while serving in the Israeli army. In other words, friendship between Palestinians and Israelis is out of the question unless one makes a decent effort to not be just like any other Israeli.

But even if one succeeds in surmounting the obstacles of language and behavior, and one has an unassailable track record of active support for the rights of Palestinians, I still believe that the kind of relations that Zionism has created between the two communities make friendship improbable. Friendship, unlike camaraderie, respect or even affection, must be based on common lives, common experiences and common problems. But in Israel-Palestine, the order of the day is the *separation* of the communities. Our lives are not only radically different but completely disconnected. Encounters – except for those linked to the struggle – are too infrequent to allow any real intimacy to develop. It is no accident that Hanan Ashrawi, who knew many Israeli women, would use the word friendship only when referring to Léa. Hanan's house was just across the street from the military courthouse of Ramallah and Léa came by almost every day, had lunch there, took naps and even spent the night. That physical closeness, unique in Israeli–Palestinian relations, allowed an emotional intimacy to develop with Hanan, her husband Émile, her sisters and nieces. It was cemented by an ongoing dialogue about day-to-day life, family and emotions, and thus the possibility of knowing the Other as an individual and not merely as "other" or as a comrade in the struggle. But had Léa's presence in Ramallah been without an honorable justification – her work at the military government and court – it would have been very badly perceived or simply not existed at all. As for Hanan and her family, they rarely came to visit us in West Jerusalem because Palestinians feel ill at ease in Israel even if they belong to that very small privileged minority that has the right to enter. Can one speak of friendship when one does not even know the homes of one's friends or how they live their daily lives?

After the start of the Intifada in 1987, Talila and Zeina no longer participated in those picnics recounted by Hanan because those kinds of pleasures became totally inappropriate in the political situation. The establishment of the Palestinian Authority and the absence of good reasons for going to Ramallah put an end to the regular get-togethers. The unique friendship between our families is fading. I say it with regret but without bitterness: political reality is simply stronger than friendship. The border is a place of struggle from which camaraderie can emerge, but the space for real closeness is extremely limited.

There was a basic difference between our Arab friends and ourselves: They were a society with its own norms, its community, holidays, national symbols and cultural references, whereas we were excluded, expatriates, who for the most part had chosen to break our cultural ties to the community we came from. It was particularly extreme for someone like me who had become an agnostic after having lived as a religious Jew.

At that time Israeli culture was a mixture of militarist nationalism and religious references. Having rejected the one and recanted the other I found myself without any cultural reference, and without any sense of belonging except to that which I had chosen: the international working class. My culture was global culture; my holidays were May Day and the commemoration of the victory of the Red Army over fascism; my symbols, the red flag and the raised fist. In my eyes everything else was a residue of reactionary tradition or dishonest compromises with chauvinism.

In 1974, taking a train to a political congress somewhere in Europe, I met a Trotskyist leader of Jewish origin. He was reading a book by Gershom Sholem on the Cabbala. Astonished, I asked him why the Jewish Cabbala interested him more than Zen Buddhism. He replied that it was part of his personal culture, his Jewish culture, and with a wink, he pulled out the traditional Jewish *shadai* medallion from under his shirt. Back in my compartment I thought to myself that the French Trotskyists still had a long way to go to grasp proletarian internationalism and to become the worthy heirs of the founder of the Red Army.

It was not until the beginning of the 1980s that my comrades and I began a process of reappropriation of Jewish culture and rerooting in a national tradition. For some of us it was the Bund and the epic of the Jewish working-class movement of Eastern Europe that served as reference; for others it was the Jewish Diaspora in the Arab world; for others yet, the Nazi Judeocide. We felt the need to root ourselves in a history and to defend an identity other than the one imposed by belonging to the tribe of Israel. We needed a narrative that would furnish us with the foundation of a collective identity different from that which Zionism wanted to build on the ruins of Palestine and the Jewish Diaspora.

8
Prisoners and banished

At the heart of the border there is a special space, which, although often located on Israeli territory and totally controlled by the Israeli authorities, was for a long time the first autonomous Palestinian territory. This space is hermetically sealed but it extends into the life of almost all Palestinian families and its political importance has long been decisive. It consists of prisons, detention centers and other internment camps where Israel locks up those who are fighting for the freedom of their people. There is not a single Palestinian family that has not had a son, a sister or a parent in prison. The number of Palestinians who have experienced imprisonment is calculated at more than 250,000, that is, 10 percent of the entire population of the occupied territories. This figure alone demonstrates the centrality of prison in the social as well as political reality of Palestinians during the course of the last three decades.

Two generations of leaders were developed in these prisons. They continue to play a key political role in the Palestinian national movement. It is rare to meet those who do not refer to their prison experience as their "university," often without knowing that they are using one of Maxim Gorky's favorite definitions. Prison is in fact a political university where daily training classes are conducted along with debates between the different factions of the national movement; a university of the people where the better-educated prisoners provide an education to those with limited schooling; and a language school, particularly for Hebrew, which the prisoners are obliged to practice in order to communicate with Jewish common criminals and with their jailers. When he was released, my friend Atta Queimeri, who had been arrested at the age of 16 and sentenced to 30 years in prison, spoke and wrote in three languages in addition to Arabic. It was thanks to the perfect Hebrew that he used in petitions submitted to the authorities that Léa, who served as a mediator during the course of one of the numerous prisoners' strikes, asked to meet Ghazi Abu Jiad, leader of the PFLP prisoners in Gaza. That meeting marked the beginning of a friendship that has lasted to the present day. Like Atta, Ghazi is now a professional translator.

Paradoxically, prison is an opening in the wall that separates Palestinians and Israelis, one of the rare places where they can rub shoulders and get to know each other. Of course, the Israeli that the Palestinian detainees meet is not the average Israeli, but even so can help them understand the Israeli mentality, the weakness hidden behind the apparent power, the fears and the fantasies that inhabit the collective unconscious. After the signing of the Oslo agreement, Israeli politicians often spoke of the "prison graduates," who, in contrast to the "Tunisians" (the leaders coming from abroad), were able to communicate readily with the Israeli negotiators without every word having to be spelt out.

One can hardly begin to understand the Palestinian liberation struggle, its great moments, its heroes and its myths, or understand the political and social reality of the occupied territories, if one tries to gloss over what is called the "community of political prisoners," its players, its struggles and its legends. To a large extent it is prison and the prisoners that have fashioned Palestinian policy, its current leadership and its outlook in the West Bank and Gaza. But aside from the guards and the agents of Shin Beth, a few lawyers and a handful of activists, how many Israelis have had the occasion to encounter this reality during 35 years of occupation?

It was the arrest of Palestinian activists from Israel in the beginning of the 1970s and, in particular, a few of my comrades implicated in the "Jewish–Arab network," that brought me into the world of Palestinian political prisoners. While visiting my detained friends, I met Omar el-Qassem, sentenced to several life terms for having been the chief of a fedayin commando of the DFLP* which, in 1969, crossed the Jordan and fought a courageous battle against far more numerous and better-equipped Israeli forces. His heroism earned him the respect of some Israeli generals as well as that of his own compatriots. His intelligence, his political insight, his wisdom and, above all, his human qualities made him a leader of the prisoners, including those belonging to other organizations. Our political discussions, through letters and conversations, had a profound effect on me, and our paths crossed several times until his death in 1988. His burial took place during one of the court sessions of my trial. Accompanied by thousands of Palestinians, proudly brandishing the banned flag and about 30 Israeli activists who had suddenly left the courtroom, surrounded by a spectacular security contingent of the DFLP, his remains passed right under the windows of the courthouse, to the sound of drums. In front of our astonished judges, Léa and

I stood to salute our friend one last time. It was the only time that we wept in front of our judges, indifferent to their surprise. We felt distant, very distant from the pathetic questions that the prosecutor tried to put to me.

That is how I also got to know Youssef Mansour, a young activist from the village of Tira in Israel. He had been condemned to death for having placed a bomb on a bus in Kfar Saba in 1969. Contrary to what is often believed, the death penalty does exist in Israel (and not only against Nazi criminals), even though official policy has always been to quash death sentences on appeal.

Some years later Youssef met up with his military judge in prison. A banker by profession, the reserve colonel Yehoshua Ben Zion had received a heavy sentence for corruption and embezzlement.[1]

It is mostly thanks to Léa that I came to know the Palestinian political prisoners. Starting in 1972, my companion had put all of her professional skills at the disposal of the Palestinians.[2] Until that time, Felicia Langer, a tireless communist militant, was the only Jewish lawyer representing the Palestinian fighters. After 1972, the two of them alone, with a few Arab lawyers, led the legal and administrative struggle in the military courts, the Supreme Court, in the prisons and the countless offices of the military administration.

I met Léa when she was a law student at the Hebrew University in Jerusalem in the spring of 1968. During one of those innumerable scuffles between Matzpen activists and other students, a smallish, young woman in boots and miniskirt drove off the counter-demonstrators by twirling an impressive bunch of keys attached to a long, thin steel chain, while shouting a string of curses that would make a whole barracks blush. I was fascinated. "What? You don't know her? That's Léa Tsemel, a real character." Three years later, after having shared many political adventures, we decided to live together.

I often accompanied her in her work. I served as translator, journalist or guide for delegations of human rights activists or foreign jurists. Since the Israeli Communist Party had barred Felicia Langer

1. Yehoshua Ben Zion would be quickly pardoned and freed. A false medical certificate had persuaded Prime Minister Begin that he was dying. Twenty years later the banker was still doing very well.
2. Léa Tsemel, her personality and her work are portrayed in a book by David Grossman entitled *Yellow Wind*, New York, Picador, 2002, in the chapter "Catch 44."

from representing people implicated in attacks against civilians, it was Léa who pleaded most of the cases linked to the big attacks of the 1970s and 1980s. It was through those trials that we began to understand the contradictory accounts of events taking place on the border of two communities. Massacres of innocents for some, courageous military operations for others – those who were terrorist assassins in the eyes of the Israelis were heroes for the Palestinians. They often were in our eyes as well.

The prison conditions were inhumane, at least until the hunger strike of 1981, but the authorities never succeeded in breaking the prisoners' organization, their strict chain of command and the rules of conduct to which they adhered. From the Nafha prison in the Negev desert to Damoun on Mt Carmel, the Palestinian political prisoners had established a virtual self-rule, an autonomous power coordinated throughout the entire country. It did not take more than a few hours for the idea of a strike to get around to all the prisons, be negotiated among the different political currents and then unfold on the basis of a practical and unanimously respected decision.

The hunger strike of the prisoners of Nafha in 1981 was one of the powerful moments of their struggle. Unlike the Irish nationalists who were conducting a strike at that same time to win recognition as political prisoners, the Palestinian prisoners were demanding equal rights with common criminals, such were the conditions at that isolated penal colony deep in the desert. For a period of several weeks, together with the families of the prisoners, we organized solidarity actions under the slogan "Long Kesh–Nafha = same struggle: respect the human rights of the prisoners!" We publicized the demands of the prisoners and informed the Israeli public on the daily progress of the strike, thanks to the news we got from the lawyers' collective set up by Léa and Felicia.[3] Although the Nafha strike did not end in a slaughter, as was the case in Ireland, it nonetheless did result in two deaths: Ali Jafari from the Deheisheh camp and Rassem Halawa from Gaza, suffocated by a nurse who did not know how to apply the tube used in force-feeding. A third death was barely avoided when Léa happened on a man dying in the solitary confinement section and was able to alert the emergency services. The prisoner was named Ishak Mghara, better known as Abu Jamal, brother of Abu Moussa (a prestigious military commander of Fatah, who rebelled

3. See Felicia Langer, *Going my Way* (Hebrew edn), Tel Aviv, Dvir, 1991, pp. 110–17.

against Yasser Arafat in 1982 and became an agent of Syrian policy within the Palestinian movement). Abu Jamal was one of the oldest leaders of the PFLP in prison, revered by the activists of his party as well as by the other prisoners for his courage, his uprightness and kindness. First arrested in 1969, he was freed two years later only to be sentenced to prison for 27 years in 1972. He died there as a result of a weakening of the heart brought on by the hunger strike. On the day they were freed in May 1985, the PFLP prisoners gathered to meditate at his tomb in Jerusalem.

May 1985 signaled the end of a chapter in the struggle of the Palestinian political prisoners. Several times during the course of the preceding years some prisoners had been freed as the result of hostage taking by Palestinian organizations. During the occupation of Lebanon three Israeli soldiers had been captured by the PFLP-CG*, an organization led by a veteran officer of the Syrian army, Ahmad Jibril, whose operational effectiveness commanded admiration. Having had his fingers burnt by the maneuvers of the Israeli authorities during the previous exchanges, but also aware of the unpopularity of the Lebanese war in Israeli public opinion, Jibril had presented the Israeli authorities with a list of more than a thousand prisoners, demanding that those who were originally from the territories occupied by Israel should be free to go back to their homes and not deported, as had been the case in previous exchanges. Various third parties such as the International Committee of the Red Cross would be the guarantors of the exchange. Having not forgotten that in earlier exchanges Israel had sent common criminals in place of the specifically named political prisoners, Ahmad Jibril had sent lists containing precise descriptions of each of the prisoners to be released.

During weeks of top-secret negotiations, Léa served as an intermediary between the prisons, the authorities and the Palestinian negotiators. We studied the lists day and night, correcting errors, passing along suggestions to the committee of united prisoners in order to make sure that all the elderly and those with the heaviest sentences would be freed, and communicating with the Palestinian negotiators by way of international organizations. As she needed help, Léa was allowed to involve the Alternative Information Center, which I had founded a year earlier with a small group of Israelis and Palestinians.

The name of Omar Al-Qassem was missing; surely that was a mistake? We were told that the Israelis had used their veto, wanting to exchange him later for the body of a soldier held by the DFLP. Some prisoners who were to be released in the coming months insisted on being replaced by others who still had lengthy sentences to serve. Towards the end of the negotiations we got permission to talk to some Israeli journalists who, until the very last minute, did not believe that Israel would really free more than 1,000 prisoners, some of whom were responsible for particularly bloody attacks, and what is more, not insist on deporting them.

On 5 May 1985, one of the most beautiful days of my life, 1,115 prisoners were freed, 600 of them inside the country. I was eager to see in the flesh all those who previously had been only a name, or those I had met only briefly in the course of hearings before the military court, but I was forced to stay in the AIC's office in order to provide information to journalists who wanted details about such and such a prisoner or where they could meet them as, this time, they were going home. That day, we were truly at the border post between Israeli society, stunned by the brilliant Palestinian victory that this exchange represented, and a jubilant Palestinian population celebrating the return of their heroes. We were providers of information but, above all, we were trying to explain the feelings of the Palestinians, what the political prisoners meant to them, the place they held and the role they would play in the future within their society.

I was able to make a quick visit to El-Bireh to greet Adnan Mansour Ghanem, who had infiltrated at the head of a commando coming from Syria. He had asked to be sent to his aunt's house, a revered lady from Palestinian high society, whose kitchen would become, until the deportation of her nephew, one year later, a sort of club of PFLP fighters. To my daughter Talila, whom she showered with gifts and for whom she knitted sweaters, she quickly became *hadoda* (auntie). But she was never able to understand why intelligent and educated people like us continued to believe that the Protocols of the Elders of Zion was an anti-Semitic forgery, whose usage was doing great harm to the Palestinian cause.

I spent the night that followed that memorable day at the "slaves' quarter," that courtyard alongside the esplanade of the mosques of Jerusalem, where a community of Palestinians of African origin lived in abysmal poverty. They were celebrating the return of Ali and Mahmoud Jedda, both arrested in 1968 for having been part of a PFLP commando that had thrown grenades in Jerusalem one Saturday evening. Since the first days of the occupation that little community had been a breeding place for activists, men and women alike. A few years earlier Israel had freed Fatma Barnawi, a Fatah militant responsible for the attack in the Zion cinema in Jerusalem, but she had not had the good fortune of being allowed to go back to her home. It was only in 1995, following the Oslo agreement, that she returned to become the commander of the women's units of the Palestinian police in Gaza.

In prison, where he had learned to speak fluent Hebrew, English and French, Ali Jedda had expressed the desire to work with the left-wing Jews, whose activities he followed with a passion from his cell. Two months after he was freed he joined the team of the Alternative Information Center.

Abdelaziz Ali Shahin, better known under the name Abu Ali, was the undisputed leader of the Palestinian prisoners' community as of 1967. I have not mentioned him previously because even though his reputation was well known to me, I only met him after he was freed in 1984, in the midst of a long campaign we were conducting to prevent his banishment.

Banishment? Deportation? Expulsion? Over the years I had used all those terms to translate the Hebrew word *guirouch**, which also means divorce, but divorce in the biblical sense of a unilateral act on the part of a man renouncing his wife.[4] I searched for a word that might best express the horror of the act I considered to be the worst of the repressive measures used by the Israeli occupation forces, one that made me want to kill every time I witnessed it.

Expressly forbidden by the Fourth Geneva Convention, the expulsion of residents of the occupied territories beyond the borders of these territories was practiced on a large scale after June 1967 and until the middle of the 1970s. The practice became less used as international protests mounted. Banishment was the ultimate measure that the Israeli occupation forces had found to neutralize political officials, municipal leaders and trade unionists. Clandestine activists or those involved in military actions were tried and sentenced

4. "The Palestinians mostly use the English term 'deportation.' Is it really what that is? Not in my opinion. The term 'deportation' has a very strong connotation in our memory, recalling the extermination camps, and it has absolutely nothing to do with that... It seems then that 'banishment' might be the proper expression to characterize this form of selective repression. In the *Larousse,* the definition is quite clear: 'Banishment: punishment consisting of barring a citizen from living in his own country...'" Maurice Rajfus, *L'Ennemi intérieur*, Paris, EDI-La Brêche, 1987, p. 165.

to lengthy prison terms. The less clandestine political activity became, the more the person involved was likely to be expelled, without any hope of coming back to his country, his home or his family, except after the Israeli occupation might end.

Since most of my Palestinian friends and comrades were involved in more or less public activities I had the sad privilege of knowing many banished people. My friends were systematically expelled, to the extent that I began to wonder if I was not the cause of their misfortune. I trust that it was my political instinct that led me to collaborate with those who made up the convoys of deportees and whom, later on, Yitzhak Rabin would call the "authentic leaders."

The first banishment I was involved in was that of Riad Abu Awad. Léa had decided that it was legally possible, if not to prevent his deportation, at least to delay it by forcing the authorities to argue the case and thus gain time to mount an international and domestic campaign. Until then all the lawyers could do was to appeal after the implementation of the deportation decree. That legal battle would, in the future, change the policy of deportation: the long judicial procedure reduced the immediate effect of the deportation and allowed us to make Israel the target of international campaigns to protest against that flagrant violation of the Geneva Convention. The price paid by the Israeli authorities became higher and higher, as Yitzhak Rabin would learn in 1992 with the expulsion of more than 400 Islamic (or at least supposed Islamic) activists and the huge mobilization, even in Israel, to put a stop to that barbaric practice.[5] As a result, after 1992 there were no more banishments, the occupation forces preferred... to have the leaders killed by special units.

During the weeks preceding the expulsion of Riad, we were able to lead our first campaign to raise public opinion against the deportations. The experience we had gained, although unsuccessful, would help guide future campaigns. After Riad, it was the turn of several prisoners who were freed during the exchange of 1985, among them Adnan Ghanem and Younès Rajoub. Their expulsion was in violation of the agreement with Ahmad Jibril. The protest campaign was even more significant than the one we had organized against the banishment of Riad, but it was the case of Abu Ali Shahin that caused people to mobilize on a massive scale.

Abu Ali belonged to the original Fatah hard core, and he was arrested in the first few months of the Israeli occupation, during the course

5. Regarding our modest role in those events, see Ashrawi, *This Side of Peace*, pp. 221–4.

of his countless border crossings between Egypt and Gaza, where he lived with his family in the Rafah refugee camp. Endowed with a rare charisma and an extraordinary capacity to persuade whomever he was talking to, he nonetheless did not hesitate, when he thought it necessary, to use expedient means to force those who were reluctant to join in. He soon became the undisputed leader of the Fatah prisoners. His political influence extended well beyond the walls of the different prisons where the prison authorities were vainly trying to isolate him. His recommendations were increasingly perceived as orders by the Fatah activists in Gaza and the West Bank.

Word of the presence of a young Jewish lawyer, whose courage and fighting spirit began to be recognized in the prisons, reached him and aroused his interest. Quickly won over by him, Léa became his lawyer, or rather his *consigliera.* Abu Ali was freed in 1984 (having been sentenced to only 16 years in prison, he had refused several times to be released in the prisoner exchanges in favor of those with much longer sentences) and immediately assumed a key role in Palestinian political life. He was particularly involved in the beginning of the development of Shabiba, the semi-public youth organization of Fatah. The authorities decided to limit his freedom of movement and then to banish him to Dahaniyé, a village housing collaborators on the border of the Gaza Strip. But they never managed to isolate him. Even the Israeli soldiers were unable to resist his charm, and the jokes he told in the Hebrew working-class slang that he had learned in prison. The authorities were forced to prohibit the soldiers from talking to him. Finally, they decided to expel him.

Léa and Avigdor Feldman, the great human rights lawyer who had, after the war in Lebanon, agreed to argue before the Supreme Court to denounce the violations of the Geneva Convention, led the legal battle against the expulsion of Abu Ali for almost a whole year. At the same time, an Israeli–Palestinian committee organized a huge campaign to rally public opinion against the expulsion of Abu Ali Shahin. Well-known personalities took part in it, as did the Kibbutz Kerem Shalom, which was separated only by barbed wire from Dahaniyé where Abu Ali was confined.

At the courthouse I was always fascinated by the respectful, even servile, attitude of the high-ranking Israeli officers towards this little man with a gray beard, whose eyes were both smiling and hard, who used a cane to walk – a consequence of spending long years in prison – and who always had a good word for his friends or for the armed guards that accompanied him. Several times, I saw Colonel

Ahaz Ben-Ari, the legal counselor for the Gaza military government, bring him a cup of tea while bowing slightly towards the man he had decided to deport.

On the day of the verdict the atmosphere in the court was tense. The family, some Palestinian and Israeli activists, and a large delegation of foreign jurists sent by various human rights organizations, waited side by side. That morning we had organized one last demonstration in front of the Supreme Court, where we announced that, no matter what the verdict was, we would all gather again the following Saturday at Kerem Shalom to continue to demand an end to the policy of deportations. The lawyers managed a small victory: they got the judges of the Supreme Court to agree that, if Abu Ali was to be deported, the authorities would negotiate with the lawyers and request the help of the CICR on the country to which he would be transferred, since deportation to Southern Lebanon, under the cruel domination of the militias of the SLA,[6] might put his life in danger.

The deliberations dragged on through the afternoon and, having to find a baby-sitter for our four-year-old daughter, I took advantage of a break to say goodbye to Abu Ali. He gave me a long hug and I had a feeling that this would be the last time. I didn't know that I would be the only one able to say goodbye to him: violating the Supreme Court's decision, the army chartered a helicopter that flew him to Lebanon in a matter of minutes, while his family and lawyers were waiting in front of the prison to meet him, as they had been promised. The following day, I wrote an open letter to Aiman, the son of Abdelaziz Shahin:

> A few hours ago, we were side by side in front of the Moskobiyé, unable to grasp that it was all over. It hurt to see your mother crying and it hurt even more to watch the fixed stare of your grandmother, mixed with suppressed anger and immense pain. But hardest of all was to watch you trying to hold back your tears. When I met you, your father was still in prison, but you knew that within a few years he would come back to your family. You knew it because that was what was stated in the official documents.
>
> But he only stayed with you a few months and then was taken away once again. To Dahaniyé. This time they did not tell you for how long but at least you knew that he was not far away and

6. The South Lebanon Army, created by the Israeli army after their retreat from Lebanon in 1985.

that sooner or later he would come home. You believed it because common sense required you to.

Today Abu Ali has been thrown out of his own country and it is hard for you to believe that you will be able to live together in your home again one day. You don't believe it anymore because that is what your experience, as the son of a fighter who refused to get down on his knees, has taught you.

I had the good fortune denied to you, your mother, the other members of your family and your many friends, to take leave of Abu Ali and to say "Goodbye, until we meet again." I had the feeling that they would not let him say goodbye to his family so during the break I went to embrace him one last time. I promised him that we would meet again, in Jerusalem, and he replied: "Of course!" Those are the words that I must convey in his name – I swear to you that we will meet again here, in the homeland. I know it because that is what the history of our peoples teaches us.

Aiman, my brother, stay here because Abu Ali is the stones, the olive trees, the children of Rafah, of Beit Ur and Zbeidat. Stay here because, if you leave, Abu Ali will no longer have a reason to come back. But if you stay and if the children of Palestine cling to their country, Abu Ali and all the other deportees will find the strength necessary to come home.[7]

After the deportation of Abu Ali Shahin there were several more convoys of deportees. The Intifada was in the air. People's committees were multiplying. Semi-legal, semi-public actions, in which women's organizations, youth and trade union groups were playing an increasingly important role, were becoming routine. The movement had to be smashed. More friends were banished to the other side of the border: Hassan Abdel Jawed from the Deheisheh camp; Jibril Rajoub, Abu Ali's successor as head of the Fatah prisoners and after his liberation, the right-hand man of Feisal Husseini; the trade unionist Ali Abu Hilal; Bashir El-Kheiri, a lawyer at El-Bireh and author of a fine book about the life of a refugee. Then, with the start of the Intifada, it was the turn of the physicist Taissir Aruri from Bir Zeit; Muhammad Labadi and his brother Majid; Jamal Faraj from Deheisheh; Abdel Hamid el-Baba from the El-Amari camp; Bilal Sharshir from Nablus as well as so many other activists with whom we had collaborated, often for years. Only the activists from Jerusalem were spared, the

7. *Matzpen*, no. 151, March 1985.

Begin government having, ten years before, amended the law in such a way that it had become impossible to deport residents of Israel, including of East Jerusalem.

In 1988, when the Intifada was at its peak, the PLO decided to charter a boat to try and bring home 135 Palestinians who had been expelled, deported or banished since 1967. A group of Israeli activists and journalists decided to go to Athens from where the boat was supposed to leave. I could not join them because at the time I was in the middle of my trial and confined to my residence in Jerusalem. On the eve of their departure I wrote a short text – a variation of a popular drinking song that began "...cheers to the ship that heads out to the open sea..." which I gave to my friend Haïm Hanegbi to pass on to my expelled comrades. It read as follows:

> Cheers to the ship that heads out to the open sea.
>
> Cheers to you, Riad Abu Awad, expelled from Bir Zeit in 1978, thrown right into the arms of the Saad Haddad militias.
>
> Cheers to you, my friend Abu Ali Shahin, you who even after 16 years in prison, six months of house arrest in Rafah and a year of banishment at Dahaniyé, continue to torment the dwarfs that govern in our name. Even the olive trees that we planted at Bashit after your expulsion frighten them: several hours after our departure they were torn up by the inhabitants of Asseret who have the nerve to call themselves farmers. When we said goodbye in the courtroom, I swore that we would meet again in Jerusalem, and we both know that this day is getting nearer.
>
> Cheers to you, Adnan Mansour Ghanem, whose torture shocked the entire world. From time to time I see your aunt who brings us some fish and sends you her love. They are doing much better at their home in El-Bireh, as it has now been two months since they got a taste of freedom.
>
> Cheers to you, Mahmoud Fanoun and Ali Abu Hilal: we promised that for each deportee 1,000 new leaders would come forward and they are now legion.
>
> Cheers to you, Doctor Azmi Jueibeh.
>
> Cheers to you, my dear friend Hassan Abdel Jawad and cheers to the inhabitants of the Deheisheh camp who tore down the fence one night and chased out the collaborators.
>
> Cheers to you, Younès and Jibril Rajoub. You were freed from prison on the same day but deported two and a half years apart. You belonged to rival parties and defended opposing strategies

> – but the occupier does not discriminate and he brought you together. Jibril, your departure left a big hole in the Committee Against the Iron Fist, but, don't worry, none of us has lost faith in the common struggle.
>
> Cheers to the hundreds of those who were banished and the millions of refugees who do not forget their homeland and whom the homeland does not forget.
>
> Cheers to all of you, my dear friends. For reasons beyond my control I will not be able to shake your hand and I doubt that you will see me among the thousands of Israelis who will be waiting by the shore in Haifa to welcome you. The navy will not let you approach the coast and, like Moses, you will only see the Promised Land from a distance. But unlike him, one day you will lead your people in your homeland. That day we will be able to live together, you and us, like two free peoples in their land.

The boat would never arrive. The Israeli secret service destroyed it in Larnaca. But the banished did re-enter their country in the wake of the Oslo agreement. Bashir El-Kheiri is a lawyer in Ramallah. Hassan Abdel Jawad opened a new press center in Bethlehem, Taissir Aruri got his job back at Bir Zeit University, Mahmoud Fanoun and Ali Abu Hilal resumed their activities as activists, Marwan Barghouti leads Fatah in the West Bank, Azmi Jueibeh became minister of sports for the Palestinian Authority and Jibril Rajoub is the commander in chief of Palestinian preventive security in the West Bank.

Abu Ali, who often phoned us from various places in exile to get the latest news, did not want to come back on the basis of an accord that he considered catastrophic for the future of his people. In 1994 while Léa was visiting Tunis, he told her again about his wish to remain in exile rather than support what in his eyes was taking shape as a capitulation. Imagine my surprise, a few months later, when I learned during a seminar co-sponsored by the Alternative Information Center that Abu Ali had returned to Rafah. I took a taxi and, in a city covered with flags and slogans celebrating its most popular son, I shared with him the joy of his homecoming. After having been elected overwhelmingly to the Palestinian Legislative Council, Abu Ali was appointed as minister of supply to the Palestinian government. Often, on his way to his office in Ramallah he comes through Jerusalem and phones us: "Get the coffee ready, I want to find out what is happening in Israel..."

Riad Abu Awad is the only one who did not come back. The Israeli authorities did not give him permission so he stayed in Cairo from where he calls us from time to time. Sometimes we see his daughters when they come to visit their grandmother in Bir Zeit...

PART TWO

Cracks

Interlude: The two rabbis

The Talmud recounts that Rabbi Akiba and his colleagues went up to Jerusalem one day. Arriving at the former site of the Temple, they saw a fox running away from the place of the Holy of Holies. Rabbi Akiba's colleagues burst into tears. But Rabbi Akiba burst out laughing.

"Why are you laughing, Akiba?"

"Why are you crying?"

"This is the holy place where nobody except the Grand Priest can set foot upon pain of death. And now even the foxes are running over it. How can you help but cry?"

"But that is exactly why I am laughing. Two prophecies were handed down to us about Jerusalem. The prophet Micah said: 'Therefore because of you Zion shall be plowed like a field, Jerusalem shall become heaps of ruins, and the mountain of the temple like the bare hills of the forest.'

"The prophet Zachariah said: 'Thus saith the Lord; I am returned unto Zion, and will dwell in the midst of Jerusalem: and Jerusalem shall be called a city of truth; and the mountain of the Lord of hosts the holy mountain. Old men and old women will again dwell in the streets of Jerusalem, every man with his staff in his hand because of old age. The streets of the city will be full of boys and girls playing in its streets.'"

"Akiba, you have comforted us."

The Babylonian Talmud, Makoth Tract, 24b

May 1976. Léa Tsemel and her secretary Samira Khatib are coming back from a trial at the military court in Gaza. They stop the car on a hill overlooking the settlement of Yamit, north of the Sinai. Yamit is already a real city. Léa cries and Samira smiles.

"How can you laugh when you see this settlement being developed at such speed? They will never give back the occupied territories."

"Don't be silly! Let them build more and more. It will all be ours when they give back the territories."

Somewhere behind them, God whispered: "My daughters, you are both wrong."

In 1982 Israel gave the entire Sinai Peninsula back to Egypt. Before pulling out, Ariel Sharon issued an order to leave no stone standing in the twenty-odd settlements that had been built in the Sinai. It is said that God cried that day.

9
Earthquake

For six years Israel lived in the euphoria of the June 1967 victory. The National Unity government included the left. A pervasive self-righteousness was fostered by the deceit that the occupation of the territories was the "most liberal in history."

Two slogans were particularly fashionable, mentioned almost every day in political discourse and in newspaper editorials: "Our situation has never been better" and "Don't worry about anything." They silenced the questions of those rare few who attempted to see behind the fog that the generals-turned-demigods had created. As for God Himself, He seemed to have taken a seat in the government, where He generously distributed property deeds to "ancestral lands." The fact that the place was also inhabited by a number of ministers who were keen on the forbidden fruit – bacon, ham and other non-kosher delights – banned by the Torah but made readily accessible by the new prosperity, didn't seem to bother Him, at least for the time being.

But there were storm clouds on the horizon: on the Suez Canal a war of attrition had cost the lives of many soldiers; the Palestinian resistance had begun to be noticed and supported, especially in Third World countries; international opinion had started to change and Israel had to announce officially that it was ready to pull back from the territories in exchange for peace. There were also important changes sweeping the Arab world. Egypt made a rapprochement with the United States, and the oil-rich states became aware of their economic weight and their ability to influence the regional political stakes. As incredible as it might seem, this reality was sublimely ignored by Israeli public opinion, by its political leaders, by the intelligence services and the think-tanks.

The Syrian–Egyptian offensive of 6 October 1973, which the West also called the "Yom Kippur War," caught the Israelis by surprise and was likened by them, for a long time to come, to an earthquake. Even though our analysis had already concluded a year earlier that war was inevitable, Matzpen activists were also surprised. When some young people who were part of a group I was leading told me early that October afternoon that Arab countries had unleashed a war and that they wanted to put out a leaflet calling for brotherhood, I told them that it was undoubtedly an Israeli military initiative that would be all over within 48 hours. The dominant ideology is often stronger than the most convincing political analysis, and I too found it hard to believe that the Arab states had dared to attack Israeli power. Above all, I thought it impossible for Israel to suffer military defeat.

For Israelis the 1973 war was a hugely traumatizing surprise. Surprise to be suddenly at war; surprise that the Egyptians had succeeded in crossing the Suez Canal (and the Bar-Lev Line, which, like the Maginot Line in an earlier war, was supposed to be impregnable); surprise that the Syrians had reconquered the entire Golan Heights in under two days... Had they wanted to, the Syrian tanks could have advanced all the way to Haifa without encountering resistance. We know today that the panic was such that Golda Meir contemplated the use of nuclear weapons. Of course, the massive support of the US (which rearmed the decimated units by means of an airlift) allowed the Israeli army to regain superiority within a few weeks, but the great majority of reservists remained mobilized for several months.

Even before the signing of the ceasefire the press was speaking of a "debacle"[1] and of a "collapse of the system,"[2] expressing the mixture of humiliation and anger of the soldiers. It marked the abrupt end of the euphoria and of the fantasy of the omnipotence and invincibility of Israel.

Beginning in December, tens of thousands of Israeli soldiers, some discharged and others still in uniform, led by reserve captain Moti Ashkenazi (whose small fortress had been the only one to stand firm under Egyptian attacks) demonstrated every week. They were asking the government and the general staff for an explanation, they wanted the ones responsible and they would no longer accept glib assurances. The press spoke about the "protest movement," an expression that captured the serious challenge represented by the demonstrations. Unanimous in its denunciations of the "system," the movement was too disparate to provide real political solutions. After six years of dreaming, it was time to start thinking again.

I had not been called up, and the Matzpen activists who had been were usually the first to be discharged because the army was afraid of their influence on the morale of the troops. Of course, I was happy

1. In Hebrew: *ha-mehdal*, which means both a grave error of judgment and the great crisis that follows it.
2. In Hebrew: *ha-shita*, which means a philosophical–political concept rather than a body of institutions and practices.

not to have had to fight against soldiers whose struggle was legitimate in my view, so I threw myself into the only battle that mattered to me, that is, unbridled militancy.

The blindness we had warned against for years was gone and our predictions had been so unrelentingly true that we were now getting considerably more attention. Suddenly there was a mass movement in the streets demanding radical change. It was a real earthquake, and we had to adjust our activity in accordance with this new reality: the national consensus would finally crack and new opposition forces would emerge.

To calm things down, the government agreed to set up an independent national commission of inquiry, which laid the blame on the military and ignored the responsibility of the political class. The process was so effective that subsequent Israeli governments would use it whenever they needed to curb any anti-establishment uprising, for instance, after the massacres at Sabra and Shatila in 1982 or the bloody repression of the demonstrations by Arab citizens that led to 13 deaths in October 2000.

As with all earthquakes, the aftershocks continued to be felt for several years. In 1977, a first groundswell put an end to three decades of Labor dominance and brought Menachem Begin's rightists to power. A second one, brought about by the peace initiative of Egyptian President Sadat, gave rise to a massive and popular peace movement, "Peace Now!,"[3] which managed to mobilize up to 100,000 demonstrators to force the government into a total retreat from Sinai and the dismantling of the settlements there.

It was the end of consensus. Israel began to discover a sort of normality, at least as far as the clash of ideas about political and strategic choices was concerned. It would be either peace or the territories; a territorial compromise or the permanent danger of new wars, real ones, not six-day outings that cost few Israeli lives.

However, this new and healthy awareness had its limits. By putting the conflict back in its Israeli–Arab context, the war had suppressed

3. On 7 March 1977, a group of reserve officers sent an open letter to Prime Minister Begin, in which they declared: "We beg you not to launch any initiative that would risk provoking, in time, a tragedy for our people and for our country [...] A government that prefers a State of Israel within the borders of a Greater Israel, as opposed to a State of Israel that enjoys good neighbor relations would cause a serious calling into question..." On 1 April more than 10,000 people demonstrated their support for this appeal under the banner of "Peace Now!"

the Israeli–Palestinian dimension. Founded by a group of reserve officers around the slogan "Peace is worth more than Greater Israel," the "Peace Now!" movement, which defined itself as Jewish, Zionist and consensual, would serve for fifteen years as a rallying point for all those elements of Israeli society who wanted peace on the basis of a withdrawal from the occupied territories. For a long time its leaders believed a consensus existed around their basic demand while the supporters of the settlements were at best a marginal minority. Born into the second generation of the Labor elite, of Western origin and secular, they did not take seriously the outside fringe that had just brought the right to power. For them it was only a setback, a punishment for the debacle of the Yom Kippur War, a parenthesis that would soon be closed. "Peace Now!" saw itself as the "true Israel," patriotic, Jewish and Zionist, but also pacifist and moderate, and, above all, in perfect harmony with American preferences. For its founders, Washington played the same role as Moscow did for orthodox communists. But Washington, which was already projecting itself as the new and only architect of the Middle East, did not include the Palestinians in its plans. Zbigniew Brezinski, Jimmy Carter's advisor, had shouted from the rooftops: "Bye-bye, PLO!"

In this context it was imperative to show that the PLO remained an essential element. It unleashed a wave of attacks at Maalot, Kiryat Shmona, Avivim, and, later, the operation along the coastal highway that cost the lives of 35 Israeli civilians. I was on that road that day, en route to Tel Aviv, after a meeting at Nazareth. The following day I wrote in a French far left daily[4] for which I was a contributor that those who had dared to say "Bye-bye, PLO!" had made a terrible mess, and that the operation in Tel Aviv, by forcing the Israeli authorities to put all the northern districts of the city under curfew, would force all the would-be pallbearers who had predicted the end of the Palestinian national resistance to think again.

That article provoked some vicious reactions, accusing me of supporting terrorist operations against civilians. To that accusation I can only reply, even today, with platitudes that have been repeated a thousand times by so many others: that terrorism is the weapon of the weak when there are no other means of making oneself heard; that the responsibility falls on those who perpetuate the occupation and the repression, pushing the Palestinians to resist by all means at

4. *Rouge Quotidien*, no. 599, 3 March 1978.

their disposal; that the Israeli government, responsible for so many crimes and systematic violations of law, is not competent to judge the forms of struggle adopted by those whom it oppresses; that even I myself can only criticize the Palestinians if I am able to offer solutions that might achieve striking political results.

No, the end does not justify the means. But what would I have done in their place? Yes, if I were a Palestinian I would have a lot to say about the political and ethical propriety of a whole series of tactical choices made by the PLO. But, as an Israeli, I have chosen not to judge. What right have I to give lessons in morality to the refugee in Ein el-Hilwe, in Lebanon, who suffers permanent aggression from the Israeli air force and sees his homeland disappear under Jewish settlements, without any serious Israeli opposition to the occupation and state terrorism? What right I have got to demand that he find less bloody means of struggle, and what can I offer him in its place? Tell him that attacks on military targets would make his struggle less unpopular among Israeli public opinion? At that time at any rate, such a statement would have been an outright lie.

That is not to say that I am not concerned about this question, which I often discuss with Palestinians. In 1997 I interviewed Mamdouh Nofal, a close political advisor to Yasser Arafat. As operational commander of the DFLP, Mamdouh was responsible for the Maalot operation, where 24 Israeli schoolchildren, taken hostage for an exchange of prisoners, were killed in the military attack on the Palestinian commando group. He told me:

> You know, our mistake at Maalot, like other operations of that type, was primarily a political error. We did not fully grasp just what Zionism is. We did not imagine that they would rather risk the lives of their own children – their children, not ours – than free our prisoners. It was a big mistake, an unforgivable mistake that caused the death of so many children, something that we did not want under any circumstance. Basically, now I think, after the fact, and based on experience that we did not possess at the time, that purely military targets were possible and therefore preferable. I am not ashamed of what we did, but, *a posteriori*, I think we should have cut back on operations of the Maalot type.

At the time when the Palestinian organizations decided to launch an escalation of the armed struggle, we felt that our principal role was to underscore the reality of the occupation and the urgency of a solution to the Palestinian question. This was despite the breakthrough represented by the Camp David agreement and the signing of a peace treaty with Egypt. That was the setting for the establishment of the Committee for Action against Settlements at Hebron and then the Committee for Solidarity with the University of Bir Zeit. We were still rowing upstream, but political debate had become legitimate again and tens of thousands of Israelis were questioning government policy. Those who were beginning to understand the reality of the occupation and the rights of the Palestinians were more and more numerous.

The decision of the Begin–Sharon duo to invade Lebanon would put the finishing touch to the effects of the October 1973 earthquake.

Rather than experiencing the peace with Egypt as an historic accomplishment in the process of acceptance of Israel by the Arab world, the Begin government and a section of Israeli public opinion saw it as a political defeat, which had to be balanced by a new show of force. That is when the vote for the Law of Jerusalem took place: this law formalized the annexation of part of the West Bank, and then at the end of 1981, the annexation of the Golan Heights, with the attempt to impose Israeli citizenship on some 12,000 Syrian citizens who had not been expelled in 1967. At the same time a new upsurge of repression in the occupied territories left scores of deaths within three months. On Ariel Sharon's initiative – he was then minister of defense – the number of new settlements increased dramatically, with the setting up of urban colonies close to big Israeli cities. Many Israelis, not necessarily right-wingers, found in this the economic solution to their severe housing problems. But that was not enough: Sharon wanted once and for all to crush the Palestinian national movement in its Lebanese fortress. He also clearly wanted to use the occasion to bring to power the Maronite far right with which some Israeli services had very close relations.

Nonetheless, Sharon had a problem: the PLO scrupulously respected the ceasefire accord signed a year previously under pressure by the United States, after a long series of bombings on both sides at the Lebanese border. A suspiciously opportune assassination attempt (never cleared up) against the Israeli ambassador to Great Britain would finally provide the green light for an invasion that had been in preparation for a long time.

For more than six months *Matzpen* had run headlines reading "No to war in Lebanon!" and had urged the Committee for Solidarity with Bir Zeit to launch a campaign against an invasion that seemed inevitable. We were, of course, called alarmists by the "Peace Now!" activists.

On 5 June 1982, the committee was supposed to commemorate the fifteenth anniversary of the occupation with a demonstration in Tel Aviv. We expected between one and two thousand demonstrators. The day before, after the attempt against Ambassador Argov, the army had started to mobilize the reserves. Yet, to our great surprise, about 4,000 motivated and spirited demonstrators marched behind the great banner "Stop the war in Lebanon!" It was the first demonstration against the war, even before the first shots were fired. Two days later we renamed the Bir Zeit Committee the "Committee Against the War in Lebanon."

The opposition Labor Party supported what they were still daring to call operation "Peace in Galilee." Along with the party, the majority of the "pacifists" parroted all the falsehoods about PLO arsenals in South Lebanon, the shelling in northern Galilee (which, of course, had come after the violation of the ceasefire by Israeli artillery) and the limitations in time and scope of the "operation," and so on. At first glance, it seemed like National Unity all over again. But there were a few of us who surmised that this would not last and that the breach opened in 1973 would lead to a real break. We were calling for a general demonstration in Tel Aviv, even as the fighting raged in the outskirts of Beirut, way beyond the 40-kilometer limit announced by Begin and Sharon.

We had made the right call: before the city hall, more than 10,000 demonstrators, many of them soldiers in uniform, heard reserve General Matti Peled call for "making war on war" and for opening negotiations with the PLO immediately. The poet Yitzhak Laor asked the soldiers to refuse to cross the border. Many of the demonstrators were "Peace Now!" activists, horrified by what they had seen in Lebanon and by Sharon's lies. In the end, one of their leaders asked for the floor and announced that "Peace Now!" was calling for a demonstration against the war the following week at the same time and place. We had done it! We had succeeded in putting in motion a mass movement against the war, which would continue to grow. For the first time, Israel was conducting a war without a consensus. The long trek through the desert was definitely behind us.

One week later 100,000 people responded to the "Peace Now!" appeal.[5] The slogans were not as radical as those of the previous week, the demands were more moderate, but we were elated. A new

5. See Mordechai Bar-On, *Peace Now!, The Portrait of a Movement*, Tel Aviv, Hakibbutz Hameuhad, 1985, p. 56.

era, one that acknowledged the centrality of the Palestinian question, had begun. After the "Bye-bye, PLO!" of the Americans and faced with the government's desire to eliminate the Palestine national movement, the PLO had succeeded in securing its place in Israeli public opinion just as it was suffering a grave military defeat with its leadership forced to leave the Middle East.[6]

Born in 1982, our daughter Talila never experienced the isolation her brothers had known growing up. She was never ashamed of her parents nor did she try to renounce her mother. For her, opposition to the occupation would be a normal thing, and even a commonplace among her classmates and their families. Her parents' friends were no longer limited to a handful of slightly weird activists. Through her and through the different ways in which she experienced both current events and our militancy, I became aware of the profound change that had swept through Israeli society. The worst had passed; nothing would ever be the same as before. Who would have thought that, a few years later, Léa would be a regular guest on Israeli television or that *Maariv,* the country's second newspaper, would include me, in 1998, in the carefully chosen list of "Israelis who symbolize Israel's jubilee...?"

The Israeli presence in Lebanon would last a few more years; the army sustain many casualties. But the Israelis learned an important lesson: military superiority, however overwhelming, did not guarantee victory when faced with a people ready to die for their freedom, especially when the objectives of the war and its legitimacy were not supported by a strong consensus back home.

Operation "Peace in Galilee" was, according to its planners, designed to put an end to the Yom Kippur War syndrome. Instead it gave rise to a new, even more traumatizing, syndrome: the Lebanese syndrome, which continues to haunt Israeli public opinion and to challenge the high command whenever it contemplates new ventures.

6. On the war in Lebanon and its effects on Israeli society, see Zeev Schiff and Ehud Yaari, *Israel's Lebanon War*, New York, Simon & Schuster, 1985.

10
There is a border!

In 1982, my friend Marcello Wexler, then a worker, activist and member of the Matzpen leadership, was also a sergeant-major in the reserve supply corps. Called up on the eve of the invasion, he refused to rejoin his unit. Before announcing his decision to his commanding officer he wrote: "One has to set an example, because this time others will follow us. This war has nothing to do with what the men expect of it and they will quickly realize that. No, I will not be alone in prison for long."

That same day a group of reserve soldiers and officers published a petition demanding that the authorities not call on them to participate in the invasion of Lebanon:

> We, officers and soldiers in the reserves, demand that you do not send us to Lebanon, because we will not be able to obey that order. This war and the lies that surround it do not have the support of the nation! We have taken an oath to protect the existence and security of the State of Israel and we remain loyal to that oath. We therefore demand that you allow us to serve our reserve duty on Israeli and not Lebanese territory.

That first petition was signed by more than 600 reservists, headed by Lieutenant Colonel Dov Yirmiya, a hero of the 1948 war, who was to become the guiding spirit of the mobilization against the war in Lebanon.

The petition was headed with two simple words: *Yesh Gvul*, meaning "There is a border" – the Israeli–Lebanese border – that the soldiers would not cross. But it also means: "There is a limit," not everything is permissible. The principles of order, the power of the law, that guide a democratic society are not absolute, and disobedience, in certain circumstances, can become a duty. The invasion of Lebanon was not a war of self-defense, but a military operation aimed at crushing the Palestine national movement and at changing the regime in power in Lebanon. It was a political decision to do what was not only unnecessary but also something for which there was no consensus among the population. "It is not a matter of a war in which one had no choice,"[1] declared Prime Minister Begin with honesty, marking a break with the discourse and rationale of all previous wars. Given this "choice" by the government, we have the choice, therefore the duty, to say no. That was the message of the petitioners, who little by little, filled up military prison No. 6 in Atlit, near Haifa. *Yesh Gvul* – which rapidly became the name of the refuseniks' movement – also meant "Enough!," "We're fed up." This became the most popular meaning, especially after a year in the Lebanese quagmire, when refusal to serve in Lebanon extended beyond the relatively modest ranks of reservists motivated solely by moral or political considerations.

To understand the extraordinary importance of the *Yesh Gvul* phenomenon and its significance in the restructuring of Israeli political and ideological discourse, one must first grasp the significance of the army's role and function in the previous three decades. The quip "Israel is not a State that has an army, but an army that has a State" was only a mild exaggeration of Israeli reality from the 1950s to the 1970s. The army was the parent of the State, born in a war of colonial conquest experienced by the Jews as a war of national liberation. Confronted with an Arab environment that rejected its existence, the army was the protector and the guarantor of national existence. As such it was all-powerful: protected by defense secrecy and by a blank check authorized by the whole of civilian society, it could do as it pleased, without effective parliamentary checks and balances. Until the war of 1973, the army was beyond reproach or debate. To criticize was taboo. Criticism was even more improbable because the army was "us": everybody did military service (three years for boys, two for girls) and, after serving, all men remained in the reserves until they were 50 years old. They did two and sometimes three periods of several weeks of reserve duty every year, not to mention emergency mobilization exercises, training days and, of course, wars. Until the end of the 1980s, one could not leave the country without the prior authorization of the army. The army was the people in arms, although, unlike the Swiss, reservists must turn in their weapons when they are demobilized.

In those days, refusing to do one's military service amounted to excluding oneself completely from society. In some circles, not

1. "One has no choice," in Hebrew, *ein Breira*, was, until the war in Lebanon, a popular expression to justify the deeds and misdeeds of various Israeli governments and the army.

belonging to a combat unit was a disgrace. The literature of the 1980s is full of novels and stories about the tragedy of those young Israelis who, for health reasons, were unable to rejoin the glorious paratrooper corps and, feeling devalued, marginalized and excluded, sank into depression and even suicide.[2]

The victory of June 1967 had further exacerbated the cult of the army. In 1968, when I was called up to do my basic training, the idea of refusing to serve – even if only in the occupied territories – had not even occurred to me or my comrades in Matzpen. If some found justification in the texts of the communist movement about the role of the revolutionary in the army (the need to be with the people wherever they might be), for most of us, the need to justify ourselves simply did not arise. In Israel, doing your military service was like paying taxes, obeying the law or sending your kids to public school.

Nonetheless, even without being in a combat unit, one was party to the occupation. In September 1969, my company was put in charge of upholding the curfew in the town of Beit-Shahour, south of Jerusalem. It was the longest curfew imposed by the army after the firing of rockets at Jerusalem. We had come to the end of the first month of the curfew, and our orders were to make life impossible for the inhabitants until they denounced those who had fired the rockets. "You are the last ones: either they crack, or we have to give up," the colonel explained to us.

Was it the word "curfew" that reminded me of other times, or was it the admiration I felt for the resistance of the population of Beit-Shahour? In any case I told my captain that I was refusing to take part in what I considered to be an unacceptable collective punishment. Surprised, the officer put me under arrest before deciding what he was supposed to do in a situation for which he had not been prepared. My friend Yonatan solved his predicament: in the temporary camp where the army was stationed, there was neither a kitchen nor a cook. Yet the army needed to eat three times a day. Yonatan casually informed the captain that, in the entire company, there was only one man capable of organizing a good canteen for around a hundred soldiers. But as you could not order anybody to be a cook, you had to negotiate. That soldier-cook, capable of preparing tasty little dishes, was me, having learned how to run country kitchens in the boy

2. See, for example, Yehoshua Knaz's novel, *Hitganvut Yehidim*, Tel Aviv, Am Oved, 1986.

scouts. In exchange for volunteering for my new post I was relieved of guard and patrol duties. Nonetheless, the captain gave me to understand that I still was going to get it and that my time would come. In fact, it came sooner than expected, and Yonatan also played a role in this story.

My friendship with Yonatan Shem-Ur sheds some light on the Israeli army and its methods in reinforcing the tribal character of Jewish society. Yonatan was a student at the Hebrew University where, like me, he did his service in what was called the "university reserve," a privileged unit mobilized during school vacations and intended to train officers with degrees. But unlike me, a Matzpen activist, Yonatan was the secretary of the student union of Herut*, Menachem Begin's party, and his family belonged to the old aristocracy of the Israeli right.

His mother, Ora, wrote a weekly column for *Yediot Aharonot* in which she attacked the right from the right. After the Camp David agreement she organized a group of wives known as "The Mad Women of Windsor" who demonstrated regularly against Begin's treason, accusing him of having "sold the fatherland to the Egyptians." His sister, Miri, was a mediocre writer and journalist for *Maariv*. Highly educated and a lover of French literature, Yonatan and I became friends through innumerable discussions at the university cafeteria. I was not impervious to his personality. His limitless Israeli cheek allowed occasional glimpses of a sensitivity that was rare among Israelis of his generation. It was the army that would bring us closer together. Yonatan, the Sabra of the urban aristocracy, knew the rules of the game and always came up with the tricks needed to save the dignity that low-ranking officers were charged with destroying. It was thanks to him that I, new immigrant that I was, was not constantly taken advantage of. As for me, a Diaspora Jew who found nothing wrong in lowering my eyes in the face of a stupid warrant officer, I often rescued Yonatan from the trouble his arrogance led him into. During the many hours of guard duty that we always did together we spoke about philosophy and literature, and also continued the political discussions that had begun in the university. In the course of those long nights I learned a lot about the Israelis, their mentality, their fears, and what they were hiding behind their legendary self-assurance. As for Yonatan, I think those conversations were the beginning of a rethinking that continued after the war of 1973, during which he was seriously wounded. He eventually cut his ties with the ideology in which he had been raised, and during the war in Lebanon we often found ourselves on the same side at demonstrations.

Thus my friendship with Yonatan enabled me to understand the role of the army as an effective mechanism for the development of tribal solidarity, which made any break with the consensus extremely difficult. The brotherhood that develops between young people who have spent three very intense years together and who have often risked their lives for each other is strengthened by another 25 years of service in the same reserve unit. Two or three wars fought together, not to mention nights of patrols or ambushes along the border – that means a lot more than ideological differences.

If I managed to turn a deaf ear to the lures of army camaraderie, and particularly to its ability to undermine political and moral conviction, it was owing to an incident beyond my control – but probably orchestrated by Yonatan – that singled me out as a rebel even in the army.

During the summer of 1969, we were in a training session for admission to the non-commissioned officers' school at a military base near Ramallah. The few dozen Matzpen activists had just covered the walls of the big cities with the slogan "Down with the occupation!" illustrated with an arrow pointing west, symbol of the retreat from the occupied territories. The press made a big story out of the event, calling it vandalism, and we were discussing it after maneuvers. One Friday morning, all shaved and shined before going on leave, we were ready for inspection by the colonel. The waiting dragged on, and there were murmurs that something serious must have happened that threatened to deprive us of the leave we had been dreaming of for three weeks. The administration building was in turmoil, officers were running in every direction and many MP jeeps were pulling up.

In the middle of all this commotion the captain came to see me and asked me what I had been doing the night before. I told him that I had been on guard, with Yonatan of course, then had showered and slept for the three hours that I had left. He demanded to see my hands and added: "If you've done nothing, you have nothing to worry about." I had no idea what he was talking about, but I heard a roar from the colonel – a giant covered in medals (won in the battles of the Red Army against Hitler) and held together with the pins and plates that stitched his many war wounds: "If I catch the bastard I'll bump him off, I'll pull out his eyes, I'll break his b..."

I was ordered to go to the colonel's office, where I stood outside, trembling. Finally his second-in-command came in and asked me the same questions the captain had put to me, and I gave the same answers. He then asked me if it was true that I belonged to Matzpen and if I knew of other members of the group at the base. I answered that I was in fact a member and that I did not know all the others (which was not true), but that I doubted that there was another militant at the base. With the tension subsiding a bit, I asked permission to ask a question: "Can you tell me what I am suspected of having done so that I can tell you whether in fact I actually did it?" He ordered me to follow him and showed me, on the wall behind the headquarters, a huge freshly painted graffiti, the paint still wet, about two meters high: "Down with the occupation!" followed by the little arrow...

I did not feel like smiling, but I sighed with relief as I had up to that moment thought that they were going to charge me with an act of espionage or high treason! I repeated to the military police investigators that I had nothing to do with the sign, that it was in fact a Matzpen slogan but that I did not know anybody who could have done such a thing. Once again, I wasn't telling the whole truth: I had figured out that Yonatan was the author of the joke – he would have had the time while we were on duty and, anyhow, it was his way of making his feelings known to the army without necessarily agreeing with the contents of the slogan itself.

Finally, I was able to go on leave and see my wife and my son Dror, who was only four months old. But in the weeks that followed, the military police came to get me several times while we were on maneuvers, to take me to different interrogation centers around the country, to question me about my political activities, my opinions, and so on. Yonatan always denied being the author of that farce, but, for me, it was the beginning of a long divorce from the army: I didn't finish the non-commissioned officers' school, I didn't get into the officers' college, I was transferred from one unit to another for several months, and finally got myself discharged. It was not until after the war of 1973 that I rejoined the army as a reservist.

Until the end of the 1980s the Israeli army was first and foremost an army of reservists. For a long time, they performed most of the essential military activity both in wartime and peacetime, leaving the most spectacular operations, as well as logistics and supply, to the ones who were drafted, the sub and regular career officers. With reserve units remaining relatively constant, the soldiers and officers got to know each other quite well and would often see each other between reserve call-ups. The Israeli male citizen (not the women, who were rarely if ever in the reserve) is a citizen soldier who wears the uniform seven or eight weeks a year and the army is part of his daily life.

Made up of adults, the reserve units function more on the basis of self-discipline than military discipline. The soldiers know each other and will not cheat their comrades by shirking their duties. They are highly motivated to ensure their own safety and that of their family, so no coercion is required to persuade them to perform. They often volunteer to replace a buddy or lend an extra hand to the unit. Likewise, the reservist knows that he will get help if he finds himself in a tight spot. Inside the group everything is settled amicably, just as in a family. In 1987, when I was arrested and accused of "supporting terrorist organizations," then temporarily released while awaiting trial, I was, paradoxically, called to rejoin my battalion, which was going on maneuvers. All the soldiers there gave me a warm welcome and the battalion commander decided to testify on my behalf. Throughout the trial, in which I was accused of the worst betrayals, I continued, as if nothing had happened, to command occasional patrols and small strongholds in the Jordan Valley. I showed up at the trial several times in uniform, making the judges smile and driving the prosecutor into a rage. During that same period my colonel tried to send me to a training course for reserve officers.

This feeling of brotherhood is what makes the army both strong and weak.[3] When I refused to leave for Lebanon with my battalion in July 1983, I knew I was not taking a serious risk, because during the previous year almost 80 defiant reservists had already been sentenced to jail terms ranging from 21 to 35 days. It was not really much of a penalty for insubordination in time of war. But the army was conscious of the popularity of the refuseniks in the heart of their units. Even if, at the beginning of the war, most of the soldiers and officers did not share their views, at the very least, they respected them. During the two training days that preceded the battalion's departure for Lebanon, I ran a sort of permanent political forum: from the battalion commander to the cook, everybody tried to convince

3. On the role of the army in Israeli society, see Claudia Grad and Michel Warschawski, *The Role of High-ranking Officers in Israeli Society*, London, Ithaca Press and the Alternative Information Center, 1985.

me to change my mind. The arguments ranged from the respect due to decisions made by a democratically elected government to the disgrace of serving time in a military prison. But after a year of campaigning against serving in Lebanon, the activists of Yesh Gvul were well versed in these debates. The book that we had just published on the right of disobedience had already become a bestseller.[4] The only argument that might have made us relent – and many of those who disobeyed confirmed this to me – was that we were letting our comrades go off to the front while we would be safely in jail.

The last attempt by my battalion mates to make me stay with them was to tie me up and carry me by force into the vehicle that was leaving for the Lebanese border... they wanted to keep me out of jail while allowing me to obey my own conscience. But I got out of the truck a few kilometers from the border, with my rifle and equipment, and wished them a healthy and safe return. The following day, my colonel sentenced me to 28 days in prison and gave me a new mobilization order for the fall... to Lebanon.

In the military prison, the refuseniks – the popular name for the draft resisters – were treated with a great deal of respect. It should be noted that, within a year, every single unit had been affected. In July 1983, there were 18 reservists serving time, most of whom were soldiers and officers who refused to return to the Lebanese quagmire after having already been there. Most of them did not belong to the radical left, far from it: some were kibbutzniks from "Peace Now!," others were ordinary citizens disgusted by what they had seen or what they had had to do. Older than the other prisoners – mostly draftees sentenced for minor disciplinary infractions – and than the military police who were guarding us, we enjoyed a great deal of autonomy and received many informal visits. Our section was surrounded by a simple barbed wire enclosure, which did not stop our encounters with our relatives, or prevent the entry of an impressive quantity of contraband, beer and cartons of cigarettes, which we hid in holes in the ground underneath our tents! My son Nissan, who was spending his school vacation about two kilometers from the prison and came to see us almost every day, specialized in tossing over beer cans until, one day, one of them fell on a guard's head. In exchange for a few packs of cigarettes the guard ignored what he had seen.

4. *The Limits of Obedience*, ed. Yishai and Dina Menuchin, Tel Aviv, Yesh Gvul Publications, 1985.

Among the more official visitors I must mention my captain. On leave from Lebanon, he felt obliged to come and see how I was doing and to tell me that there had been no casualties in our battalion, an increasingly rare exception.

We prisoners passed the time discussing politics (among ourselves but also with the young draftees, both guards and prisoners), and we felt that our main task was to set an example so that others would refuse to cross the Lebanese border. Every case of insubordination was widely covered in the media, and the popularity of the Yesh Gvul movement and that of the disobedient soldiers grew as the army got bogged down and the war became unpopular.[5] I myself was ordered to go to Lebanon three times, and three times I refused to cross the border. All in all, I was jailed for 63 days, not a lot of time considering the significance.

Ever since the war in Lebanon, the senior military staff had been aware that the time when soldiers obeyed without discussion was definitely past. For every military operation that does not give rise to consensus there will be insubordination. That is exactly what happened less than three years after the end of the Lebanese adventure when reservists were called up to try to repress the Intifada, the Palestinian uprising in the occupied territories. Between 1988 and 1990 there were about a thousand refuseniks, but fewer than a hundred were sentenced to prison terms, because the army had learned its lessons from the Lebanese experience, the most important one being not to give too much publicity to insubordination. That is why, as also happened with many of my comrades, instead of bringing me before a military court, my commander had me sent only to what he called my "kosher zone."

But where was the border? It was an issue that every soldier had to decide for himself. Unlike Lebanon, where the border of obedience was the one marked by the armistice lines of 1949, the occupied territories posed more problems. Some refused to enter the occupied territories in uniform, others refused to obey certain orders, such as firing on demonstrators or accompanying agents of the security services on their night-time raids. Some soldiers simply refused to carry a truncheon, that oh so significant addition to the ordinary equipment of a soldier in regular service. For us they were all part of Yesh Gvul, each one creating his own border in his soul and conscience.

5. See Sarah Helman, "Militarism and the Construction of Community," *Journal of Political and Military Sociology*, no. 25, Winter 1997, pp. 305–32.

As for myself, I had decided to stick to the line I had followed since joining a reserve unit, of refusing to serve inside the occupied territories, except on the border. Since my regiment was generally posted in the Jordan Valley this refusal did not have much practical significance. During the entire Intifada I served my reserve call-ups on the Jordanian border, a zone for which I became without a doubt one of the best specialists in the Israeli armed forces. There was not a single patrol route, strongpoint or bunker that I was not familiar with, from the Bissan Valley to the Dead Sea. And from the observation post where I was frequently stationed, about 100 meters from the River Jordan, I liked to look over to the other side, towards Jordan, and dream about what the region might be like if there were no wars or conflicts...

11
Together

The war in Lebanon resulted in two upheavals: in Israel, it marked the end of the national consensus and the emergence of a mass extra-parliamentary movement, and on the Palestinian side, the defeat of the PLO in Lebanon had created a political void in the occupied territories that favored the emergence of a new generation of local leaders and new forms of struggle. Each of these political developments would have important consequences for the other society, to the extent that they were aware of it.

The fact that hundreds of thousands of Israelis had rallied against the war in Lebanon and that tens of thousands of them had begun to understand that the "liberal occupation" was only a deceit, could not fail to have an impact on the Palestinian national movement. A potential political ally existed in Israel, and it was necessary to find the ways to link it to Palestinian objectives. At the same time, the political upheavals in the West Bank and Gaza Strip and the beginnings of a new approach towards the Israeli population would sooner or later affect the perceptions and positions of the Israeli peace movement.

Two new imperatives began to take shape: to keep each society informed about developments on the other side, and to show that a common perspective could be fashioned without in any way compromising the integrity of either side.

The establishment of the Alternative Information Center corresponded to the first imperative, the formation of the Committee Against the Iron Fist to the second. Why the "Iron Fist"? Because Yitzhak Rabin, defense minister in the National Unity government of 1984, had declared that he would use an iron fist to smash the resistance in the West Bank and in the Gaza Strip. Rabin felt he had free rein for two reasons: the last Israeli troops had been pulled back from Lebanon, and the peace movement, having achieved its main goal – the withdrawal from Lebanon – had mostly subsided. And Labor was back in power.

The Committee Against the Iron Fist was not merely a new organization fighting against the occupation. We wanted to unite Palestinians and Israelis in protest actions that would allow a joint struggle, a goal that was by no means self-evident. For the Palestinians, fighting against the occupation meant inevitable confrontation with Israeli forces. The act of addressing Israeli public opinion was in itself a significant turn, motivated by awareness of the fissure in 'National Unity.' The Palestinians had been pleasantly surprised by the hundreds of thousands of Israeli demonstrators against the massacres in Sabra and Shatila in September 1982, but those who understood that it was necessary to incorporate this new development into Palestinian strategy were few indeed. Feisal Husseini was one of those few.

Son of Abdelkader el-Husseini, a legendary hero of 1948, Feisal had been one of the first Fatah activists in the occupied territories. A member of one of the oldest and most prestigious Arab families of Jerusalem, he was head of a whole series of semi-legal organizations, which he led from his offices at the Arab Studies Society (SAS). The SAS was in the heart of what the police called Jerusalem's "Fatah-land,"[1] a block of buildings located between the Ministry of Justice and the American Colony Hotel. A program of feverish political activity was carried on in that limited space by organizations that were more or less tolerated by the authorities: women's movements, trade union organizations, Islamic groups, the editorial offices of several newspapers and the famous Hakawati Theater, directed by François Gaspar (Abou Salem). Léa's office had been there since 1984.

As its name suggests, the SAS was a study center, where university scholars and activists, Palestinian and foreign, conducted research on Palestine, its history and geography. But it was a lot more than an academic institution: it was the general headquarters of the Palestine national movement in the occupied territories, where hundreds of activists met to plan their activities or people came to seek redress for the hassles of the occupation. I remember countless meetings, before and after the formation of the Committee Against the Iron Fist, in a house the whole world would come to know as "Orient House," where Feisal Husseini, acting as official spokesperson for the Palestinians of Jerusalem, would receive foreign diplomats.

In 1988, in the course of my trial, the attorney-general accused me of having been the ... initiator of the Intifada! It implied granting me powers I obviously did not possess. It was also a typical colonial preconception: for the public prosecutor, only a Jew could have taken the initiative for a movement that had upset an occupation that had

1. A region of Southern Lebanon, which during the 1970s was under the control of the Palestinian resistance.

been in place for twenty years. But there was a tiny element of truth in that otherwise ridiculous accusation: the Committee Against the Iron Fist, which I led alongside Feisal Husseini, and in which there were activists from different Palestinian organizations and a couple of dozen anti-Zionists Jews, had developed a political strategy and forms of struggle that less than four years later would characterize the originality of the Intifada: public activities, non-violent demonstrations, the use (through Israeli militant intermediaries) of Israeli legal means in Jerusalem to organize demonstrations and public initiatives, regular press conferences and a systematic program of documentation and information in the form of reports and communiqués. This new strategy was the result of the situation created by the war in Lebanon, the emergence of a new generation of Palestinian cadres from the interior, the appearance of semi-public mass organizations, cracks in the Israeli consensus, and the need to find a new balance between armed struggle and popular mobilization.

The Palestinian activists of the committee all became known and recognized leaders of the Intifada. The committee did not limit itself to preparing analyses and strategies. It was above all an action group: daily demonstrations at Jerusalem's Damascus Gate, gatherings in front of the Moskobiyé, exhibitions about the prison situation, press conferences where, for the first time, substantial reports were presented on different aspects of the repression in the occupied territories, and, in 1987, the first big Israeli–Palestinian demonstration along the entire length of the green line in Jerusalem. Israeli–Palestinian is an exaggeration: there were in fact about thirty Israelis there to accompany – and protect simply by their presence – more than a thousand Palestinians, who did not yet understand that a demonstration without high pressure water jets and tear gas could be useful. Without Feisal's presence there is no doubt that this first demonstration would have ended, like all previous demonstrations, with confrontations, injuries and arrests. Feisal thought it was important to convince the population that it could protest and express itself without being shot at or imprisoned. This alone made the participation of Jews, however modest, so important. In his eyes it was equally important to address the Israeli population in its own language while mindful of its concerns and preconceptions.

Four years of intense political activity side by side with Feisal Husseini allowed me to get to know him very well. Without really being friends, we were close. There was great trust between us, even after his official duties had diminished our relations. An aristocrat by birth and an uncontested national leader, Abu el-Abed (the father of Abed, as the Arabs called him) was and continued to be a militant until his premature death. A few weeks before his death in June 2001, I met him at a demonstration outside a house that was being demolished near Jerusalem. He spoke to me with nostalgia of the "good old days" before he became a spokesperson for the Palestinian Authority to foreign diplomats and the Israeli "caviar left." I can attest that he did not feel at ease in his new role. Abu el-Abed was not one of those leaders who were happy sending others off to fight for the cause. Between 1984 and 1987 one could see him every week at the Damascus Gate or outside the prison, a poster in hand like a regular activist. He was often stopped for an identity check. It was not common in those days, and it's impossible nowadays.

Even after becoming Yasser Arafat's minister of affairs for Jerusalem, Feisal Husseini rarely missed a demonstration, small or large, the only difference being the presence, after the early 1990s, of his loyal bodyguards. The last time we confronted the Israeli army together was the day after Benjamin Netanyahu's decision to build the Har Homa settlement on the Abu Ghneim hill, to the south of Jerusalem. As we were trying to get past the cordon of soldiers, with the help of his efficient bodyguards, I caught a happy wink from him, as if the "good old days" were back...

Feisal Husseini was the Palestinian leader who, more than any other, believed in and worked for a real reconciliation. There are many Palestinian leaders who support peace and coexistence with Israel; the majority among them are ready to meet with Israelis, to enter into dialogue and to cooperate with them. Some of them will even tell you that several of their best friends are Israelis. But I know only a few Palestinians who wholeheartedly embraced a vision of coexistence and reconciliation. Not as a lesser evil or for purely pragmatic reasons, or because it was good for the Palestinian public image, but because it was fair and right in and of itself. Feisal Husseini was one of them. In 1984 there was no practical need to organize, with a handful of Israeli radicals who represented only themselves, the Committee Against the Iron Fist. Our committee had no prospect of changing Israeli or Palestinian public opinion, in the short or medium term, or of creating a new public image for the Palestine national movement. But for Abu el-Abed, it was a matter of giving concrete and immediate expression to his long-term vision. It was a struggle waged in the present, which would help to develop in people's minds the idea of a common future for the two peoples living on this land.

Although Feisal Husseini was one of the pioneers of meetings with Zionists, starting from the obvious principle that it was imperative to reach out to the center of Israeli society, he had a rare ability to win the trust of Israelis (which his interlocutors too often confused with friendship), and he was always able to distinguish between allies, partners and moderate enemies, between cooperation, dialogue or semi-negotiations, and between militancy based on a common political perspective and diplomacy. Abu el-Abed could make these distinctions because he had a thorough knowledge of Israeli society and also a very clear vision of what coexistence could mean. He foresaw a coexistence where there would no longer be two sides, but only one, composed of men and women of different national, ethnic and cultural origins. It was no accident that he coined the slogan "Our Jerusalem." [2] Jerusalem did not belong to the Israelis or to the Palestinians, the Christians, the Muslims or the Jews. The city belonged to all of us, a unified bi-national collective.

Abu el-Abed never hesitated to use his Israeli partners as mediators or as counselors, nor to undertake initiatives that would be more likely to succeed if they were led by Israelis rather than by Palestinians. He did it because he knew that he could trust them. As partners, they never felt exploited or manipulated.

It was that immense faith in a common future that pushed him to devote body and soul to the Oslo peace process, even though it was no secret that he was skeptical about the outcome, and his differences with Yasser Arafat were known, especially on the question of Jerusalem. But he was also aware that failure risked closing forever what the American diplomats called the "window of opportunity" and provoking a "Balkanization" of the Israeli–Palestinian conflict. His optimism was shattered, however, after the fiasco of Camp David in July 2000 when a great number of the peace movement activists rallied around the new consensus.

While we were organizing the Committee Against the Iron Fist with Feisal Husseini, Sari Nusseibé, Jane and Samir Abu Shakra, Mahmoud

2. In a speech made in 1996 during a demonstration organized by Gush Shalom, Feisal Husseini had spoken of the day when Jerusalem would no longer be claimed exclusively as an Israeli, or Palestinian or Christian or Muslim city, but would be "Our Jerusalem, for us." It became the title of an international petition on Jerusalem, capital of two sovereign states.

Jedda and Jibril Rajoub, Matzpen and some activists of the Palestinian left decided to create the Alternative Information Center (AIC). The stated objective of the AIC was to make available to the communities on both sides of the border information that was not otherwise readily available to them. The Palestinians knew little about the Israeli political, social and cultural scene, and the Israelis ignored everything that was going on in the occupied territories. The Palestinian press, which often wrote about Israeli political life, did not then always know how to distinguish between the essential and the anecdotal. It gave the same importance to a demonstration of "Peace Now!" against the settlements as it did to a gathering of a few dozen anti-Zionists. On the other hand, in the peace movement, when the PLO became known and indeed recognized, no one knew what was going on five minutes away from West Jerusalem or ten minutes from Tel Aviv, or if indeed anything important was happening.

So our first objective was to get information across: to write in Arabic about Israel and in Hebrew about the Palestinian reality. To do it we needed a mixed group, which, on the basis of solid political trust, could summarize information and circulate what seemed most appropriate for the two communities, as well as for the outside world. Since the Israeli media had long ago lost interest in what was happening in the occupied territories, our news quickly filled a void. There were daily news bulletins as well as more substantial and analytical weekly reports on the use of torture, the systematic demolition of houses and administrative detentions as well as the emergence of ethnic and social divisions in Israel. Thanks to the network of contacts we had in the West Bank and in the Gaza Strip, as well as among lawyers, our information would rapidly prove to be valuable and original.

The second objective of the AIC was to make widely known the activities and political positions of new Palestinian resistance organizations as well as the Israeli left and peace movement. We felt, before many others did, that communication required tools that were separate from the activists' organizations and that they needed a degree of professionalism. Without ever claiming an "objective" neutrality, we worked hard to serve as spokespersons for all the participants in the struggle against the occupation, racism or exploitation.

But important as these first two objectives were, the real *raison d'être* of the AIC was the desire to work for a common strategic vision, capable in due course of mobilizing Palestinians and Israelis in the same struggle for the future. That is what made our experience so special: to develop a common strategy, we needed to put together a team of men and women belonging to both communities, sharing the same ideological presuppositions and the same values. It was a gamble that had never been tried and the odds were very long. The experience of joint struggle during the course of the previous fifteen years had created a capital of trust, and a broad political agreement had been achieved through many political discussions; but as for achieving real unity, it was a big leap indeed! In 1984 the project seemed totally utopian. Fifteen years later, when, during a hike in the desert of Judea, three colleagues of the Alternative Information Center – a Palestinian former political prisoner, an Israeli ex-kibbutznik, and a religious Jew from New York – perished accidentally, the whole of Israeli public opinion was moved by this completely new reality. For several weeks the media devoted numerous articles and commentary to the AIC and to our having chosen to create a new arena of struggle, but also of life that transcended community boundaries.

> It was not just a curiosity about the unaccustomed that fascinated the local media and made thousands of Israelis and Palestinians dream, but what they sensed as the promise of another reality infinitely more reassuring than the highest wall or the most powerful ghetto.[3]

Fifteen years later I can say that our gamble paid off, but not without problems: in the context of the cooperation between the occupiers and the occupied, between people of very different cultures, who often had to use a third language to communicate, we could not avoid misunderstandings, tensions and even crises.

Who were those men and women who gambled on creating a common political space on the border? First of all, activists: Although some of them had experience as journalists, most were not professionals. As for the Palestinians, almost all of them had served time in prison, many for years at a stretch. One day I started to calculate the total years spent in jail by the members of the staff and executive board of the AIC. I stopped counting when I got to a hundred. They were known and respected leaders in their community. The younger ones, who had joined the AIC in the early 1990s, were

3. Simone Bitton, "Chronique," *Revue d'études palestiniennes,* new series, no. 9, Spring 1999.

all graduates of the famous Ansar III[4] prison camp in the Negev desert. Most of them belonged to Palestinian organizations on the left, although they often defended unorthodox views in their own groups.

At the outset, the Israelis were Matzpen activists, but little by little they were joined by activists from feminist and student organizations, social movements and the radical wing of the peace camp. The executive board included several well-known intellectuals ranging from the old communists to 'New Historians.'

What enabled this community of several dozen people to work together was above all that they shared the same values. They believed, in spite of everything, in internationalism, and for them, in the Israeli–Palestinian context, this internationalism meant the uncompromising struggle for Palestinian national liberation. To retain credibility in the eyes of Palestinian activists, that support could not simply be a matter of making oral statements or expressing one's position in written documents. It required concrete actions that often led to confrontations with the state, its police and its courts. Based on this political trust, one then had to learn how to behave in ways that demonstrated real respect, something that was neither easy nor self-evident. Can you imagine what was going on in the mind of Zyad, a refugee of Deheisheh, when he heard Tikva, a former Palmach* fighter, tell a journalist how, in 1948, her unit captured Zakarya, the village home of Zyad's parents? Or Elias, recently freed after several years in prison, when he saw Reuben, in reservist's uniform, popping into the office during a short leave? Or what Sergio was thinking, having just lost his childhood kibbutznik buddy in South Lebanon, when he heard Abir trying to justify Hezbollah?

When one is on the border, it is necessary to have the courage to hear the other as he really is, to understand him without paternalistic condescension, and at the same time to learn how to change one's ideas and behavior. For example, when one is an Israeli and accustomed to speaking first and loudest, it is knowing how to make the effort to wait for the Palestinian to take the floor, and how to decipher his restraint or silence, which might be politely concealing real anger or profound disagreement.

4. Name of the prison camp at Ktsiot in the Negev desert where, during the first Intifada, the Israeli army had interned up to 12,000 persons, most of them without trial.

Crises did occur. Although they never divided the AIC between Jews and Arabs, cultural differences and the sensibilities produced by the dominator/dominated relationship did appear. When we were discussing the professionalism of the AIC, and the need for greater objectivity in order to strengthen our credibility with the media, several Palestinian members thought this position reflected a certain weakening of the militant spirit of the Jews. The desire by some to open the pages of our Hebrew publications to members of the Zionist left also provoked a difficult debate. Even more difficult was the argument over salaries. We had established a salary equivalent to that earned by a skilled worker, as was the custom in the communist left, and of course, the same salary for all. But since the salary of a trained worker in Israel was higher than the salary of an executive director of a ministry in the Palestine Authority, what to do? Sacrifice the principle of equality or, in an association that wanted to be close to the people and their problems, pay salaries that seemed scandalously high in the eyes of the Palestinian population?

To be in a working collective on the border, to manage not only ideas or common actions, but a living association with its day-to-day difficulties, its differences, its problems of salaries and working conditions, not to mention crises of internal relationships, was, in a way, to experience the beginnings of a real coexistence.[5] We never tried to be a microcosm of the utopia that we dreamed about. At best, we were attempting to break down the walls of separation, a promise of another possibility.

Operating right at the limits of legality, the Center put its small technical infrastructure at the disposal of a new network of Palestinian people's organizations, printing leaflets, designing brochures and laying out the Palestinian newspapers *al Mara* ("The Woman"), *al Taqadum* ("Progress"), and *Gesher* ("The Bridge"), the first journal published in Hebrew by a Palestinian organization. This aspect of the AIC's activity actually took place at the geographic boundary line between East and West Jerusalem. It was the main meeting place between Palestinian and Israeli activists who were looking for technical assistance at a reasonable price or, when necessary, free of charge.

The services rendered were not only technical: after the authorities decided in 1986 to close down the Palestinian newspaper *al Mithaq,*

5. In this regard, see Isabelle Avran, *Israel–Palestine: les inventeurs de paix*, Paris, Éditions de l'Atelier, 2001, pp.153–7.

the AIC put its own publications at the disposal of the banned newspaper's staff. Beyond this demonstration of support, the AIC facilitated links between Palestinian organizations and the solidarity movement, which, after 1986, began to show new signs of life. These links took the form of an increased cooperation on the ground, in particular solidarity with the Deheisheh refugee camp, some of whose residents were on the board of directors of the AIC or were active in its network.

By January 1987, three years after its creation, the Alternative Information Center had managed to carve out a small niche in the political arena and among the media. Some dramatic successes, such as the coverage of the 1985 prisoners' exchange, the publication of the first report on torture (which showed that, after having temporarily disappeared, it then reappeared with the return of a Labor government!) and the campaign for Abu Ali Shahin, had given the AIC visibility and credibility both as a source of information and as an effective tool to promote solidarity, and made it the main facilitator of interaction on the border between the two communities. It was only a matter of time before the authorities would try to set things straight.

12
No man's land

I had just taken a group of British visitors on a tour through Yad Vashem, the museum and documentation center of the Nazi Judeocide. Before heading to the nursery school to pick up Talila I stopped by the AIC office to pick up some papers. I had barely entered when a bunch of strangers burst into the apartment that served as our office. At first I thought that it was a gang of the Kach fascist group, who, a few weeks earlier, had painted racist slogans and death threats on the door. I was trying to pick up the phone to warn some friends who worked in the Communist Party office in the same building when one of the invaders stopped me. I was momentarily reassured when I recognized Commissioner Schneitcher, chief of the investigation department of the Jerusalem police. They were not fascists, just the police – accompanied by agents of the notorious Shin Beth, the general security service.

For an hour they searched the office from top to bottom, seizing every single document they laid their hands on. Since paper was the main "instrument" of the AIC, and the written word virtually an obsession among all leftist activists on the planet, they carried off more than forty boxes, two computers, a printer, a fax machine and a mimeo. All of this took place without a word spoken, except to order us to sit at our respective desks and be quiet. Nonetheless I asked for permission to warn my sister, so that she could pick up Talila from the nursery school, and the man who seemed to be in charge agreed. Thus, Léa's secretary, Fathyié, found out from my sister what was happening to me. Accustomed to dealing with such situations, she alerted my companion.

With the search completed, Schneitcher took charge of the operation and read me an official document. This stated that in accordance with the 1950 Anti-Terrorism law,[1] the commissioner general of the police

1. The Anti-Terrorism Act, inspired by similar legislation from the British Empire, was enacted in 1950 in view of the risk that extreme right Zionist organizations might undertake a policy of destabilization against the young Jewish State. It complemented the Emergency Regulations of 1945, imposed by the British mandate authorities in Palestine – and still in effect – which were described at the time by the man who would become the Minister of

had decided to close the Alternative Information Center because of "links and services rendered to a terrorist organization: the Popular Front – George Habache (sic)." He added that I was being arrested for questioning and asked me if I had anything to say. Somewhat ironically, I told him that I knew of no organization of that name (the name of the organization led by Dr George Habash was the Popular Front for the Liberation of Palestine), that at any rate we had no ties to that organization or to any other terrorist organization. I was then taken off to the Moskobiyé with the other six members of the staff. As we left the Center, television crews and an impressive number of journalists were standing around, invited by the police who – I would later find out – had told them of "a big scoop."

In his autobiography, Carmi Guilon, the former boss of the Shin Beth who was responsible for this "big scoop," explains:

> When I joined the Shin Beth unit whose mandate was to deal with the extreme right and the far left, I found a rather indifferent attitude regarding the far left. They were regarded as salon communists against whom it was not worth wasting important resources. Personally, I thought it was urgent to define clear boundary lines and to stand by them. They had to be regarded as clandestine networks and I decided to provide us with the means [...].
>
> The members of the staff of the Alternative Information Center had official press cards, a print shop, and they published a monthly review. At first sight their activity was legal, but they were within our sights because of their extremist political positions. That's when we discovered the intensity of their collaboration with terrorist organizations, in particular with the Popular Front of George Habash, who is until this day the leader of the opposition to the Oslo accords. That's why Shin Beth must keep an eye on fringe groups. As long as their action is legal, Shin Beth does not want to nor does it have the authority to intervene. But when we find that they are systematically carrying out illegal and harmful activity, we decide to put a stop to their activity [...].
>
> The Alternative Information Center was closed in February 1987 because it was rendering services to the Popular Front

Justice in the 1970s, Yaakov Shimshon Shapira, as "worse than Nazi laws." The Anti-Terrorism Act and the 1945 Emergency Regulations required a suspect to prove his own innocence.

> and because it was being financed by it. "Mikado" was arrested, tried, and sentenced to three years in prison. "Mikado" was my personal target. In the Shin Beth one learns not to have any qualms regarding an objective: it's not professional and does not serve the cause. I got to know "Mikado" through systematic intelligence work and it is no exaggeration to say that I was able to penetrate to the depths of his soul before we decided to arrest him.[2]

Léa rushed over to the jail after receiving the phone call, persuading the duty officer to let us exchange a few words by convincing him that my arrest was for some harmless offense. We knew that this time it was a lot more serious, and we decided on a strategy. I was then taken to the sinister cell number 20, which in fact was a passage to a large warehouse completely cut off from the rest of the building. In a brilliant article, which stirred up considerable attention at the time, the lawyer Avigdor Feldman baptized this place "the Kingdom of Shin Beth." It was not run by the police or by the rules of the prison and the jails, but by Shin Beth agents and their despotic whims. It was there that, until 1999, torture was practiced daily and legally. Several dozen Palestinians had lost their lives there since the beginning of the occupation.

This warehouse 'kingdom' was divided into tiny individual cells, each no larger than four to five square meters, and interrogation rooms. I had the rare privilege of being moved around without the infamous stinking sack that was tied over the heads and faces of Arab prisoners, often for days at a time, so I was able to see other prisoners, heads covered with the sack and tied in various ways to a pipe that ran the length of the building.

I was not tortured, and for the most part my interrogators were polite. I was allowed to see my lawyer regularly, I had cigarettes, toiletries and even sheets. Nevertheless, the 15 days I spent in cell number 20 were the hardest days of my life. On two occasions, I almost thought I was losing my mind. If I hadn't had the extraordinary privilege of frequently seeing Léa, who kept on telling me that they do not torture Jews, that everyone knew I had been arrested, and that by law they must take me to court by some predetermined date, that this imprisonment could not go on indefinitely – in short, if I had not been dragged back to reason every two or three days by

2. Carmi Guilon, *Shin Beth between the schisms*, Tel Aviv, Yediot Aharonot Publishers, 2000, pp. 65–6.

my lawyer wife – I think that I might have confessed to anything. Anything to put an end to those long days of solitude in a dismal cell where I became acquainted with the most degrading levels of filth and squalor, with rats running in all directions, a soaking wet mattress, a faucet that I used to brush my teeth and wash that was only 20 centimeters off the ground. The worst was the total lack of anything to do, until my brother Daniel, who was part of my legal team, had the idea of asking for a Bible, the only book they could not deny me. Twenty years had gone by since I had opened the Book of Books and I now savored every page…

At the very first interrogation I stated that, as director, I was solely responsible for whatever was going on at the AIC. As a result, the other members of the staff were freed within 48 hours, but not before one of them – a young pregnant woman, who during the first night had to be rushed to the hospital – had signed a statement that seriously threatened to incriminate all of us. Interrogations could last for hours or just a few minutes. Sometimes there were two or three sessions a day, then two or three days passed without any questioning. That's when one increasingly felt the need, well known to those who have undergone interrogations, to see and speak to another human being. I also had confrontations with some people with whom I was suspected of being in contact. With the arrest, towards the end of the interrogation phase, of a close friend who had nothing to do with the AIC, the work of Shin Beth was over.

Contrary to their public image, Shin Beth agents are not merely brutes who only know how to beat people up. Although most of them have practiced torture – with the explicit authorization not only of governments of the right and the left, but of the Supreme Court as well, at least until 1999 – they are often educated men who think of themselves as left-wingers. After their retirement, three of their chiefs, Yaakov Péri, Yossi Genossar[3] and Carmi Guilon,[4] all met up again in

3. Yossi Genossar was accused of having used torture against Izzat Nafso, a Circassian officer of the Israeli army, of secretly contacting the enemy, and of having deliberately prevented a national commission of inquiry into the torture practices of the Shin Beth from finding out the truth. He nonetheless served as intermediary between Yitzhak Rabin and Yasser Arafat during the many crises that befell Israeli–Palestinian negotiations.
4. After having been responsible for the "non-Arab department" and therefore in charge of the closing down of the AIC, Carmi Guilon became head of the Shin Beth in 1995. His recent defense of the practice of torture provoked a crisis between Israel and Denmark, to which he had just been named ambassador.

the left wing of the Labor Party where they backed rather moderate policies. Although at first I was in the hands of a brute who threatened and insulted me, he was quickly replaced by a much more subtle and polite pair. Both used the language of the left and arguments that made it clear each had had a solid university education.

The interrogations began to resemble living room conversations, erudite and relaxed. It was undoubtedly a trap, and it required a good deal of effort on my part not to forget that we were on different sides of the fence and that there was a real war going on between us. Was it their method of choice or was it simply an expression of the dubious tribalism that characterizes our society? Maybe it was a bit of both. It seemed that my interrogators were doing everything to establish a "we," a common identity that I needed to distance myself from at any price. One day, the interrogator who called himself Alon received a phone call in the middle of a session. I realized that he was talking with his daughter, who, I had learned from a previous conversation, was a high school student. After a few minutes he asked me if I could lend a hand. She needed to write a report on parliamentary commissions and she needed some documentation. He knew that I could help and, in fact, I told him where, at the back of our office, there was a documentation center that distributed pamphlets of civic interest, where he could find one on the workings of Parliament. He just about handed me the phone so that I could tell his daughter how to write her paper! Another time he told me that he was going to be hiking in the Golan for the weekend with his friends, and he asked me what routes I might suggest in that region where I so much liked to walk. He even promised, with heavy irony, that after my release from prison we could go for hikes together, in ten or twelve years' time!

For those 15 days I was obsessed with re-establishing, at any cost, a border between them and me. It was not an easy task. In the total isolation of cell 20, who would not have looked forward to a friendly rapport with men who appeared to want to do their utmost to establish some kind of familiar contact? Who would not be distracted by rambling discussions on the Leninist theory of the right to self-determination or the advantages and disadvantages of the Freinet method in the schools that each of our daughters attended? At the same time I was anxious to avoid any unnecessary antagonism and concerned about keeping my dignity and a sense of equality with my interrogators despite the situation and my physical appearance, which was really disgusting. I was trying to remain within the boundaries of the community and its legitimacy without falling into the trap of the tribal mirage. I had never been in a position that required so much mental and intellectual tension.

It went something like this:

> You see, Mikado, you have crossed the line. You've been active on the far left for twenty years, defending radical and anti-Zionist positions, but aside from a little harassment, you have never been bothered. Do you agree with me?
>
> Yes, more or less...
>
> And you know why? Because Israel is a democracy, and in this democracy, our role is to defend democracy, (including) for the likes of you and your friends...
>
> ...
>
> But over there (pointing to what I thought was East although the interrogation cells had no windows), there is no democracy, there is occupation. And we have a problem with people like you: where are you? Here, protected by democracy, or on the other side? On the one hand, you're one of us, active in the community, a soldier respected by his superiors, or member of the parents' committee of your daughter's school, but on the other hand, you bring with you Ali [a Palestinian colleague who had spent 17 years in prison] and Hamdi [a leader of the Deheisheh refugee camp], and they are not protected by democracy. So you have to choose: to be on this side of the border and be protected by democracy, or be with them and be treated the way we treat them.
>
> But as long as we're acting within the law...
>
> Don't be an idiot; you know very well that over there there is neither law nor democracy. It's your choice... I like black and white, not gray...
>
> And if we choose to be together?
>
> No man's land does not exist for us. Do you understand me? It's very important.
>
> Let me think about it...
>
> Think as much as you like, we've got all the time in the world.

After that I was taken back to my nauseating cell. We had reached the heart of the problem. After a week of questions about supposed meetings with Palestinian leaders in Cyprus, and other mostly false allegations, my two interrogators had changed the thrust of the discussion. They wanted us to give up our joint activities with Palestinians and to help them re-establish a clear border between "them" and "us." The information that we published and the solidarity actions we organized did not bother them as much as the fact that we had created a common space, a breach in the wall, which must, at all costs, separate Israeli democracy from the arbitrary nature of the military occupation.

If they insisted on my giving them the names of the Palestinians with whom we were cooperating, of leaders of the student movement, of trade unionists, of activists in women's organizations, and so on, it was not because they needed the information but because they wanted to discredit us in the eyes of the Palestinians. They told me: "Why do you insist on covering up for them, since they are happy to talk and have no scruples about giving you up…" My lawyers had told me that they had arrested several Palestinian activists close to the AIC, but these were people I knew and trusted.

At any rate, I was not a rat. Refusing to name names was a matter of principle, deeply anchored in my political tradition, in the memories of the resistance, and more so, in the values my parents had taught me. Jewish tradition views the informer as the worst of criminals, and during the Middle Ages, the rabbis had authorized the killing of informers without trial. In Strasbourg I had been shown a spot, along the banks of the Ill, where they used to drown them…

Two years later, at my trial, I persisted in refusing to name names, which resulted in an additional charge of contempt. But I had told the court of my intention of pleading my case based on the texts of the Jewish tradition, and faced with the impressive pile of rabbinical books and Talmudic exegeses that I had brought, the Chief Judge Tal, himself an erudite and practicing Jew, decided to overlook the matter, adding that it might well cost me when it came time for the verdict. We shall see how I would pay for this attachment to Jewish tradition and the memory of Jean Moulin.

Two days after having raised this question of the border, Alon put the matter back on the table.

Well, have you thought about it?

Yes. I fully understand what you explained to me, but I feel like you've brought it up too late. The no man's land has become a reality, with or without the AIC. You will not be able to close the breach that has been opened in the border between the two communities.

There was a bit of bravado in my response, but the news that was reaching me through my lawyers – about solidarity with the AIC, the daily demonstrations in front of the Moskobiyé, the petitions, the criticisms expressed by Labor deputies and well-known intellectuals against the closing of the Center and my arrest, as well as the dozens of people who came to express their support every time I was brought before the court, dirty and chained, to prolong my custody by the police – all of that gave me new confidence and comforted me with the sense of a change in attitude by a part of the Israeli left towards the Palestinians, and those who cooperated with them.

After 15 days, the judge refused to extend my time in police custody and my interrogators allowed me, for the first time, to shower and shave because I was going to appear before the district court where a formal indictment would be made along with a motion that I be detained until the end of the trial. It was in the detention cell of this court that I was visited by District Judge Dov Eitan, whom I knew by reputation. He was no longer a judge, but simply a lawyer, having been forced to abandon a promising career for having signed a Yesh Gvul petition while he was a lieutenant colonel in the reserve. Known for his great intelligence and erudition, he was the only judge who refused to believe the police when they denied the use of torture, and he had acknowledged the bona fides of the testimony of a seriously wounded Palestinian who insisted that he had not bumped into a door.

"I have good news and bad news," he said. "The bad news is that it is my colleague Bazak who will decide whether you are to be kept in prison, which is to say that you will be, no matter how good your lawyers are. The good news is that since Bazak is sitting today, he cannot serve on the bench that will try the case against you. Good luck. Léa and Avigdor know that they can count on me if they need me."

We were not able to count on Eitan after all. He committed suicide during my trial, as a result of a hate campaign conducted against him. He had agreed to defend Ivan Demanjuk, accused of being Ivan the Terrible of Treblinka and condemned to death after his trial. Dov Eitan was convinced that the accused was not Ivan the Terrible and that a horrible and irreversible judicial error was about to be committed. But the allegation, loudly trumped up by the media, that he was defending a Nazi criminal for money, drove this courageous man out of his mind. He was not around to hear the verdict of the Supreme Court, which let Demanjuk go free.

Dov Eitan was right. When I came into the courtroom, Judge Bazak could not conceal his disgust, even though for once I was all cleaned up and shaved. This judge would become famous a few years later, for having requested the quashing of proceedings against a network of settlers who were sowing death in the occupied territories and had tried to dynamite the El Aqsa mosque. After having systematically covered up the torture of Palestinians, he was horrified by the pressure used by the Shin Beth during the interrogation of the settlers and ruled that such conduct invalidated all the charges. Needless to say, my case was heard for a few minutes, and the following day I left for the prison at Ramlé, which, after the 15 days spent in cell number 20, seemed like the George V Hotel.

Fifteen days later, in a pleading that is taught nowadays at the Law School in Jerusalem, Avigdor Feldman obtained my conditional release by the Supreme Court, establishing a precedent that would be used later for the provisional release of Palestinian suspects also accused of crimes against the security of the state.

13
The trial

The trial, which was presided over by three judges of the district court, a jurisdiction that tries murders and other serious crimes, lasted more than two years, with occasional interruptions of several months. Three main themes ran through the arguments and contradictory testimony, all linked to varying notions of limits or borders: what is legal in the context of the arbitrariness of the occupation? What is legal in support of the struggle of the Palestinians? What is solidarity?

It's a fact that the media coverage of the trial prevented any attempt by the public prosecutor or the Shin Beth to go beyond the charges and examine the real activities of the AIC. At one point, when the prosecutor tried to go further, he was called to order by the presiding judge, who said: "Mister prosecutor, we are not in a military court in the occupied territories. Here our work is based on proofs and the penal code!"

One of the charges against the AIC had to do with the production of the journal *al-Taqadum,* published by the Federation of Palestinian Students, which was linked to the PFLP. Questioned by my lawyers on whether he knew whether this journal was distributed "openly or clandestinely," the Shin Beth expert was honest enough to answer, "openly," thus confirming what we had maintained, namely that the journal was in fact tolerated by the occupation forces and that we did not have to be more Catholic than the Pope.

The key question was this: was a student, trade union or women's organization, which had ideological affinities with the PLO or one of its components, automatically a terrorist organization? To answer in the affirmative was to declare illegal every form of Palestinian organization, not only unions but charities and cultural groups. Every form of solidarity with the Palestinians, even a mere meeting, would become impossible. From our point of view it was totally unacceptable. But then, where was the border? Using a rabbinical precept, which caused Chief Judge Tal to smile, I replied: "Everything that is not categorically and explicitly banned by the law is kosher, strictly kosher." Organizations that are not explicitly declared terrorist are, in our opinion, legitimate organizations, whatever their ideological affinities or the more or less discrete links with other associations. "We refuse to be the handmaidens of the Shin Beth and to investigate what lies behind the public and permitted expression of Palestinian popular organizations."

In addition to *al-Taqadum,* we were accused, during the three years prior to the closing of the AIC, of having printed, designed or laid out 31 other journals, brochures or leaflets "linked to illegal organizations." We were likewise accused of keeping in our offices "material belonging to or useful to illegal organizations." It had nothing to do with bombs or chemicals that could be used to make explosives, but written materials: journals, brochures and articles.

Of all the incriminating material, the one that aroused the greatest anger on the part of the Shin Beth was a brochure, designed and laid out by the AIC staff for a student group at Bir Zeit, which the prosecutor insisted on calling a "training manual." It was in fact a collection of accounts by Palestinian activists who had been arrested and tortured, and it described in detail the interrogation methods of the Shin Beth. The Shin Beth was convinced that the purpose of this brochure was to train activists to stand firm during possible future interrogations by providing them with information about the traps set for them by the Israeli secret services.

The trial revolved around two very different questions: could the content of the texts published by the AIC be defined as "support for terrorism"? And were the organizations we collaborated with and for whom we published this material "terrorist organizations"? The first of these questions was at the heart of lengthy testimony I provided during three long sessions. It was virtually an exercise in Marxist education on the class struggle, the struggle for national liberation and the right to self-determination. The media coverage of this kind of "workers' university" helped draw a much bigger audience for the second day of testimony. My presentation of the debates between Lenin and Rosa Luxemburg on the national question and the Marxist theory of the state was a big success! I was beginning to feel as if I were Althusser teaching at the rue d'Ulm... My cool-headed lawyers knew that the court was far less impressed with my rhetoric than the journalists and the audience of sympathizers filling the courtroom. Furthermore, several of the texts signed by me, and endorsed by Matzpen, were extremely virulent; we did not mince words in rejecting Zionism.

For the first few months, we were pessimistic about the outcome of the trial: how to persuade the court that it was perfectly legitimate to support (including material support) organizations fighting the occupation simply because they were not directly implicated in the armed struggle? Would it not be better to accept a deal with the prosecutor who was ready to reduce the charges substantially in order to cut short a trial that would be long and expensive and put an end to media coverage that was sympathetic to the AIC?

One event would change everything. On 9 December 1987, that is, a few weeks after the trial began, the Intifada started. The Palestinian population of the West Bank and the Gaza Strip rose up, and the uprising entered into history as a powerful appeal from the occupied to Israeli public opinion: "You thought that we were resigned to the occupation," said the rebels in effect, "but our patience has run out. We are ready to live alongside you in peaceful coexistence, but for that to happen you must withdraw from the territories occupied in 1967, dismantle the settlements and allow us to establish our independent state. So long as that does not happen we will fight you, and you will not be able to continue your normal lives."

When the Intifada began, two decades had gone by during which the Israelis had not noticed the Palestinians who lived ten minutes away. They noticed them as waiters in restaurants, maintenance workers in hospitals and mechanics in garages. Even if they shopped from time to time in this or that town in the West Bank (where everything was cheaper) or if they went to eat shish kebab in Jericho, the life of the Palestinians in the occupied territories remained invisible and inaudible to them. At best, one spoke of the "Palestinian people," the "territories" and the PLO, in a sort of abstract way, as if removed from everyday life; even the bomb attacks – then quite infrequent – were seen as something coming from a foreign country. The green line that separated Israel from the occupied territories had disappeared from the map, but the people that lived there existed only in the form of hired hands and a picturesque décor. They were non-existent as a society, as a human and national reality. Palestinians and Israelis crossed the border every day, but whereas the former encountered Israel and the Israeli people at every step of their way, the Israelis noticed no one.

During the ten years that had preceded the Intifada, few units of the reserves were involved in maintaining order in the occupied territories, and in most cases it was not a very traumatic experience. But all that changed within a few weeks: the green line was once more etched into the Israeli unconscious and the occupation became a concrete reality for the occupier. Thousands of reservists called up to suppress the uprising brought home images of courageous resistance and of a repression that often made them ashamed; Yesh Gvul got a second wind, and a hundred or so officers and soldiers would be sent to prison for insubordination.

All of a sudden, the Alternative Information Center – reopened after six months by a court decision – was besieged with requests to organize meetings and visits in the occupied territories.

The trial had made our center into the number one calling place for all those who felt the need to see, listen to and enter into dialogue with Palestinians. The tiny crack opened by a few dozen activists in the wall that separated the two communities had become wider. Although it was not yet a tidal wave it was at least a stream that replaced the trickle of the years from the 1960s to the 1980s. Initiatives to express solidarity with the Palestinians and to organize joint activities were rapidly increasing.

One of the numerous restrictions of my conditional release banned me from going to the AIC offices. So I decided to publish a daily bulletin entirely devoted to Israeli actions of solidarity and protest against the occupation, intended to inform Palestinians of the new possibilities opening up on the other side of the border. The idea for such a bulletin had been suggested to me by a Palestinian diplomat stationed in Africa who, in the course of a public meeting in Geneva,[1] had heard me describe the new movements that had come together in Israeli society and wanted these developments to become known within the ranks of the Palestinian national movement. We called it *The Other Front,* because we felt that a truly new front had been opened. Since I was not allowed to go to our office in West Jerusalem, I simply did the work at Feisal Husseini's office in East Jerusalem.

On New Year's Day 1989, approximately 10,000 Israelis, Palestinians and foreigners demonstrated shoulder to shoulder around the wall of the Old City of Jerusalem, marching behind Feisal Husseini, who had brought together not only the comrades from Matzpen and the Israeli Communist Party, but also the leaders of the Zionist party Meretz*

1. The prosecutor having mistakenly failed to ask the court to take away my passport, I had, on several occasions during the course of the trial, made short trips out of the country, until the authorities got wind of this and tried to oppose it. The Supreme Court, which heard the matter, ruled at that time: "The suspect is not someone who would flee, so we see no reason to bar him from leaving the national territory."

and of "Peace Now!" For once, Palestinian and Israeli demonstrators experienced without discrimination the same violent repression by the police, who were totally baffled by what was going on (an Italian pacifist lost an eye that day).

The AIC action became an example for thousands of Israelis. My trial, which was based on an indictment drawn up before the Intifada, became meaningless in the eyes of an increasingly large section of Israeli liberal opinion.

The verdict, handed down in October 1989 was a victory; we were found not guilty of support for terrorism; as for the possession of materials intended to serve illegal organization, the court ruled that possession of written materials could not be considered a crime. As for the 31 counts that alleged we were providing services to illegal organizations, we were found innocent of 30: the court agreed with our argument that the organizations in question had never been illegal, even though their ties with declared terrorist organizations were a matter of public record. One count remained: the production of the famous 'Training Manual.' In contrast to other publications produced by the AIC, this one, although coming from a student organization, included an introduction that made direct reference to an illegal organization – the Popular Front for the Liberation of Palestine – which it referred to as "*our* organization." The majority of the court agreed that we did not know what was written there, but ruled that we were guilty nonetheless of having "closed our eyes" to the links that tied this brochure to the PFLP. My refusal to give up the names of the Palestinian who provided the manuscript was cited as the reason for determining my guilt.

The reading of the verdict provoked an explosion of joy throughout the courtroom. For several hours the radio spoke of the "victory" of the AIC. When the sentence was announced – 30 months, including 20 behind bars, plus a heavy fine – there was general astonishment. Even the prosecutor could hardly believe what he had heard. Never before had a Palestinian been sentenced to prison for more than four months for printing banned materials even with his eyes wide open, while I was being jailed for 20 months for "having closed my eyes."

The next day, the journalist Gidon Eshet explained that this 30-month sentence was a way of punishing me for the 30 charges that the court could not sustain. I did not agree with this analysis, widely circulated in the media, which saw the court's sentence merely as small-minded vengeance. On the contrary, the verdict by Judge Tal and his confederates had a very specific purpose: to warn the Israeli peace movement not to get too close to the border.

A few days after the verdict, the journalist Lili Galili described, in *Haaretz,* the new state of mind prevailing in Israel at the time, a reshuffling within Israeli society and new alignments. The solidarity meeting organized on the eve of my incarceration served as her model. It took place (is this a paradox or a symbol?) in a Jerusalem synagogue.

> The Kol Haneshama synagogue had already known some strange moments. A few months ago, it hosted the first public appearance by Feisal Husseini after his release from prison. For well over an hour, his back to the tabernacle holding the scrolls of the Torah*, Husseini, nephew of the former Mufti*, spoke to the Israeli public, thanks to the intercession of the Jerusalem far left. Michel Warschawski, better known as Mikado, accompanied him to that event. Last week the roles were reversed: this time it was Husseini accompanying Warschawski for an evening of solidarity a few days before the latter started serving the twenty-month prison term to which he had been sentenced for laying out a brochure for the Popular Front at the Center he runs. When the organizer of that very special evening announced that Husseini would have some words for Mikado before his incarceration, there were a few seconds of hesitation: who was going to prison and who was getting out?
>
> An unusual audience filled the room: old battle horses, those veterans of the left who always give the impression of bearing the suffering of humanity on their shoulders and were showing the signs of wear and tear after twenty-five years of being the "Israeli left", yet managing both the blasé look of those who have seen everything mixed with worries about the warnings of things to come. Seated next to them were the youth. The last twenty-five years had given birth to a new generation of contenders, strange, enthusiastic and exhibiting an unshakeable belief in their capacity to change the world.
>
> Only the events of the last two years could have brought together this mix of people to the same place for the same event: the remnants of Warschawski's anti-Zionist organization Matzpen side by side with those who have recently quit "Peace Now!" Not too long ago, they were oceans apart, those who were at the fringes of society and those who were deeply rooted in it. This evening, even a deputy mayor was present: Ornan Yekoutieli, chairman of the Ratz*group in the Jerusalem City Council. Not too long ago Yekoutieli had had some problems during a council session because he was sporting a button showing the

> crossed flags of Israel and Palestine. A few months later Warschawski was arrested for the same reason. His friends joked that the police did not understand that what was new for Warschawski was not the wearing of the Palestinian colors, but the Israeli ones…
>
> The rather odd evening reached its peak with the entry into the synagogue of an aged couple: he with a beard and skullcap and she with the traditional wig of Orthodox Jewish women: Mireille and Max Warschawski, Michel's parents. Their arrival was greeted by an excited murmur… they did not fit into this human landscape… The next day Rabbi Warschawski told me that he was sorry, not about what Michel was doing, but on the contrary, about the fact that he was no longer a practicing Jew. He added: "Having said that, he's a lot more of a Jew in his soul than all those here who claim to adhere to Judaism."
>
> In the course of the evening Warschawski's remarks tended to confirm that. This former Talmudic school student defended his refusal to reveal the names of the Palestinians who wrote the Popular Front brochure that had been typeset at his organization based on the religious ban against the 'mosser'. It's a sacred principle, explained his father, to refuse to be a 'mosser', meaning an informer. Of all the arguments available to him, that's the one his son chose.
>
> In another part of his moving speech, devoted mostly to the boundaries of legality, Mikado said: "What is not explicitly illegal is strictly kosher." He pronounced the expression "strictly kosher" as do only Orthodox Jews of Ashkenazi origin. But in the ambience of that evening there was no longer any contradiction between the context in which the words were used and the speech they were a part of. I was nonetheless curious to know how Mikado's wife, Léa Tsemel, who is also his lawyer, resolved the linguistic problem of "strictly kosher", as she was simultaneously translating Warschawski's words for a Palestinian colleague!
>
> To wrap it all up, at the end of the evening Warschawski got two particularly warm hugs: one from Feisal Husseini, the other from Daniel Boyarin, a religious Jew who teaches Talmud at Bar Ilan University.[2]

The sentence of the district court was so severe that the prosecutor agreed that I could remain out of jail until the Supreme Court ruled on the appeal that our lawyers had immediately filed. On 27 June 1990, three judges of the Supreme Court confirmed the verdict, but reduced the sentence to 20 months, with eight behind bars. It was still more than a Palestinian would have received, but this time the border had specifically treated a Jew more severely than an Arab.

2. Lili Galili, "Solidarity from all sides," *Haaretz*, 20 November 1989.

14
The left-wing colonizer

Since 1992 the Israeli peace movement has aroused great interest internationally. In a country at war, the fact that dozens, indeed sometimes hundreds of thousands, of people rally against the policy of their government is not a run-of-the-mill phenomenon, especially because, unlike the France of the Algerian war or the United States of the Vietnam war, it was often the very existence of Israel that was challenged by its enemies.

After the huge demonstration that followed the massacres of Sabra and Shatila, the Palestinians themselves attached great importance to this rebellion at the very heart of the Israeli population: it was not merely an unexpected ally in the midst of the enemy camp, but a reality that challenged the Palestinian national movement's idea of Israel – perceived until then as entirely homogeneous and totally united in its hostility to the Palestinians and their rights.

Nevertheless, the Palestinians were quickly disappointed. The protest movements against the repression of the Intifada did not mobilize the hundreds of thousands of demonstrators that had filled the streets during the invasion of Lebanon. "Is Palestinian blood not as red as the blood of Lebanese?" asked a former Palestinian prisoner during a meeting with peace activists in 1989. In fact, the difference between the reaction of the Israeli left to the war in Lebanon and the Intifada does not reflect a greater or lesser empathy towards the respective victims of those two events. It is rather a product of the nature of this left, its ideological contradictions and its cultural characteristics. These contradictions go back to the early days of Zionism, as shown for example by this enlightening paragraph by David Hacohen, leader of the Zionist workers' movement in Palestine in the 1930s and 1940s:

> When I joined the socialist students' club (in London) there were English, Irish, Jews, Chinese, Indians and Africans – all under English domination. Already at that time I had to fight with my close comrades around the issue of Jewish socialism, to justify the fact that I would not accept Arabs in my union, the Histadrut, that we urged Jewish households to not buy anything at Arab stores,

> that we organized guards around the orchards to keep Arab laborers from working there, that we tossed gasoline on Arab tomatoes and broke Arab eggs in the baskets of women who had bought them. The Jewish National Fund sent Yehoshua Hankin to Beirut to buy lands from rich absentee landowners and we then kicked out the farmers. It was all right to buy dozens of hectares from an Arab, but to sell, God forbid, one Jewish hectare to an Arab, was forbidden. It really wasn't easy to explain![1]

To work "for Zionism, socialism and friendship among the people," as proclaimed for half a century by *Al-Hamishmar*, the Hashomer Hatzair* daily, was no easy task. The left Zionist must manage a never-ending schizophrenia that is not only ideological but existential. This schizophrenia requires him to provide a rationale for everything he does and to lie to himself constantly, all of which can only make things worse.

There is no need to elaborate on the internal contradiction between a socialist or at least humanist ideology, and a colonialist project, which, under the worthy guise of building a refuge for persecuted Jews, denies not only the most elementary rights but the very existence of an indigenous community, deprives it of its lands and its access to work in order to provoke its eventual mass exodus. To live with this contradiction the left Zionist must deny reality; literally erase it from his memory.

One day, I went to Tel Aviv with two comrades: Mahmoud, a Palestinian archeologist who had worked for many years for the Arab Studies Society on a map of pre-1948 Palestine, and Tikva, a veteran of the Palmach shock troops, who had joined the ranks of the radical left in the 1980s. As we passed near to the *moshav** Shoresh, Tikva told us that her unit had camped there during one of the truces of 1948. Mahmoud added: "Yes, and that's where the village of Beit Mahsir used to be," to which Tikva replied: "No, no way, there was no village there." Taken aback, Mahmoud reminded her that he had just finished a detailed investigation of that region, but Tikva was certain about her memory: "I was there, I know what I'm talking about!"

I suggested that the two of them reread the appropriate documents and we went on to another subject. Several weeks later, when we were working together on the proofs of the journal, Tikva cried out: "But of course, the ruins!" And then: "Do you remember that discussion

1. Published in *Haaretz,* 15 November 1968.

with Mahmoud several weeks ago? Well now it comes back to me. There were ruins 200 meters from the camp where I used to go to write my daily letter to my mother. But now that I think about it, they were not the remnants of an ancient village, but those of a village that had just been emptied of its inhabitants and destroyed. And to say that I didn't see it! And to think that for more than forty years I buried that memory!"

The amnesia of the left Zionist is accompanied by an image of reality that has nothing to do with historical facts: since his intentions are pure and the values he defends noble, he can never be held responsible for the crimes he has committed. If he killed or stole or expelled it's because he was attacked, and he is twice a victim: for being attacked and for being forced to do a bad thing to defend himself. The schizophrenia of the left Zionist is supported by a shrill paranoia that beholds the Jew as Jew, an eternal and absolute victim. The right, which does not share the universal humanist values that adorn left Zionism, was, for that reason, often more honest than the left on matters of historical fact. In 1970, in the course of a debate before the students of the WUJS,[2] invited to Israel by the Jewish Agency, Ezer Weizman – who was no longer a general but not yet president of the state, provoked an outcry, as he was wont to do, by stating (and I paraphrase):

> I won't waste time discussing the statements by MP [from Mapam, the left Zionist party] Elazar Granot: Haim Hanegbi of Matzpen is completely justified in saying that it is a tissue of lies, and I have no substantial differences with him on the facts, based on what he described. What differentiates Haim and me are the conclusions that we draw. For him it's a matter of a 180-degree turn and renouncing Zionism so that we may be forgiven for our crimes. For me it's all about being prepared for permanent war in order to keep, by force, that which we have taken by force.

After the war of 1973, the same Weizman would make a major political U-turn, which led to the right accusing him of treason for having conducted secret negotiations with Yasser Arafat long before the left Zionists.

The left Zionist believes in democratic values and wants to live in a democracy. But above all, he wants a Jewish State. Thus he becomes

2. World Union of Jewish Students.

the promoter of the philosophy of separation, not simply as a means but as a fundamental value. That is why his discourse is often more segregationist than that of some right-wing currents.

In the introduction to his *Portrait du colonisé,* dedicated to the "Portrait of the Colonizer," Albert Memmi writes about what he calls the "colonizer who rejects himself" or the "colonizer of the left," whom he describes thus:

> He is confronted with another civilization, customs different than his own, men whose actions often take him by surprise and with whom he feels no great affinities. And there you have it – even if he refuses to side with the colonialists – he cannot stop himself from judging that civilization and its people. How can one deny that their technology is seriously retarded, their customs strangely ossified, their culture outdated? Many of the traits of the colonized shock or irritate him. He is repulsed in ways that he cannot hide and which show up in remarks that curiously resemble those of the colonialist. In truth, the time has long gone since he was sure, *a priori,* of the universal identity of human nature in all parts of the world. He still believes in it, of course, but more as a universal abstraction or an ideal for the future.[3]

Memmi was talking about the French in Tunisia but his words apply perfectly to left-wing Zionism.

The Zionist wants separation to maintain a state that is as Jewish as possible; the left Zionist also wants separation in order to protect democracy and progress, that is to say, his European, modern, liberal and secular civilization, when faced with the Arab world, which frightens him. Memmi again:

> He discovers that, if the colonized have justice on their side, even if he can give them his approval and some help, his solidarity stops there. He is not one of them and has no desire to be. He vaguely foresees the day of their liberation, the restitution of their rights, but he doesn't seriously dream about sharing their existence, even a liberated one.[4]

Yossi Sarid, spokesman of the left in Parliament, has incessantly repeated words to the effect: "We have to make peace, because it is

3. Albert Memmi, *Portrait du colonisé,* Paris, Gallimard, 1985 [first published 1957], p. 52.
4. *Ibid.* p. 51.

the only way to separate ourselves from them and it's with the Arabs that we have to make peace. What do you want? If it was simply a matter of personal preference, I would prefer something else, but they, not the Swiss, are our neighbors..."

The left Zionist is tied to the West, which his parents left behind when they chose to solve the Jewish question in the East. Europe is his real metropolis and New York his Mecca. Therein lies the source of another contradiction for the left Zionist: he is profoundly pro-American and sees US policy as the only guarantee for the preservation of civilization. The support of Latin American dictators by the US government is hardly a serious problem for him, so he does not understand why he is treated as a reactionary and pro-imperialist by the intellectuals of the European left, whose friendship and respect he claims. To resolve this contradiction, the left-wing Zionist has recourse once more to anti-Semitism: hidden behind every criticism of Israel lurks a more or less conscious anti-Semite. Since "the entire world is against us," we have to stick together because we cannot afford the luxury of tearing each other apart. National unity is more than a duty justified by a situation of permanent conflict, it is a way of being, intrinsically linked to the position of the settler face to face with those whose rights and homeland are despoiled by our very existence. Like it or not, Zionism provokes a conflict with the Arabs, and that conflict leaves little room between the two camps. So it is a matter either of choosing to join the right wing of the Zionist camp in its war against the Arabs or of accepting renegade status.

But it's not easy to be a renegade, even if it's only in terms of moral support and acts of solidarity, because it means alienating yourself from those you live and work with, from those with whom you do your military service, without being able to feel solidarity with the Arabs, whose culture is completely foreign to the left-wing Israeli, who rejects it in any case as reactionary and threatening.

Thus the left Zionist chooses to "shoot first and cry later,"[5] to participate with his brothers in the repression of the other, and then bemoan the fate that forced him to commit the crimes he committed.

5. "Shoot first and cry later": an expression commonly used to describe the heartache of the Israeli soldier forced to fight in spite of himself, revived in the 1980s to criticize the hesitations of the well-meaning left. The editorialist of *Yediot Aharonot,* Nahum Barnea, devoted a series of articles to a denunciation of this attitude. These articles were published well before the war in Lebanon in a collection called *Shoot first and cry later* [Tel Aviv, Zmora, Bitan, Motan Publishers,1981].

As one can see, this attitude leaves no room for the other, the victim. It's a matter for Israelis only, or even more so, for the left-wing Israeli and his tortured conscience. If the other were present, one would have to consider his rights, and then challenge one's own Zionism.

Nonetheless, the left Zionist wants sympathy for the tears he sheds – not for the fate of his victim, but over his tarnished conscience and the lost innocence of his youth. He even expects the Palestinians to love him for all the sacrifices he is ready to make on their behalf. Moreover, that love is, to him, the only proof that the Palestinian can provide of his desire for peace and coexistence, because, in the eyes of the left Zionist, reconciliation precedes peace. Could it be otherwise, since he believes that the conflict is only, or at least mainly the result of the refusal by the Arabs to coexist with neighbors who have never done them any harm?

In typical colonialist fashion, the left Zionist already knows all about 'the Arab,' what motivates him, and what is characteristic of his conduct and his reactions. Since he knows, he thus has no need to listen, to try to understand: he creates 'the Arab,' in order to give coherence to his own discourse and keep a clear conscience. Memmi writes:

> Who the colonized really is, is of little consequence to the colonizer. Far from wanting to understand the colonized in his real dimensions, he is concerned with making him undergo that essential transformation. He attributes ulterior motives to each and every one of them according to what suits him, recreating a colonized subject that fits his every whim; in short, he makes up stories.[6]

But since reality is not a fairytale, the left Zionist is always caught short by it and surprised by the unexpected reaction of the Arabs: he was surprised by the war of 1973, he was surprised by the resistance to the invasion of Lebanon, he was surprised by the Intifada! This surprise then turns to anger: the Arab is not performing the role assigned him in a scenario that was supposed to provide for him and, who knows, one day even give him his independence. So it is too bad for him: confronted with such ingratitude, and with this latest non-acceptance of the only conceivable (to him, of course) peace offer, he moves over straight away... and joins the right.

6. Memmi, *Portrait du colonisé*, p. 59.

The left-wing Zionist shares with the right-wing Zionist what the Israeli columnist Doron Rosenblum calls the "didactic method": he does not talk with the Palestinian, he makes him understand, he explains to him. He explains about the world and its constraints, about what is in the domain of the possible and what is utopian; what is good for him and what threatens to cause him harm. From the Prime Minister to the "Peace Now!" activist, from a top general to the sergeant at a roadblock, Israelis explain, warn and threaten when it appears that Palestinians don't want to understand. "It's in your interest to understand. Don't make the same mistake you made in 1948, which got you where you are now. As long as you refuse to understand that it is impossible to dismantle all the settlements, to demand your right of return, or to recover Jerusalem…" Whether he belongs to the right or the left, the Israeli is constantly giving someone a lecture, pointing his finger, his billy-club clearly visible. The only difference is that the left-wing Zionist thinks that he is doing it for the good of the Palestinians.

Above all, what differentiates the left colonizer from the right colonizer is, in fact, paternalism: "The paternalist is one who wants to see himself as being generous and above and beyond racism and inequality. But his is, if you like, a charitable racism. Because the one who is most openly paternalist rebels as soon as the colonized demands his rights." [7]After he has condescended, at the risk of getting into trouble with the members of his own group, to recognize the existence of the Palestinian – and that took him more than four decades – the left-wing Zionist cannot accept that the latter still wants his rights: he needs to be trusted; one day he'll find a solution, especially since everybody knows that he does not like being the occupier and that he has always advocated separation. If the occupied, the dispossessed and the refugee insist on fighting for their rights, they are only proving once again that they're not interested in peace and therefore they deserve to be repressed.

Beyond the left-wing Zionist and in conflict with him are the men and women who have broken with the national consensus and its values. But has the colonizer of the far left (of which I am one) succeeded in breaking with the behavior and character traits of the dominant community, which his privileged existence is likely to have imposed upon him? Not always.

7. *Ibid.* p. 97.

Just like the left-wing Zionist, the anti-Zionist activist often knows, better than the Palestinian, what's best for him. He has read Lenin and Bauer, sometimes even Fanon and Césaire, and that training gives him the authority to understand what is right and what is wrong. On the other hand, he's read nothing of the political literature of the Arab national movement; but is that really necessary, since he already knows in advance what the Palestinian liberation movement must be like to deserve his support?

His difficulty in identifying with the Palestinians often derives from an ideological differentiation. Of course, he supports the struggle of the Palestinian people, sometimes unconditionally, but it is more of an abstract struggle, not the real battle unfolding right in front of him, because that one is not left wing enough, or too nationalist or not nationalist enough. It matters little why he separates himself from the real struggle of those whom Israel oppresses; what does matter is that, often, his total and unconditional support becomes critical non-support. Although he recognizes the right to self-determination of the Palestinians, the far left colonizer does not "recognize" the PLO, which is to say the Palestinian national movement such as it is. Often he treats it as if it were a group of collaborators, and he would prefer a mythical national movement, which in fact would be no more than an imaginary reflection of himself. He also has a tendency to fashion the colonized in his own image, namely that of a European revolutionary ready to sacrifice every single Palestinian in order to obtain his own utopia. In so doing, he provokes either rejection or indifference on the part of the Palestinian nationalist, who rightly sees in this far left-wing militant just another variant of colonial paternalism.

Again, as Memmi says:

> Wanting to compete with the least realistic nationalists, he speaks like a demagogue, whose excesses only increase the mistrust of the colonized. He suggests obscure and Machiavellian explanations for the acts of the colonizer, or, to the irritated astonishment of the colonized, he loudly justifies the behavior that the latter has just condemned.[8]

If he does not make a conscious effort to remind himself where his words and actions come from, if he does not behave modestly,

8. *Ibid.* p. 68.

the far left-wing settler runs the risk of finding himself in the same boat as the left-wing Zionist, whom he believes he is fighting against. He will oppose the emancipation movement of the Palestinians or he will not give it all the support that it has the right to expect from those who believe in anti-colonialism and the right of the colonized to self-determination (which is to say, the right to decide for themselves, including the right to make the compromises they judge necessary).

A few months after the signing of the Oslo accords, in 1993, in the course of a discussion that included activists of the Palestinian and Israeli far left, I heard an Israeli woman militant explain, like a teacher presenting a lesson to her students, that accepting a Palestinian state in the West Bank and the Gaza Strip was pure and simple treason.

She received a curt response from a Palestinian militant who had been in all the battles and had spent years in prison: "Why do you take it upon yourself to refuse us an independent state, even a tiny one, in less than 22 percent of our national territory? Are you going to endure fifty more years of occupation and violence?"

But it was the insensitive response of the Israeli militant that needs to be pondered: "I see that even the Palestinian left has lost the desire to fight..."

PART THREE

The internal borders

Interlude: M. Dankner and M. Shemesh

A few days after the signing of the Oslo accords, the daily *Hadashot* published a report in which several dozen personalities of the Israeli political, media, university and artistic worlds were asked: "What does the peace that will soon be signed with the Palestinians mean to you?"

Most of the replies were routine. However, the answer given by the journalist Amnon Dankner drew my attention. Dankner is almost a caricature of a Western, liberal, secular Israeli, and clearly in favor of peace. He hates the religious bloc and abhors the Jewish Arabs: he reveres the army and thinks of himself as the guarantor of the national consensus, for which he is willing to work overtime on the talk show he co-hosts with the representative of the right, Tomi Lapid.

To the *Hadashot* reporter, Dankner explained that for him peace meant that soon he would be able to get into his car in Tel Aviv and drive non-stop to Florence.

The next day, on the way to the grocery store in my neighborhood, I ran into my neighbor, M. Shemesh. This septuagenarian is the antithesis of M. Dankner. An immigrant from Iraq, he worked for 30 years as a sales clerk in a supermarket, barely making ends meet to feed his seven children and give them a minimum education. M. Shemesh is deeply religious, and, like the majority of the inhabitants of the neighborhood, votes for the right. Some of his children supported the fascist extreme right before joining the Shas Party, which became their new home base.

Of course, we spoke about the peace. Before leaving he clasped me in his arms and with tears in his eyes told me: "Now that there is going to be peace, you think that I'll be able to return to Baghdad, not to live there, but at least for the summer, on vacation?"

That was when I was reminded of Dankner. Peace for the liberal and pro-peace journalist, and for most of his kind, meant the opening of the borders, all of them without distinction: that opening would confirm Israel's ultimate integration with the West, thus turning its back on the Arab world with which it was supposed to be reconciled.

For M. Shemesh, and maybe for a majority of Israelis who are usually labeled as rightists, peace is also the opening of the border, but not the one that leads to Florence or London. Peace is the possibility of reconciliation with the Arab world, from which they came, the opportunity to re-establish links with that culture and, above all, the chance to tear down the wall that had cut them off from their own Arabness, their own beleaguered identity.

These two different, even contradictory, reactions, of the typical liberal, secular and pro-peace middle class on the one hand, and the traditionalist working-class sectors with their Arab culture and often their right-wing discourse on the other, reflect two worlds, which, in Israel, are increasingly turning their backs on each other. Is one of these worlds the bearer of hopes for peace? And if so, which of the two?

15
Separation at last?

As is often the case in national liberation struggles, the Intifada gave rise to two parallel processes of wear and tear. After three years of struggle and enormous sacrifices, the Palestinian population was exhausted. In a number of ways the uprising started to generate its own decline. But the ravaging effects on Israeli society would prove to have even greater impact: as Israeli repression began to bear fruit, under the combined pressure of American diplomacy and a weary public opinion, Labor ended up involved in a process of negotiations with the PLO, at first indirectly, and then, after the election of Yitzhak Rabin in 1992, without intermediaries.

The Oslo accords, solemnly ratified on 13 September 1993 on the White House lawn, marked an historic turning point in the attitude of the Zionist movement and the State of Israel towards the Palestinians: for the first time an Israeli government recognized the existence and legitimacy of a Palestinian people in the land of Palestine and committed itself to allow it, gradually, to express its national self-determination. In exchange, the Palestinian national movement announced a ceasefire in its struggle for national liberation and renounced its claim to 78 percent of its homeland.

The "Declaration of the Principles" of Oslo was far from fair to the Palestinians. Although it mentioned "one hundred years of conflict," in effect acknowledging that the conflict began with the start of the Zionist venture in Palestine, it carefully refused to pronounce in favor of either side or make any assessment of historical responsibility. Unresolved issues got the upper hand over concrete measures, and the ultimate objective, which was supposed to be negotiated in the second phase of the process, was left unclarified. Thus, rather than heralding Palestinian independence, it hinted at it. Despite the many obstacles and the risk of impasse, many of us were nonetheless – moderately – optimistic: things were moving in the right direction and we counted on the common sense and, above all, the good faith of the signatories.

In those euphoric days, we should have paid more attention to the skeptical remarks of General Matti Peled – who, along with Uri Avnery, Haim Hanegbi and myself, a year earlier, had founded Gush

Shalom ("The Peace Bloc") to compensate for the disappearance of "Peace Now!" after a left government had returned to power. In the course of a discussion on the significance of the Oslo accords and the tasks awaiting the peace movement, the former general warned us (and I paraphrase):

> Stop dreaming, the implementation of the accords is not a done deal, and I know what I'm talking about: Rabin and I are from the same generation, we ate in the same mess. No Israeli government will ever agree to withdraw from the occupied territories or to dismantle the settlements on its own, unless it is forced to. There has to be immense pressure for it to agree to respect the accords as the Palestinians and we ourselves understand them – international pressure as well as pressure from the Israeli peace movement, without which they will do everything to strip these accords of their meaning.

We did not really take his pessimistic predictions seriously. Rabin had signed an agreement with the Palestinians with the whole world watching. How could one believe that he would dare not to respect it? But the old general gave us a lesson that day that would quickly prove to be of great relevance: less than six months after the signing of the Declaration of Principles, Rabin had begun to sabotage it, first declaring that he did not intend to respect the timetable ("There are no sacred dates," he announced in February 1994), then stating that there could only be a partial withdrawal from the Gaza Strip.

Nevertheless, both peoples believed in the peace, the majority being ready to pay the price for it by renouncing many of their dreams. For two months, I witnessed dozens of acts of fraternization, including some with soldiers, especially near the checkpoints that had separated Israel and the occupied territories since the end of the Gulf War.

At the institutional level the reaction was more varied. When, in November 1993, our "Peace Bloc" wanted to organize a joint demonstration with Fatah, in Nablus, to demand the immediate release of Palestinian political prisoners, the army opposed it: "You know full well that demonstrations are forbidden in the occupied territories," explained the military commander in the West Bank, "and especially with an illegal organization!" For the first time, the Supreme Court rejected the arguments of the army. Judge Levine authorized the demonstration, stating: "Times have changed, and as of now, public liberties have to be taken into account on a par with questions of security and public order."

Several thousand Palestinians and Israelis duly demonstrated in Nablus – a city that was virtually unknown to most Israelis. My role was to provide liaison for the march's security squad, made up mostly of Palestinians who two months earlier were still being sought by the Israeli security service for "terrorism". During the preliminary meeting between the organizations and the governor, the latter refused to talk to the representatives of Fatah, and acted as if they were not present. However, many of his soldiers fraternized with the Palestinian security squad.

During that time, I was collaborating with a French TV broadcast team on a program about the settlers (who were presented as the victims of the agreement). After having interviewed several dozens of them throughout the occupied territories, we concluded that they, including the most hard-line extremists among them, were all preparing to leave.

But, as Matti Peled had predicted, Rabin and the army were not ready to take the necessary measures to launch the peace process. It was impossible for them to treat the Palestinians as equals, or at least with a minimum of respect. Furthermore, the old generation could not believe that the Palestinians were ready to turn over a new leaf. As another general, Rafael Eitan, a former minister and head of the far right party, Tsomet*, often said: "If they had done to us what we did to them in 1948, we would never forgive them, and that is why I do not believe in the peace."

Thus, right from the beginning, two factors combined to prevent the implementation of the Oslo accords: first, the certainty that Israeli–Palestinian relations would remain in conflict for a long time, possibly forever; as Camille Mansour[1] so aptly pointed out, that certainty led to a strictly security-based reading of the accords; second, the extreme difficulty if not the total inability of the Israelis to question their classic colonial relation with the Palestinians and the territories they inhabit.

Should one conclude that the signing of the accords by Rabin resulted only from international pressures pursuant to the Gulf War? I don't think so. For the Israeli government as well as for the overwhelming majority of the Israeli population, the Oslo Declaration

1. Camille Mansour, "L'impasse coloniale d'Israel," *Revue d'études palestiniennes,* no. 28, Summer 2001.

of Principles was welcome because its hidden message was the promise of separation – a separation that, in their dreams, had replaced the expulsion of the Palestinians.

Could the Oslo accords have led to something else? Undoubtedly, as Camille Mansour wrote:

> An Israeli reading of the Oslo accords based on their true intent, according to the rules of good faith and Israel's best interests, meant that the settlement process not only had to be frozen, but de-legitimized, that security had to be understood in the broadest political terms, that the political, economic and psychological dividends of the peace process had to be realized as soon as possible, and that Israel should not go too far in pressing its advantages based on military supremacy. Otherwise, an Israeli reading of the accords based on the balance of forces in strictly military terms implied that Israel had only signed the accords because the occupation army, after the Intifada, found the management of the day-to-day life of Palestinians in the big urban centers of the West Bank and the Gaza Strip extremely expensive, and that it would be best to withdraw from those centers in favor of a Palestinian authority that it could hold responsible for what goes on there. Faced with these two possible readings of the Oslo accords, or rather, two possible alternative paths, immediately after the signing of the Declaration of Principles in Washington on 13 September 1993, Yitzhak Rabin unveiled the mechanisms and policies that indicated that the second reading would prevail.[2]

Matti Peled had sensed it: only political pressures, international and domestic, could have imposed a different reading. But the international community revealed its great cowardice, arguing with all the hypocrisy its chancelleries are capable of to bring the protagonists together for face-to-face discussions. As for the peace movement, its overwhelming majority decided that the Declaration of Principles embodied all its objectives. In spite of its obvious limitations? No, in fact, because of those limitations.

A few days after the signing in Washington, "Peace Now!" organized a party at a Jerusalem square to celebrate what seemed to it the beginning of the end of the conflict. I met Mossi Raz, secretary general of the movement, who insisted that I participate.

2. *Ibid.* p. 22.

I politely refused. In the end it was my daughter who persuaded me to join him. She and her friends wanted to celebrate the peace and to express, as openly as possible, their joy and their hope for a future without war and without conflicts. But Mossi and his friends from "Peace Now!" were not only celebrating peace and the hope of reconciliation. They were also celebrating their victory over the Israeli right and indeed over the Arabs, because they considered that this agreement, which necessitated enormous compromises on the part of the Palestinians, exonerated them and, above all, gave them the promise of separation.

For Talila and her friends, peace was its own reward, but for my friends in "Peace Now!" it was the means of guaranteeing, in good conscience, the "Jewish and democratic" character of Israel. I shared with Talila the naïve hope of a land reconciled with itself, but I knew that one would have to engage in many more struggles for that hope to be realized, that one had to insist on respect for the accords already agreed to, the immediate dismantling of the settlements, the release of Palestinian prisoners, the rule of law... And I feared that, as far as the essential struggle for the implementation of the agreement was concerned, Mossi and his comrades, for whom the Oslo agreement was good enough, would once again let us down.

In fact we found ourselves alone again. First, we were the only ones to demand an immediate start to the dismantling of the settlements, the release of political prisoners and the return of Palestinians expelled between 1967 and 1993, as promised by the agreement; and later, we were the only ones to demand adherence to the supplementary agreement that had been signed. In the eyes of our friends in "Peace Now!" we were, once again, dreamers, visionaries who refused to accommodate their objectives to the new realities of the "process."

But the disappearance of the peace movement, which blindly trusted the Rabin government and the internal dynamic of the "process," left the field wide open for the settlers and the extreme right, who, seeing that the Rabin government had no intention of proceeding with anything resembling the beginning of the dismantling of the settlements, stirred themselves again. Soon, their mood was transformed into arrogance and an unprecedented belligerence, which led eventually to the assassination of the Prime Minister and with him, of the entire Oslo process.

For the Palestinian people the Oslo accords meant the beginning of the implementation of international law, the imminent prospect of an eventual end of the occupation of the West Bank and the Gaza Strip, and the hope for a long-awaited independence. For the majority of Israelis, it meant, above all, the possibility of separating from the Palestinians and freeing themselves of the constraints of an increasingly costly occupation.

After 1991 and the Gulf War, the Israeli government had set up a measure known as "closure." Well before the Oslo accords, the closure of the territories reflected two conclusions arrived at by the majority of the Israeli leaders: on one hand, the good old days of the "liberal occupation," which did not require mass repression, were over, and on the other, short of a miracle, the "transfer" option – the expulsion of the Palestinians to Jordan – was no longer on the agenda. They needed to find a way to get rid of the Palestinian population without calling into question the settlement process in the West Bank and perhaps also in the Gaza Strip. It turned out to be the "sealing off" of the territories, meaning the confinement of the Palestinians in what were in effect reservations, of which the Gaza Strip is the biggest and most tightly sealed.

The closure started with one of the most discreet operations of "ethnic cleansing" in the last few decades: in the space of a few weeks, Tel Aviv and its surroundings were emptied of some 20,000 Palestinian workers, most of them from Gaza. Most of these would never again see the city that for twenty-five years they had helped to build, entertain and develop, only 50 kilometers away from their own slums.

By cutting the territories into four zones, completely separated from each other, the closure created a total upheaval in the social, cultural, family and economic life of the Palestinians. It meant the end of their freedom of movement, one of the rare liberties that Israel had not challenged during the first twenty-five years of the occupation. With the exception of some political activists and former prisoners, Palestinians had been able to circulate without hindrance inside the occupied territories as well as in Israel itself. The peace process ushered in the end of that basic freedom. The occupied territories were encircled by military checkpoints, and the military government issued travel permits as it pleased to certain privileged individuals, to essential workers and Palestinian VIPs. The scope of the closure would increase from time to time, occasionally becoming total closure (with cancellation of all permits), then an internal closure (a state of siege in the Palestinian autonomous zones) and, since the end of 2000, an "encirclement," the confinement by the military of all the cities and dozens of villages of the West Bank.

As a result of the closure and its drastic measures, many Palestinians came to regret the period before the Oslo agreement, regarding the "peace process" as the worst feature of the occupation since 1967. Yet, for the majority of Israelis, the closure was the very essence of the process: "They're in theirs, we're in ours" became the Labor Party's electoral slogan. The party even refused to dismantle the settlements set up at the very heart of the Palestinian population, as at Hebron or at Psagot, near Ramallah. Ehud Barak liked to say: "Tall fences make good neighbors." The word "separation" (*hafrada*) entered the lexicon of sacred concepts, alongside the "Jewish State," "Jewish immigration" (*aliya**), and "security" (*bitahon*).

Very few Israelis understood the depravity of this unilateral and compulsory separation. In June 1995 I asked Naomi Hazan, a Meretz member of parliament, what could be done to stop the closure of the territories. She seemed surprised and replied: "Nothing. The closure is the beginning of the separation, a step towards a Palestinian State. This is how to accustom public opinion to the future borders." What blindness! The majority of Israelis saw more clearly than the Meretz deputy that closure was not a border but a prison.

The concept of a border implies a minimum of reciprocity, each side being able to decide at any given moment who comes in and who goes out. It implies negotiating with the other side the procedures, conditions, indeed the numbers allowed to enter its own territory. The closure is totally different: it is forced on the Palestinians by the Israelis, who decide unilaterally who enters and who leaves, not only to the Israeli territory but to the Palestinian territory as well. The closure imposes separation on the Palestinians, and a separation imposed unilaterally is called *apartheid* in Dutch. As Ilan Halevi wrote:

> It is significant that the Hebrew word used is *hafrada* [separation], which expresses the idea of an external action, of a coercive act, and not *hipardouth*, from the same root, which refers to the notion of self-separation, that is, secession. Thus it really is *apartheid* in the most classic sense.[3]

As in South Africa of the 1950s, it is a real segregationist obsession, consistent with the goal of a Jewish State as being as ethnically pure as possible, which allows the separation of populations while keeping

3. Ilan Halevi, "Apartheid is not socialist," *Revue d'études palestiniennes*, no. 22, Winter 2000, pp.116–17.

control of space, borders and natural resources in the hands of the Israelis. The Palestinians are free to police their reservations and to administer their education, health, social services and municipalities – provided, of course, that they can find the needed funds.

As long as closure was the system adopted during the transition period only, the Palestinians and their leadership were made to suffer its devastating effects. According to Oslo, the system would disappear within five to six years at the latest and give way to an independent state possessing territorial continuity, real borders, and thus, sovereignty. At the Camp David summit in July 2000, the Palestinian negotiators discovered, to their great surprise, that the Israeli government wanted to make the apartheid system, namely the fragmented territories, the control of the borders and natural resources, into the final status and ultimate solution of the Palestinian national question. This offer, described at the time as extremely generous by the media, which made no effort to grasp its real meaning, was perceived by the entire Palestinian community as a slap in the face and proof of an insufferable arrogance on the part of a government that had promised to "bring one hundred years of conflict to a conclusive end."

That was when the second Intifada started. A few months later, negotiations were renewed at Taba, where the Americans offered entirely new proposals that would have led to real progress. For a variety of reasons, the Taba talks failed to change the course of events. The Oslo process was buried for good and, with it, what the Americans had called the "window of opportunity" was closed. For in the meantime, Israeli public opinion had also changed. In less than ten years, a veritable social revolution had drastically transformed the Israeli political landscape, allowing Ariel Sharon to be elected prime minister of a society that had changed completely since the beginning of the negotiations process.

Developments within the "internal borders" of Israel had little by little taken precedence over the dynamic of Israeli–Arab relations, and had become decisive in the evolution of the reality of its external borders.

16
Jews and Israelis

The first time I ever heard an anti-Semitic remark was in Tel Aviv. I had never been the target of such remarks in Strasbourg, even though I had spent 16 years there as a practicing Jew, displaying my religion with the skullcap I wore on my head. (I had only taken that cap off once, during a gathering of the far right, at which the anti-Semite French politician Tixier-Vignancourt was supposed to speak. With a friend, I had planned, rather foolishly, to go and heckle him, but the presence of burly skinhead goons quickly changed our minds...)

Once in 1965, during a visit to Tel Aviv my very own cousin called me a kike. I liked Jerusalem. I had spent the summer in a Talmudic school and felt at home. In Tel Aviv, which I found impersonal and dirty, everything except the language was foreign to me. There were not many practicing Jews around, or at least not visibly so. My cousin, born in Tel Aviv, was a true Sabra, loud-mouthed, self-confident and proud of his physique. Compared to him, and in his view, I looked very much like a Jew: rather puny, my back slightly stooped, with my skullcap, white nylon shirt and polyester pants. I had probably said "Sorry!" too often to the passers-by who bumped into me on Dizengoff street (the boulevard that was then the pride of Tel Aviv because of its anonymous modernism). That was when my cousin told me, with the contempt of someone who was ashamed to be seen alongside a bumpkin fresh from the farm: "Stop acting like a little kike, you're not in Strasbourg."[1]

The woman who was to become my companion, herself a Sabra, would describe anybody who did not seem tough enough in her eyes as a *savonette* (a bar of soap). This Israeli expression was a blasphemous allusion to what the Nazis did with the fat of the Jews massacred at Treblinka and Auschwitz. "Blasphemous" was the word that stuck in my mind the first time I heard the expression. I remember feeling

1. One shouldn't think that this was merely an isolated incident. In January 2002, on several occasions, Zvi Handel, a National Union Party deputy, called the US ambassador in Tel Aviv a yid because he had suggested spending less money on the settlements.

my whole body tremble, as if my mother had been called a whore or someone had urinated in front of the tabernacle of the synagogue. It was absolutely incredible and yet terribly commonplace in the Israel of the 1960s, where weakness was considered a flaw. Encountering that aspect of Israeli culture forced me to confront the barrier of hatred and bloodshed that had separated Jews and anti-Semites throughout history. But I was dealing with Jews like myself, who seemed to have suddenly donned the cassocks of Inquisition priests, Cossack tunics or SS uniforms. Was it necessary, in order to become an Israeli, to swear allegiance to the executioners of the Jewish people and to their ideologies? Did they expect me to spit on the charred corpses of my relatives so that I would not be considered unworthy of the new Jewish sovereignty?

The connection between Zionism and anti-Semitism had always been an ambivalent one. The Zionist movement, born in response to modern anti-Semitism that took root in Western Europe through the Dreyfus Affair, shared some of the symptoms of the disease it was supposed to cure. For numerous Zionist thinkers of Central Europe, Zionism offered a remedy to the problem of the East European Jews. These were considered to be an obstacle to the assimilation of the Jews of France, Germany and Vienna, as well as those of Budapest, England and Italy, into European modernity. The destitution and anti-Semitism of the Czarist Empire were pushing hundreds of thousands of Polish, Byelorussian and Lithuanian Jews to emigrate to the West. These embodied an image of the Jew that assimilated Jews had been trying to erase for more than a century. If these Eastern Jews could emigrate elsewhere, then assimilation might succeed; thus the idea of the Jewish State, in the beginning, was not necessarily linked to Palestine.

From its inception, Zionism always carried within it a rejection not only of Judaism, but even of the Jew himself, or at least of a certain way of being Jewish. That Jew was crudely caricatured by the ideologues of Zionism: primitive, reactionary, unproductive, parasitic, passive, effeminate – in a word, degenerate. Zionism wanted to rid Europe of these bad Jews for the greater good of modern and civilized "Israelites."

To accomplish this, Zionism clearly needed anti-Semitism. As Golda Meir said at the beginning of the 1970s (and I paraphrase): "Too much anti-Semitism is not good because it leads to genocide; no anti-Semitism at all is also not good because then there would be no immigration (to Israel). What we need is a moderate anti-Semitism."

Hence the strange relations between Zionism, and later the State of Israel, with certain anti-Semitic regimes: from Herzl, who negotiated the departure of Jews from Russia with the notoriously anti-Semitic Czarist minister Plehve, to the economic and military connections of Prime Minister Rabin's government with the anti-Semitic military dictatorships of Argentina and Chile, a country in which the Jewish Agency, charged with facilitating the immigration of Jews, enjoyed a privileged status.

After its creation the Jewish State became a goal in itself and no longer simply a means for protection from anti-Semitism. "Come to Israel to save yourself" very quickly became "Come to Israel to strengthen Israel." One of the popular slogans of the 1970s was: "From one immigrant to another, our strength is assured." During the 1980s, the campaign to free Soviet Jews was conducted solely within the perspective of immigration to Israel. Different Israeli governments opposed the policy of free emigration defended by the Austrian Chancellor, Bruno Kreisky. That battle was won by Israel at the Malta summit in 1985, when Gorbachev was persuaded to forbid transit through Vienna. Ninety percent of the Jewish emigrants arriving there opted to go to the West rather than Israel. Thanks to direct flights from Bucharest to Tel Aviv, Soviet Jews who wanted to leave their country (as well as all those who pretended to be Jews in order to obtain the much-coveted visas) became Zionists by default.

The ambivalence towards anti-Semitism is not limited to state policy; it is also found in Zionist ideology and in Israeli culture. Zionism is not solely focused on the goal of creating a Jewish State by gathering exiles from the four corners of the earth on their ancestral land. It also seeks to regenerate the immigrant Jews by voluntary means. In their national home, they lead a free, productive and modern life, and become, by a process of acculturation and assimilation, Hebrews, Israelis. In the melting pot of the new Israeli culture, the education system and the army, the roots linking the new immigrants to their own history wither, their traditions and their culture of origin disappear, and their outward appearance – often portrayed by Israeli cartoonists of the 1940s and 1950s in ways that conjure up anti-Semitic caricatures – is replaced by the image of the Sabra, big, virile, blond, with blue eyes: in short, an Aryan Jew.

In *The Seventh Million,*[2] the historian Tom Segev described perfectly the contemptuous attitude of these Sabras towards the Jewish refugees

2. Published in Paris by Liana Levi, 1998, and translated by Eglal Errera.

of Central Europe and later on towards the survivors of the Nazi genocide, who had the misfortune of being pale, undernourished and often sad-faced. In a word, they looked too Jewish – and, above all, they had failed to face up to their enemies, and had let their loved ones be massacred "like sheep going to the slaughter."

How does one explain that attitude of contempt towards the victims of Judeocide? Much has been written about the problems of the survivors, their feelings of guilt on still being alive, their great difficulty in understanding the horror, in seeing the bodies and the wounded souls of those who experienced discrimination, the ghettoes, the raids and the camps. But as far as the attitude of the Jews of Israel is concerned, before and especially after the creation of the state, at least two additional factors must be included. First of all there was the profound shame of the Jew of the Diaspora, whose weakness, individual and collective, was so starkly revealed under the Nazi yoke. Zionism aspired to be the absolute antithesis of that weakness. The Israeli is ashamed of the Jew of the ghetto, just as the *nouveau riche* is ashamed of the parents who remain what they always were: unaffected, poor, unsophisticated and strangers to the modernism that seeks to impose itself as the only standard. This shame is enhanced by a feeling of guilt and failure: the existence of a Jewish community in Palestine, modern, armed and partially sovereign, failed to stop the Judeocide, and did little, if anything, to try to stop the massacre, or even to save as many Jews as possible. In the Israeli unconscious, especially in the years following the creation of the state, the feeling of guilt was clearly pervasive. But in a perverse and banal way it was turned against the victims: why did they let it happen? Why didn't the great majority of the Jews fight? The Zionist answer is: because they were not men like all the rest, they were "bars of soap."

For months, my friends at Talmudic school had insisted: "You can write French, you must translate this book so that the whole world might know the truth." The fact that my Yiddish left much to be desired did not discourage them: it was imperative that the Francophone world should know what had really happened during the war in Eastern Europe, and assess the inglorious role played by the Zionist leadership. What an assignment for a 17-year-old!

My comrades were talking about the book *From the Depths of the Abyss* by Rabbi Michal Dov Weismandel. That remarkable man describes the immense efforts he undertook to save the Jews of

Slovakia and, later on, to convince the allied governments to take military measures that might stop the genocide. But the book is also a terrible indictment of the cynical and criminal passivity of the Zionist leadership in Palestine, which refused to mobilize international Jewish public opinion to try to convince the Anglo-Americans to bomb, for example, the railroads leading to Auschwitz.

The Zionist leader Nathan Schwalb wrote to Rabbi Weismandel:

> One should never forget that it was known that when the Allies would finally win, just like after the First World War, they would divide up the world amongst the nations, and that's why one had to do everything so that Palestine would become the State of Israel ... One also needs to know that the Allies lost rivers of blood, and if we did not have our own share of martyrs, what right would we have to sit at their table when they would be dividing up people and countries after the war? It's only with blood that we can inherit our country.[3]

That response, accurately reflecting the position of the Zionist leadership of the time, can help one understand the immense gulf that separated Zionism from the majority of the religious community in Israel. It was a gulf viewed with contempt by some and by others as a terrible indictment of complicity – or passive complacency – with the genocide.

The religious world, which deemed itself to be the repository of the memory of massacred European Jewry, accused the Zionist establishment of having viewed the genocide as a means to accelerate the process of the creation of the State of Israel. Some are even convinced that, for the Zionists, the Judeocide was a positive phenomenon that contributed to the purification of the Jewish people, facilitating the future regeneration of the survivors in Palestine.

In 1954 Israeli society was shaken by the libel suit brought by the government against Malkiel Greenwald, a member of the religious community of Jerusalem. In a little-read pamphlet he accused the famous Hungarian Zionist, Rudolf Kastner, and the Zionist leadership of Palestine, of collaboration with the Nazis during their occupation of Hungary. Although the court ruled that Greenwald was liable for

3. Cited in S.B. Beit-Zvi, *Post-Ugandan Zionism in the Crucible of the Holocaust*, Tel Aviv, Bronfman Publishers, 1977, p. 346.

damages of one cent plus interest, it concluded that "Kastner had sold his soul to the devil."

I never translated Rabbi Weismandel's book, but coming across his name again some years later in an anti-Zionist far left gathering played a part in determining my future political course. Those activists were among the rare Israelis who expressed a profound empathy with the Judaism of the Diaspora and its suffering, rejecting the manipulative attitude of Zionism towards the death of the Jewish masses of the Diaspora. The universalistic humanism of the group was not limited to the defense of the Palestinians: it was also manifest in a great respect for non-Israeli Jews, from the Shtetl and the Mellahs as well as from the Orthodox quarters of Jerusalem.

Paradoxically, with my skullcap, I felt more like a foreigner in Israel than in Strasbourg. During the 1960s, being a practicing Jew and looking like one meant that one was not yet a real Israeli, much like the relative who arrives from the country and, even though accepted in good faith by his urbanized and modern family, has to work hard to justify being considered a city person and thoroughly urban citizen. In the eyes of the new Israeli, the practicing Jew was a residue of the Diaspora who should be made to disappear.

Israel already belonged to its second generation. Hardly concealing its admiration, the first excused the second its aggressiveness, its lack of culture and its vulgarity. Above all, it admired that which gave its children a non-Jewish look. Was it a coincidence that Israel and the new Jew brought up in Israel were admired in the West as well? They hardly looked like Jews! For the Europeans, Israel was Sophia Loren in *Exodus* or those strapping blond guys driving tractors, with machine-guns slung over their shoulder.

The others were not shown, except to affirm the continuity of Jewish history with a certain sense of folklore: Yemeni immigrants stepping off the plane on to the Promised Land or Orthodox Jews in the religious quarters of Jerusalem. Continuity, but breakdown too. The "other Israel," which one hardly ever saw in the propaganda films or the enthusiastic reporting about the renaissance of Israel, was the periphery, the fringe: it was the "development cities" of the Negev and Galilee, or the agricultural villages, the wretched moshavim of the Jerusalem corridor, where fifteen years later they still did not speak Hebrew. The majority of the immigrants from Arab countries were concentrated there: religious for the most part, or at least traditionalists, attached to their culture and their rites, but compelled to change their lifestyle and their attitudes to be worthy of the new Jewish State.

Until the end of the 1980s these two realities had precise names: on the one hand, the "Beautiful Israel," Western, modern, liberal and secular; on the other, the "Second Israel," traditionalist, Orthodox, religious, Diaspora-like. To go from Second Israel to Beautiful Israel, to cross the border that separated the periphery from the center, one had to take off the skullcap, lose one's accent and choose Western and secular modernity.

Among practicing Jews, there were many who shut themselves off in their ghettoes and maintained a more or less discreet antagonism towards the new culture and what it represented; others tried to hide their faith; a minority tried to fuse their faith with their Zionism, doing their best to be worthy of the new country. I remember my Aunt Claire, who, coming out of the synagogue, pointed to Elhanan Blumenthal, in his paratrooper's uniform, telling me proudly: "You see, some paratroopers are religious too." The remark reminded me of my maternal grandfather, who was also so proud of the Jewish soldiers who had received the Iron Cross at the Verdun front!

There are countries where the internal border exists between the social classes; there are others where ethnic and national differences prevail. In Israel, the line of demarcation passes between the Israeli center and the Jewish periphery. While the great majority of the liberal and democratic left was clearly situated in the center, I naturally found myself in the periphery. Naturally, because I was also a practicing and Diaspora Jew, and naturally because everything in my childhood and in my education led me to identify with those who were different, pointed at, tolerated at best, and at worst excluded from the community.

A quarter of a century later, when the fringe decided to claim its place at the heart of Israeli society, the entire contradiction between Jews and Israelis would blow up. Contrary to the expectations of the founding fathers, the border erected between the past of the Diaspora and the modern and sovereign present did not vanish in a process of absorption of the fringe by the center. It had become a wall of hatred and of mutual fear.

17
The periphery becomes the center

The day after the election of Yitzhak Rabin in 1992, the Labor deputy Yossi Beilin (who would later be the chief negotiator of the Oslo accords) made the following comment on television:

> There is a risk that the results of this election are the fruit of circumstances that may not appear again. We must therefore take advantage and move forward rapidly in the peace process, because it may well be that this is the last time that the left has the possibility of putting its program to work.

This perceptive analysis stood out against the triumphalist statements of the entire Zionist left, which saw this return to power by Labor as the closure of an anomalous interlude that had lasted for fifteen years. The Zionist left-wingers had a tendency to confuse the State of Israel with themselves, as they were the ones who had built it in their own image and according to their view of the world. For fifteen years they had refused to see the sociological, political and cultural upheavals that had refashioned Israeli society. With each electoral defeat, every time the Shass Party grew stronger, they spoke about it with surprise as if it was a setback that would not happen again. The general trend, however, was indisputable: the Israel of Ben Gurion, the kibbutzim, and the colonels who could quote Virgil, was disappearing.

To a certain extent, Beilin's warning was already too late: the left-wing government set up by Yitzhak Rabin did not reflect the sociopolitical reality of Israel, and its policy of compromise with the Palestinians clashed with an increasingly influential sector of public opinion. Since the early 1980s a new social and political bloc had emerged, based on a deep-seated rejection of Labor, its elites, its ideology and its blueprint for society. This group was divided by profound social and cultural contradictions but its rejection of Labor created a powerful enough bond to guarantee its solidity. It was composed of those who, since the foundation of the state, had not met the criteria of the "new Jew" and were pushed to the sidelines of the new society being built. On the one hand were Jews of Arab or Oriental cultures (Jewish Kurds, Persians or Indians) who were perceived as too backward to be the standard-bearers of the modernist Zionist mission; on the other were religious Jews whose faith and practice were considered to be relics of the Diaspora. In the eyes of the founding fathers of Israel these ethnic and cultural particularities should have disappeared within one or two generations in the melting pot of an aggressive socialization designed to compel integration – or rather, assimilation – into the Western and secular model. With assimilation achieved, everybody would find their place at the center of Israeli society, even the children of those who had been pushed to the sidelines, to the geographic and social periphery.

Well, a generation has come and gone but the periphery has remained the periphery.

The massive immigration coming from the republics of the ex-USSR, hailed as capable of propelling the preceding immigrant waves upwards on the social ladder, passed right over them, leaving hundreds of thousands of children of Moroccan, Kurdish, Iraqi and Yemeni immigrants far behind. Despite school, the army and other institutions of integration, the "Second Israel" has not disappeared. However, things have changed: it can be said that if, between the 1950s and the 1980s, the periphery was excluded from the national collective, from 1980 it excluded itself, willingly rejecting the official discourse and the dominant culture.

I realized this after my release from prison when I decided to continue working on social activities around issues that I had taken up behind bars. In addition to literacy classes (I had discovered in prison that there were illiterate Israelis, Jews and Arabs born in Israel), I volunteered to work in a detox center, where I organized discussions on current affairs. I was asked to organize some activity for the day commemorating the Holocaust, a subject close to my heart and about which I was used to preparing discussions, particularly with young people. The men and women who frequented the detox center were mostly of Sephardic origin, almost all of them born in Israel. I launched into the matter and had been speaking for less than 15 minutes when one of the participants interrupted me, saying: "Michel, you are an educated guy, and we know that you are not an idiot. Furthermore, we really believe that you respect us. So why are you spinning all those yarns about six million murdered Jews? Don't tell us that you believe it!" Most of the others nodded their heads in agreement with him. Completely stunned, I asked: "And you, what do you believe?" They replied, agreeing: "The Ashkenazim want to make us believe that they and not we are the victims. But we won't fall for it." This incident was repeated every year, even after I took them to the Yad Vashem memorial, filled with its documents and horrifying photographs.

My view is that once the ruling classes are no longer able to impose their worldview and their ideology on those whom they want to control, the periphery begins to become conscious of itself, its own character and that which sets it against the power of the elites. At that point there is a revolution, or at the very least, a fracture.

During the course of the 1980s we were witness to a real seesaw between the center and the periphery, in terms of political power and in the dominant discourse. The fringe groups, in particular the religious communities and the Oriental Jews, began to support en masse the parties of the right, not so much because of ideological affinity but as a rejection of the left, that is to say the Labor Party. That coalition between the traditional right and the excluded is a winning combination, statistically and ideologically. Statistically, because the religious and Oriental communities are continuing to grow in number to the detriment of the secular Jews of European origin; ideologically, because the discourse of the Zionist left is itself impregnated with nationalism and religion, and therefore can only reinforce the doctrine it is supposed to fight in order to retain its dominance.

It is very important to understand that the common denominator of this anti-leftist bloc is not the ideology of "Greater Israel" and the settlements, but the desire to give Israel a more pronounced Jewish character, the opposite of the globalist discourse and non-observant lifestyle of the left. The zeal for the Judaization of Israel is expressly opposed to the "Israelization" symbolized by the myth of the kibbutz without morals and Tel Aviv, the heathen city. In this situation, the frequent electoral visits by Labor leaders to rabbis and other Kabbalist centenarians elicit nothing but mocking smiles.

The Yemeni families have not forgotten the children that were taken from them during the 1950s to be given up for adoption by Ashkenazi families. They also remember the side-curls that were snipped by the zealous bureaucrats of the Ministry of Immigration. The Iraqi Jews have not forgiven those who greeted them with DDT sprays, especially since a good proportion of the immigrants from Baghdad were better educated and cultured than those who were claiming to civilize them. The Moroccans, above all, do not forget or forgive the contempt to which they were subjected, and they envy the good fortune of their compatriots who, instead of "coming up" to Israel, chose to emigrate to Paris or Montreal. As for the Orthodox Jews from Poland, Bessarabia or Lithuania, they no longer want to be confined by the contempt and condescension that surrounded them. The Moroccan Jews liked Begin not only because he was not contemptuous of them but also because he attended synagogue and knew how to recite the sacred texts; the Orthodox respected Netanyahu because his political movement never publicly expressed contempt for tradition. Thus Orthodox and Arab Jews removed Labor from power and replaced it with the right. The victory of Yitzhak Rabin in 1992 was truly a digression provoked by the catastrophic manner in which Shamir had conducted Israel's domestic and foreign policy, to the point of turning his back, with archaic extremism, on the American administration as well as a chunk of his traditional electorate.

At the beginning of this alliance between the right and those excluded by the Labor state, the ideology of Greater Israel had only a limited influence over the mass of voters. Contrary to often-prejudiced superficial analyses, the Israeli populace is not "automatically right wing." At the beginning of the peace process they wanted peace and were willing to pay the price. When Deputy Meir Shitrit tried to organize the locally elected Likud officials on the eve of the Knesset vote on the Declaration of Principles for the Oslo accords, they told him that they could not campaign against the accords for fear of losing the support of their voters.

The return of the left to power did not mean any change in attitude of the elites towards the peoples of the periphery. On the contrary, the elites acted as if they had retrieved what rightly belonged to them, and re-established control of a state that they had always considered to be their private property. Their arrogance evoked that of the leaders of Versailles re-entering Paris after the crushing of the Commune, but now under the banners of privatization of the public sector and dismantling of social services. The Minister of Health decreed the payment of fees for visits to doctors; the Minister of Social Services wanted to abolish family benefits for the first two children; and the Minister of Education, Shulamit Aloni, launched the idea of schools that "would really be a lot of fun," with a great deal of curricular autonomy. The schools would be financed by parents' committees in better-off areas, while the representatives of poor districts and the development cities went begging for budgetary allocations for public schools without any resources at all.

In January 1997 I prepared a report on the crisis of the textile industry in the townships of southern Israel. One after the other, factories that had been built and subsidized to give work to immigrants sent to Judaize the country's south had closed their doors. The instructions from the IMF were clear: end government subsidies, and allow only profitable enterprises – that is to say none – to remain in operation. Anger ran high in Dimona, Ofakim and Sderot. I met Yaish Jerousi, who had emigrated in 1961 from Casablanca to Dimona, a new town springing up in the Negev dunes. He had worked for 36 years in a textile factory that had just closed:

> The country stops at Kiryat Gat.[1] Haven't you noticed that even the rain stops at Kiryat Gat? Here in Dimona, it's no longer Israel, it's Gaza. It's worse than Gaza, because the government gives plenty of money to Gaza, and they have completely forgotten us. Everything for the Arabs, nothing for us, that is the new Middle East of the left.[2]

At Dimona I realized that while the well-to-do social groups found immediate benefit in the peace process, whether economic, professional or symbolic (*vis-à-vis* liberal opinion in Europe), the working-class sector saw few improvements, except for individual security, although that too became questionable with the suicide attacks of 1996 that followed the assassination of the Islamic leader Yihya Ayash.

The assassination of the Israeli Prime Minister in November 1996, or rather the manner in which the left responded to that event,[3] would sanction the victory of the anti-Labor bloc and secure the dominance of right-wing ideology within the bloc itself. Less than one week after Rabin's murder, the telephone rang at the Alternative Information Center. The secretary general of "Peace Now!" informed me that the emergency meeting of peace organizations scheduled for the following day had been indefinitely postponed. We were to have discussed a response to the assassination and to the campaign of hatred and violence that had preceded it. "It is not the appropriate

1. A town of immigrants in southern Israel.
2. *Mitsad Sheini,* no. 7, January–February 1997.
3. On changes in Israeli society in the 1990s, see Dominique Vidal, "Troublante Normalisation pour la sociète israélienne," *Le Monde Diplomatique*, May 1996.

moment for such an initiative," Mossi Raz told me. "One should not pour oil on the fire." The next day I learned from the newspapers that the leaders of "Peace Now!" had preferred to meet with the representatives of the Council (of the Settlements) of Judea, Samaria and Gaza, the very ones who had incited the violence and challenged the legitimacy of the Prime Minister!

After a few days of confusion the right quickly realized that the assassin of Rabin and those who had encouraged him to commit his crime had won their bet: the left would never again undertake initiatives without giving the right the power of veto over their legitimacy. The reason why "national reconciliation" became the immediate post-Rabin credo is, therefore, pretty obvious. The left had ceased to have its own political line, distinct from that of the militant right. The previously minority ideas of the right had become official *policy,* particularly with regard to the settlements. Since the left had come around to agreeing the right, why would it have been otherwise for the working-class base of the anti-Labor bloc? After the assassination of Rabin the left–right divide ceased to exist. The colonization of the West Bank and Gaza became one of the components of the new consensus, the only debate being the question of the number of new settlements. It explains why so many Labor voters and activists had no problem shifting their vote to Sharon a few years later.

In 1996 the election of Benjamin Netanyahu meant a lot more than merely the return of the right to power after the Rabin–Peres interlude. With unprecedented verbal brutality, Netanyahu had formulated a new political program for Israel and marked out the limits of legitimate discourse. He had pushed the Zionist left into a rearguard battle, always on the defensive in trying to limit the extent of its decline. Under the pressure of the right-wing offensive the Oslo process was stripped of its substance, and in the end lost all legitimacy in the eyes of a large part of public opinion.

Unlike the election of Yitzhak Rabin in 1992, that of Ehud Barak in 1999 would not reflect a change in political power. Barak positioned himself openly within the national policy and ideology defined during the iron-fist years of Netanyahu. When, immediately after his election, the ex-Chief of Staff Barak paid a visit to the extremist settlers of Ofra and Beit-El, and called them "my dear brothers," he was not engaging in demagogy to neutralize the right opposition: he was truly identifying with the settlers, their politics and their ideology.

Contrary to Rabin, Barak refused to collaborate with the Arab parties that had given him 90 percent of the votes of the Israeli Palestinian population, but he immediately brought into the government the National Religious Party, the political home of the extreme right settlers. That is why the Camp David fiasco was fundamental to the basic policy of Barak and his government of national unity. That policy never questioned the colonization of the Palestinian territories, doomed to become Bantustans according to the wishes of his predecessor Netanyahu and his successor Sharon.

The rallying of Israeli public opinion, and particularly of the marginalized communities, to the right-wing discourse was not inevitable. It was the direct result of the inability of the left to defend a coherent program, distinguishable from that of the right, a program that would advocate the values of peace, coexistence, democracy and respect for human rights, while rejecting the philosophy and practice of colonization on the basis of principle rather than pragmatic opportunism. It also followed a total renunciation by the left of its social mission.

Today, the political fault line in Israeli society is no longer between settlers and pacifists, or moderates and conservatives. The divide is social and cultural, and unlike the issues linked to the Israeli–Arab conflict, around which the right and the left were always able to find the basis of a national consensus, this divide represents a fatal risk to the Zionist project and truly threatens to cut the Israeli people in two.

An iron curtain is being erected between two social blocs with antagonistic blueprints for society. On one side are those who want to follow the original plan of the Zionist founding fathers, namely, a modern state, Jewish but not theocratic, a democracy for the Jewish population, and participating in neoliberal globalization. Most of them are the second and third generations of Western and Eastern European immigrants; they enjoy a European lifestyle, and are comfortable, even wealthy. Opposing them are the children and grandchildren of the Oriental immigrants, still living in their ghettoes: the development towns in northern and southern Israel and the impoverished districts of the great cities, far from the wealth of the residential quarters of Tel Aviv. They dream of "returning to one's roots," of a lost paradise where the values of tradition, family and community solidarity would replace the liberal market and cosmopolitan modernism that is trampling them underfoot.

Each camp lays claim to a different legitimacy. For the first it is the recent past that justifies their dominance, the fruition of the work of their pioneer parents, their efforts and sacrifices in building the country and its defense; they made the desert bloom, and, arms in hand, defended the new Jewish sovereignty. The second camp looks back to a more distant past, and they question those whom their spiritual leaders have nicknamed the "Hellenized": "Did you say a Jewish State? But what do you know about Judaism? What's it to you who eat pork and oysters and have never set foot in a synagogue? It is we who are the heirs of three millennia of Jewish history, the guarantors of the Jewish character of Israel. Here, you are the strangers; you are much more at home in Los Angeles or London!"

Today the marginalized groups claim a legitimacy acquired through the ballot box: they are the majority in society and in Parliament, yet they do not have power. Economic power, the media and the state institutions are still in the hands of the old elites. It is why they hate the media ("No to the hostile media!" is a popular sticker) and detest the judicial system, particularly the Supreme Court, which tries through its rulings to safeguard the original liberal and modernist Zionist plan. In 1997 more than 250,000 Israelis demonstrated against the Supreme Court because it had dared to challenge an anti-democratic rabbinical decision.

In short, for more than a generation, the parties representing the periphery have been in office, but real power has eluded them. Those of the periphery feel that they have been robbed of what is rightly theirs, and the center fears that the "populace" – that is the word used – will tear apart its "beautiful" Jewish and democratic state. As is often the case, hatred between the two is directly proportional to the fear that each camp feels towards the other: The first fears that an ignorant and fanaticized people is pulling it once more into the darkness of the ghetto; the second that it will be assimilated by force into the global village and its Western lifestyle. Each camp shuts itself in and erects barriers to protect itself against the other.

Which side of this border should one be on? This question is more difficult than the one we had to answer during the 1960s and 1970s. The border between Israelis and Arabs was the border between occupiers and the occupied, between oppressors and the oppressed. At that time, if one had a working political and ethical compass, one knew whom to denounce and whom to support, whom to fight and with whom to stand in solidarity. But armed with that same compass pointing in the direction of human rights, justice, liberty and equality, can one choose where to stand near a divide that goes right to the heart of Israeli society?

One week after the election of Ehud Barak I participated in the opening of the annual festival of liturgical music at Abu Gosh, a beautiful Arab village near Jerusalem, with a basilica dedicated to Notre Dame of the Ark of the Covenant. The choir I sing in was due to perform Fauré's *Requiem*. The festival of Abu Gosh is one of those events where one sits among cultured and well-off folks to listen to beautiful music, drink excellent wine and to relax, far from the "other Israel" that threatens our beautiful civilization. A few minutes before the beginning of the concert, the director of the festival, Hagi Goren, raised a toast to "our" victory and to the "hope of finally rediscovering the Israel we love." The hundreds of people in attendance raised their glasses, happy to have saved the country from "Levantinization." I was outraged by such pretension and prejudice. Apparently no one attending the festival could imagine that the voters of Shass or Likud could like Fauré or Mendelssohn. I put down my glass and went back into the basilica to await the beginning of the concert.

These were the same people who a few days earlier, on the announcement of Barak's victory at the Rabin Plaza in Tel Aviv, had shouted: "Anyone but Shass!" They had no objection at all to Barak entering into a coalition with the National Religious Party of the extreme right, but rejected with disgust the religious party of the working-class groups containing Jews of Arab culture, who at that time were far more politically moderate. The conflict between the right and the left was no longer an ideological conflict, but a class conflict between two antagonistic social projects, between two ways of imagining the Israel of the future.

I confess to preferring Mahler and Australian merlot to Arabic music and arak. I regret not having learned, like so many of my friends, to enjoy both. But I refuse to belong to that Israel that thinks itself progressive because it loathes the Orthodox Jews and despises the people. An Israel whose Mecca is Washington and whose Bible is the *Wall Street Journal*; an Israel that wants peace because peace will allow it to rid itself of the Arabs, but also fears peace because it will leave them standing face to face with their Oriental brothers. That Israel is not mine, and I fight against it. But on the other side of this border, I can no longer find my place in that Israel which refashions a scorned identity by siding with fundamentalism, chauvinism and the rejection of democratic standards; or which makes up for the dismantling of public schools by sending its children to the schools of the *el ha-Maayan* network, where they are bound to become both ignorant and fanatical; and which hopes in the end to establish an Orthodox regime where women – and men – will lose the civil liberties they have won during previous decades.

Fifty years after the birth of the Jewish State, the divide that fractures Israeli society is likely to leave very little room for those who defend a vision of a society based on democracy and solidarity, who are secular but respectful of cultural diversities, who are open to the Arab world but enriched with the democratic traditions of the French and American Revolutions. There is a great risk of being toppled over one side of the border in search of the lesser evil, and the rejection of what we used to call, not too long ago, the "main enemy." Yet we have to make the difficult choice of not choosing between these two deadly perspectives. We must engage simultaneously in a struggle against those who want to make Israel the advance post of the new neoliberal crusade against the nations of the Middle East and those who want to imprison it within an armed ghetto, led by the rabbis of a new Messianism, in which fundamentalism and nationalism reinforce each other.

18
Hallel's prayer

"Must one recite Hallel's prayer[1] on the day celebrating Israel's independence, or not?" Every year this question divided the religious community of Strasbourg. My father settled it according to an old rabbinical method, by taking the middle road: one would recite the Hallel but without a blessing. Behind this problem of ritual lay the attitude of the religious world towards Zionism, and since 1948, the State of Israel. The majority of practicing Jews, in the Diaspora and in Israel, did not feel that the existence of Israel was linked, in one way or another, to the Jewish religion. Few among them considered themselves Zionists; many claimed to be anti-Zionist. In my family one did not claim either position; we were practicing Jews and that was all we needed to say.

From its beginnings Zionism considered itself a radical and modern counterpoint to religion. The latter was perceived not only as an anachronism that no longer had its place in the modern world proclaimed by the ideologues and pioneers of Zionism, but also as the principal cause of the moral and material misery of the Jews and their two-millennia-long oppression. The majority of Zionists were atheists and anti-religious. It is said that during the 1920s, Golda Meir and other pioneers of the Labor-Zionist movement celebrated Yom Kippur with a great banquet in the main square of the Petah Tikva settlement. It was their way of publicly affirming that they had finally turned the page in Jewish history, and that the legends, rites and other superstitions of their parents had been tossed onto the scrap heap of history.

The rabbis were aware of this subversive dimension of Zionism, and many of them cursed the Zionists and their movement. Even after the creation of the State of Israel, and in spite of the mass immigration of religious survivors of the Nazi Judeocide, most religious practitioners of European origin remained hostile to Zionism. Although this phenomenon was less pronounced among religious Jews of Arab culture, at that time it was Ashkenazic Judaism that set the tone.

On Independence Day in 1966 and 1967 I saw the Israeli flag set on fire in the Orthodox quarter of Mea Shearim, and posters on the

1. A prayer of thanks recited on religious holidays.

walls calling believers to fast as a sign of mourning. Of course, that extremist view was only held by a tiny minority, even in such an Orthodox neighborhood. But so was the isolated and marginalized position of the Merkaz Harav Talmudic Academy, where I was studying, and where they hoisted the Star of David and recited the Hallel with the blessing on Israel's Independence Day.

It's true that Merkaz Harav was the only Talmudic college where the majority of the students had indeed done their military service and also proclaimed their membership in the Mizrahi* (the Zionist Religious Party). One did not wear the black suit and hat there, as was found in the other Talmudic colleges. It was more the kibbutz style that prevailed, a colored shirt worn outside the pants, Jesus-style sandals and a skullcap knitted by a sister ...or a girl friend.

The Talmudic schools did not consider the Merkaz Harav as belonging to their community, even though some of its teachers commanded a certain respect in rabbinical circles. Its founder, Rabbi Abraham Yitzhak Kook, had been the Chief Rabbi of Palestine during the 1930s, and as such, had tried – with limited success – to build bridges between the Zionist movement and Orthodox Judaism. His principal theoretical contribution was to see the Zionist movement and the effort to create a Jewish State as the first steps of the Messianic era. For the majority of rabbis and Orthodox Jews, these concepts bordered on heresy. My parents' decision to send me to study at the Merkaz Harav did not, I believe, show any inclination towards that Messianic ideology but, rather, a choice favoring a certain continuity with the Orthodox Judaism of Western Europe, the choice of modernity.

A very small minority of the religious milieu in Europe before the founding of Israel, the Mizrahi, the National Religious Party (PNR), became, after 1948, one of the most important political parties in the country. For Ben Gurion it had a dual function, on the one hand, providing religious support for the young state from Jewish communities throughout the world as well as from the large minority of practicing Jews in the Israeli population; on the other, providing a politico-cultural framework to help integrate the thousands of religious or traditional immigrants from the Arab countries. The power of the Mizrahi – particularly through the ministries and the municipalities, which it controlled – was in fact a part of the dominant power of the Labor-Zionist movement, which it ceded to this satellite party. In a way, the Mizrahi played a role identical to that of some peasant parties in the people's democracies in Eastern Europe, whose existence depended entirely on the good will of the Communist Parties and the importance they attributed to the existence of such satellite parties.

The Mizrahi completely embraced the dominant ideology, apart from its anti-clericalism, which it in turn replaced with the Messianic politics of Rabbi Kook. He was like the younger brother of the Labor Party, admiring his older brother and, by imitating him, often in a ridiculous manner, trying to resemble him as much as possible, wearing a knitted skullcap in place of the *kova tembel*.[2]

The contempt in which the Zionists held religion and the Orthodox Jews was matched only by the hatred these latter felt towards Zionism, but if the first was flaunted, the second was hidden. Moreover, it was combined with a real fear of being pushed towards *shmad*,[3] of having to renounce the way of life and the very existence of the religious community. Between 1965 and 1967, I took part in numerous demonstrations organized by the religious institutions in Jerusalem against autopsies or for the preservation of the ban against driving during the Sabbath in the religious quarters. The sobs of the speakers were heartrending, and occasionally the demonstrators tore their clothing in a sign of mourning. They perceived the Jewish State as an anti-Semitic regime as dangerous as that of Plehve in Russia, and its police (especially a certain Sergeant Markovitz, or "Gestapo Markovitz" as he was called in graffiti in the Mea Shearim quarter) as Cossacks who would not hesitate to massacre them. The kibbutzniks of the Hashomer Hatzair and the activists of the League Against Religious Coercion who came on Saturdays to the Shabbat Square to beat up the zealots did nothing but reinforce the memories of the pogroms that haunted the residents of Mea Shearim and Bnei Brak. In my eyes, too, they conjured up images of the pogromists of Poland, whom they seemed to resemble more closely than their own grandparents...

The Orthodox saw the danger of conversion looming everywhere. Because I spoke French, I was even recruited to the Peilim organization, whose mission was to save Jewish children who, for financial reasons, had been sent by their parents to study in Christian schools. My job was to search for such children in Catholic institutions, although

2. In Hebrew: *kova tembel*, the pull-down cap worn by the pioneers and the first kibbutzniks. From the 1950s to the 1970s, the *kova tembel* was the symbol of the Sabra.
3. Literally: extermination. In common usage, *shmad* is the term used in the Ashkenazic Jewish tradition to describe forced conversion.

without much success. Our cultural efforts were less heroic but more effective: with a small band and bags of candy we would organize parties in the villages on the outskirts, trying to counter the influence of the secular youth movements.

Thus the Orthodox communities lived just like oppressed communities, fighting to safeguard their existence in a state, which, in their eyes, was intending to liquidate the Jewish people, as they understood it. As for the believers recruited by the PNR, they were made to feel ashamed as Jews who tried to assimilate an Israeli identity while maintaining their faith and their practice as discreetly as possible.

In 1967, everything was turned upside down, and in the space of one generation, religion and the religious communities would not only stop being oppressed by the regime, they would become one of its essential components. This reversal occurred in two complementary movements.

The war of June 1967 would awaken an unprecedented Messianic feeling, particularly in Zionist religious circles. The "miraculous" victory over the Arab armies, the "liberation" of Jerusalem and other holy places, which had previously been under Jordanian control, created a completely new atmosphere. For some, the Messianic era had arrived; for the secular, or at least those who paid lip service to secularism, it was the realization of Zionism's ultimate objective. Rapidly, these two currents of opinion would converge in a great Messianic and nationalist movement whose discourse would eventually dominate Israeli public opinion, at least in its more moderate forms of expression.

In the religious world, the trend represented by the disciples of Rabbi Kook, who until 1967 had remained marginal, began to gain momentum. Its rabbis became personalities courted by the politicians of all the Zionist parties, and its processions to the Wailing Wall, originally religious, quickly became massive nationalist and militarist parades, and degenerated finally, in the 1980s, into bloody racist pogroms, two or three times a year.

This is the movement that would give rise to the Gush Emounim* (Bloc of the Faithful) and would be at the forefront of the settlers' organizations between 1970 and the end of the 1980s. The disciples of Rabbi Kook and the tens of thousands of young people who followed him no longer tried to imitate the secular population: they set the new standard, the post-1967 one, first for the secular, but rapidly for the religious as well.

Although most secular Israelis did not share the Messianic nationalism of Gush Emounim they acknowledged its great idealism and readily referred to its membership as the "New Pioneers of Zionism." Gush Emounim would be the driving force behind the settlement of the West Bank and the Gaza Strip, dragging along with it various governments of the right and the left, the army, and little by little, the majority of public opinion. As we have seen, the Labor Prime Minister, Ehud Barak, addressing the settlers of Ofra and Beit-El, bastions of the Gush Emounim in the West Bank, a few days after his election in 1990, called them "My dear brothers." Barak included representatives of the group in his government, hastening the departure of Meretz from his coalition.

In less than a generation, Messianic nationalism became an essential component of the new national discourse, even within Labor-Zionist circles. From the right to the left, one spoke of the Holy Land, evoked the divine covenant and venerated the holy places. The Zionist movement and Israel were no longer a solution to the Jewish question, but elements in the redemption of the Jewish people and the liberation of the Holy Land.

This new synthesis between religion and nationalism had an impact on Orthodox communities, which, until 1967, had jealously separated the Zionist project from the Divine message:

> Nobody can deny that the Six Day War provoked a turn to the right among the religious and the Orthodox. The political revolution of 1977[4] further accentuated the turn...We are witness to a strange combination: on the one hand, an important part of non-Zionist Orthodox society went through an ultra-nationalist process, and on the other, whole sections of the religious–nationalist public went through a process of "Orthodoxation", inheriting from the Orthodox their hatred of the left.[5]

As the June 1967 war had demolished the traditional Labor ideology, particularly its anti-religious dimension, the electoral victory of Menachem Begin in 1977 would signify the end of Labor's political hegemony. The combination of these two factors would

4. Which saw the end of Labor's political power.
5. Levy Ishak Hayerushalmi, *The Domineering Yarmulke,* Tel Aviv, Hakibbutx Hameuhad, 1997, p. 108. See also Israel Shahak and Norton Mezvinsky, *Jewish Fundamentalism in Israel,* London, Pluto Press, 1999, especially pp. 55–96.

push the majority of the religious world into the right-wing fold, first politically, then ideologically and finally, culturally. Since the left-Zionists had adopted the religious discourse, at least in part, the religious no longer had any reason to be afraid: not only were they no longer going to be destroyed or compelled to adopt the way of life and thinking of the secular, but the latter started to borrow more and more of the cultural baggage of the religious and publicly to express their respect and their indebtedness to a culture for which, a few years earlier, they had nothing but contempt.

Support for the Likud Party was seen by the Orthodox parties as far more natural than the alliance with Labor, which they had nevertheless regularly renewed since the founding of the state. It is true that Menachem Begin and his party never shared the anti-religious style of Labor-Zionism, and the majority of the leaders of the right did not conceal their attachment to tradition, often using a language with religious connotation; nor did they desert the synagogue, at least not on holidays. If the political collaboration between the religious parties and Labor was a marriage of convenience, the new alliance with the right quickly brought about a common perspective, and each of the parties would take significant steps in the direction of the other.

For the right, little by little a plan began to emerge to create a different society from the one Labor had tried to establish. It was one in which the values of Jewish tradition would take the place of socialist pretensions and where largely autonomous religious communities would replace the Jacobin centralism of Ben Gurion. Curricula were progressively transformed in the public high schools, and ample subsidies were allotted to the networks of schools affiliated with the religious parties; the state-controlled media increased their religious broadcasts, and celebrations of religious holidays became increasingly prominent. Parliament got in on the act, passing numerous laws restricting personal freedoms in favor of stricter observance of religious codes (the ban on the sale of pork, ban on opening stores on Saturday, and so on).

One needs to recall that the *status quo,* the phrase used by Ben Gurion since the 1940s to describe the *modus vivendi* between state and religion, had been seriously undermined by the 1970s. During the 1960s, only one solitary restaurant opened (discreetly) on Saturday, and only two butchers sold pork meat, but by the 1990s, one could count dozens of restaurants open on Saturday and similar numbers of stores that sold non-kosher products. So, contrary to what the secular community claimed – and sincerely believed – the Orthodox were not challenging the *status quo*, but really attempting to restore it. For them it was a matter of taking advantage of their increasing power in the state apparatus to put a stop to the growing secularization of civic life.

This dual and contradictory perception was reflected in the fact that each side felt that their respective lifestyles were being attacked and challenged.[6] It is the backdrop to what has been called over the last decade the "war of cultures." It is nevertheless significant that the secular put up a bigger fight for the right to eat shrimp than they did over the massive introduction of religious passages in school textbooks and rabbis in the public schools.

But the alliance between the right and the religious has not only led to a greater Judaization of the state; it has also engendered a nationalization of religion and of the religious groups. Traditionally, the latter had been the defenders of a moderate policy in Israeli–Arab relations, strongly influenced by the position of Diaspora Judaism, which favored making itself inconspicuous among other peoples, avoiding provocation and trying to safeguard Jewish lives. In broader terms, nationalism, militarism and machismo are values that Orthodox Judaism has always associated, with more or less concealed contempt, with the gentiles, while ascribing to itself the attributes of the weak, but also the shrewd.

During the 1980s the political alliance with the right would result in an ideological shift by the religious parties. In an increasingly sweeping rejection of everything that could be identified with the left, the religious parties progressively adopted the analyses and ideas of the right, not only on social matters but also on issues linked to the Israeli–Arab conflict. The Habad-Lubavitcher Hasidic* group would even embrace Messianic notions that up until then had been the sole preserve of the National Religious Party. What is even more symptomatic of this ideological, indeed theological, shift is that the other rabbis had agreed to ignore what they would previously have considered a heresy, and had chosen not to break with the Messianic trends in their ongoing struggle against the power of Labor.

That was the setting for my meeting in 1994 with a team from Israeli Television that was preparing a documentary on my political life. We

6. See Tsvia Greenfield's *Cosmic Fear: The Rise of the Religious Right in Israel*, Tel Aviv, Yediot Aharonot Books, 2001. This book, written by an Orthodox Jew who describes from the inside the evolution of the Orthodox communities in Israel, is called in Hebrew *They are afraid!*

were in front of the Hebron yeshiva*, one of the most prestigious Talmudic colleges in Jerusalem. The director wanted to organize an exchange between the ultra-Orthodox and myself, at one of the sites of my own pious adolescence. We were swiftly brushed aside by a half dozen or so Orthodox of all ages ("We do not speak to media hostile to the State of Israel," "the media are anti-religious," "the media are leftists"), when a woman came over to silence the younger ones, who were becoming more and more aggressive, and agreed to answer my questions.

She was not just anybody: she was no less than the grandchild of Rabbi Zonenfeld, the highest authority of the Orthodox Jews of Jerusalem in the 1930s, a committed, anti-Zionist leader who had gone as far as putting a curse on Rabbi Kook for his support of Zionism. To gain her confidence, I told her that, a long time ago, I myself had taken courses at the Hebron yeshiva and had had the privilege of being a student of her father. I then spoke to her about the anti-Zionism that was characteristic of Orthodox Judaism and, to my great surprise, she responded: "But we are Zionists! We are in fact the best Zionists, because only we, the Orthodox, can guarantee the Jewish character of this state. Moreover, that is why we should not do military service, because we respect the division of labor amongst ourselves: there are those who fight, those who settle and there are those who study Torah. But we complement each other..." I was frankly astonished and could barely ask her: "What would your grandfather, the venerable Rabbi Zonenfeld, say about your ideas?" To which she replied: "He too would have adapted to the new reality."

While it is undeniable that rabbis know how to juggle texts and thus change the law to accommodate circumstance and interests, it is impossible to understand this ideological–theological shift without taking into consideration another factor that marked a real turning point in the history of religious Judaism, what I would call rabbinical populism. For generations, rabbis handed down the law, and the faithful followed, unconditionally. Today, two phenomena have drastically changed that model: on the one hand, the proliferation of currents, sects and rabbinical trends; on the other, government support to religious institutions that is proportional to their respective strength. It means that the rabbis must win over the maximum number of the faithful in order to increase the government subsidies that go to their religious institutions and schools. They can no longer be indifferent to their public's opinion.

It is said that on several occasions, the Chief Rabbi Ovadia Yossef – spiritual authority of the Shass Party and the majority of Jews of Arab culture – sought out a rapprochement with the Labor Party and that his wife, Margalit, persuaded him to desist by repeating the gossip that she had heard in the market about the difficulty the Shass electorate would have in understanding an alliance with the left. Little by little, the relatively moderate positions of Yossef were replaced by an extremist and grossly racist discourse.

When, a few weeks after the signing of the Oslo accords, Uri and Rachel Avnery, Matti Peled, the Deputy Charlie Bitton, Haim Hanegbi and myself led a delegation to Rabbi Ovadia Yossef, to try to convince him to throw all his weight behind the struggle in support of the peace process, we were surprised and a little annoyed by his refusal to receive us. In fact, we were there fighting a rearguard battle that we had already lost: he could not allow himself, in the eyes of his public, to be photographed in the presence of a group known for their leftist, moreover secular, positions.

The politico-ideological shift that swept the Israeli religious world was accompanied by cultural and behavioral changes: gradually, the Orthodox, Ashkenazi and Sephardi shed their humble, peaceful, indeed resigned Diaspora traits, the ones that Herzl had described as effeminate, to become more Israeli – macho, rough, aggressive and arrogant. It was a great shock for someone like me, who had grown up in that milieu, to see youngsters in long, black coats and great hats actively taking part in racist assaults! Imagine my astonishment, one day on a street in the Mea Shearim, to see a revolver under the black coat of an Orthodox Jew. A believer with a pistol? I remembered my grandfather exclaiming, when I was walking the cocker spaniel of a neighbor: "A Jew with a dog?"

Wasn't this Ben Gurion's ultimate triumph? To have finally succeeded in eliminating the humiliated old Jew, including the Orthodox periphery, and replacing him with the self-confident Israeli, even though the latter refused to renounce his faith and his lifestyle for the modernist, secular and globalist project they had tried to force on him? Were we, after all, going to become like "all the other nations"? That is what the Hebrews had demanded of the prophet Samuel but he, disappointed by their wish, promised them that they would live to regret it. My friend Daniel Boyarin, great Talmudist, effeminate Jew, as he called himself, and proud of it,[7] enjoyed repeating: "Yes, they have really become like all the *goyim*," using the biblical term with a Yiddish accent that gave it all its scornful meaning, as if to say: "They have become real rednecks..."

Far from fighting this turn by the state towards religion, Labor-Zionism did everything to help it along, even outbidding the right: bigger budgets for religious institutions and parties, more legislative concessions, and above all, a great deal of theatrics. How can one forget Shimon Peres' fawning pilgrimages to Chief Rabbi Yossef, or the blessings sought by that Labor minister from the centenarian Cabbalist Kaddouri, a simple believer turned miraculous rabbi for purely – if one can use that term – electoral reasons, or the Minister Shlomo Ben Ami kissing the beard of Rabbi Abouhazera?

Yet all the efforts of the leaders of the left-wing Zionists to prove their loyalty to Jewish tradition – wearing a skullcap to every commemoration, recalling that their grandfather was a rabbi and that they liked him a lot, swearing that they didn't eat pork and did read the Bible every night before going to sleep – had absolutely no effect and were seen for precisely what they were: hypocritical and demagogic attempts to win back the support of the social strata and communities that had turned their backs on them. The more the left paid court to the Orthodox, their parties and their rabbis, the greater the contempt expressed by the Orthodox towards the left. The Orthodox milked the left for all they could get, only to go back to the right where they always felt more comfortable. The bidding war in pursuit of the rabbis was not only pathetic but counterproductive, for it strengthened the self-confidence of the religious organizations and their conviction that they were confronting adversaries without values, without a banner and without a future.

A few weeks before writing these lines, I accompanied Léa to Bnei Brak to visit some Orthodox cousins with whom she had renewed contact some thirty years after a break owing to her politico-professional activities. The conversation, which I did not want to take part in, echoed the dialogue of the deaf between the secular and the religious, but also mirrored the evolution of the discourse between these two during the last two decades. On the one hand, Léa's need to prove that she was no less Jewish than they were, that

7. In Anglo-American: a *sissy*. See Daniel Boyarin, *Unheroic Conduct: The Rise of Heterosexuality and the Invention of the Jewish Man*, Berkeley, University of California Press, 1997, prologue and pp. 33–80.

she had a sound knowledge of Jewish culture (with some thanks to me) and a genuine attachment to the tradition, at least in the cultural sphere; on the other, and in clear distinction to her almost apologetic words, an offensive discourse, self-confident, triumphalist and condescending, which I tried to transcribe during our return to Jerusalem, as follows:

> We are winning. Your plan has failed. To give the slightest consistency to the notion of a Jewish State, you have to draw on our religious heritage. Is it by accident that your children try to find meaning in their existence through religion and that there are so many born-again Jews? Your hedonism is empty of all meaning. Your children ask themselves why they should put up with the difficult and often dangerous life in Israel if it's only to live there like *goyim*. Those who don't emigrate, turn towards us. Even the most secular among you need us, not only for your petty political schemes, but also to give coherence to your policy. We are going to become the majority because those who won't join up with us would prefer to go live somewhere else. We, however, will never leave, because we know why we live here and what binds us to this country. You no longer frighten us; we pity you. Pity you because you are brothers, whom we love, lost sheep for whom we are responsible. You have been the tools of Divine will and with your arms you created a state for the Jews. Now it's up to us to give it a proper content.

As the title of Seffi Rachlevsky's book on the rise of Messianic fundamentalism in Israel expressed it so well, Zionism had been the "donkey of the Messiah," the secular and unconscious weapon of Divine will and the redemption of the Jewish people. In his conclusion, Rachlevsky describes what the religious feel today in Israel:

> The results of the elections of 1996 were seen as a sign of victory for religious Judaism. Its way was winning, and unwavering Messianism was reaffirmed. The advance towards the final redemption by the conquest of territory and the certain coming of the Messiah[8] has been complemented by a new advance: the return to the faith by the people of Israel. Everybody feels it: sinners are doing their penance. The time of the left that encourages sin and cuts off

8. Namely, Menachem Mendel Schneersohn, the last rabbi of the Lubavitcher, seen by his disciples as the Messiah.

> the *payes** is gone; the time for a real Jewish heart has come and that heart wants Judaism. The people voted and in spite of murder and incitement against the religious, in spite of the media, the people want Eretz-Israel, want nationalism and above all, want Judaism.[9]

The Orthodox were right on at least one count in their condescending arrogance towards the lost sheep: non-religious Zionism is pathetically incapable of offering a secular and democratic alternative project to the one defended by the religionists. There is not and never has been a truly secular current in Israel, armed with a social outlook in which religion does not play an essential role.

A few years ago, after a demonstration in which almost a quarter of a million religious Jews demanded the abolition of the Supreme Court and the establishment of a "truly Jewish State," the leading television channel interviewed the former Labor Minister Shimon Shetrit, then professor of constitutional law at the Hebrew University. To the question: "What alternative do you propose to the demand for a religious state wanted by the religious parties?" the minister responded after long reflection: "A traditionalist state." He was not able to say a "secular state", or a "democratic state," without questioning the very nature of the State of Israel. And so it is with most of the parties and politicians who think they are being secular by demanding less power for the religious parties, more tolerance for non-Orthodox religious currents, the right to elect women to the religious councils,[10] or to allow women to lead services at the Wailing Wall, but never the separation of religion and the state. These "secularists" find it quite unexceptional that the Knesset deliberates about what types of conversion are valid, evaluates which type of religious divorce conforms to Jewish law and which branch of religious Judaism has the right to represent tradition and to legislate in matters of religious rituals ... so, as democracy would have it, it is Arab MPs who get to resolve questions of strictly rabbinical concern.

What is called secularism in Israel is nothing more than contempt for the religious, a lack of respect for differences that sometimes

9. Seffi Rachlevsky, *The Messiah's Donkey*, Tel Aviv, Yediot Aharanot Publishers, 1998, p. 319.
10. The religious councils are state institutions, elected by municipal councillors to manage the business aspects of Jewish-only religious affairs.

culminates in the worst anti-Semitic stereotypes. During the electoral campaign of 1999, the TV spots of the Shinui Party*,[11] in which one saw an Orthodox Jew with a big nose picking the pocket of a valiant Israeli, would not have embarrassed the *Stürmer*. In spite of this party's far-right positions on the Israeli–Arab conflict, most of the Shinui voters came from the left.

In the choir where I sing once a week there are very few religious people. However, I suspect the great majority voted for the Shinui Party in the last elections. Yet, every year, these acknowledged anti-religionists insist that the traditional candles are lit to celebrate Hanukah* without omitting any of the ritual prayers. Religious people are detested by the left, and this feeling is so commonplace that it is expressed in everyday speech: for instance, when driving and seeing an Orthodox person, to cry out: *"Dross kol doss!"*, which means: "Run down every religious Jew!" Yet it is expected that every session of Parliament starts with a prayer, with the non-believers joining the religious. It would be considered shocking if a rabbi banned a well-known non-believer from reciting the blessings at a national commemoration.

The detestation of the religious is only one of the forms of intolerance and rejection of cultural pluralism that characterize Israeli society. Israeli pseudo-secularism denies the other respect for his specificity and expresses its rejection of differences. In 1986, my friend Ornan Yekouteli, deputy mayor of Jerusalem and an important leader in the campaigns against religious coercion, organized demonstrations against the banning of cars on the Sabbath from Bar Ilan street in Jerusalem. Convinced that being on the left necessarily implied that I shared his rejection of religion, he asked me to help him coordinate one of the demonstrations, which ran the risk of becoming rather violent. I replied: "Not only do I have no intention of demonstrating with you, but it may well be that you'll find me on the other side of the barricade, defending the right of the religious to live their Sabbath as they like, in the quarters where they are a clear majority." I added, ironically, that the State of Israel was expert in building by-pass roads in the occupied territories, intended to avoid the Arabs, and there was no technical problem in building a new route that would by-pass the religious quarters of north Jerusalem.

Once again, I find myself on the other side of the barricade – with men and women with whom I do not share any values, who live in

11. A party organized at the time of the campaign. Its program was limited to a denunciation of religion and the religious parties.

a world I left behind more than three decades ago, and against those who are at least formally committed to values that are my own, like secularism, respect for women and individual freedoms. I am not being argumentative or provocative.

I deeply believe that respect for the other, as long as he is not doing harm to others, is a fundamental value, and that to be lacking in that respect or to make exceptions is to run the constant risk of indulging in a cultural imperialism. Lest one get the wrong impression: I reject the postmodern relativism in which everything is equally valid yet, without falling back on the illusions of our youth, I continue to believe in a certain idea of progress. The equality of the sexes, even though it is not much more than a pious wish, is preferable to the oppression of women. What we formally call democracy is better than the whims of dictators or priests. I consider it a duty to fight for these values, in my society and elsewhere.

But I dislike missionaries and their hypocrisy too much to agree with the crusades undertaken by those who want to impose the values of our civilization on others. This civilization of ours has too many crimes on its conscience to have the right to feel that its superiority is self-evident. Those who built their civilization on plunder and massacres, on the destruction of hundreds of cities and villages, on the expulsion of hundreds of thousands of people, those who turned institutional discrimination into a system of government, as well as all those who remained silent about the crimes of the present and those of the past, are in no position to preach progress to others, and much less to have the right to impose their way of life in the name of that very progress.

Indeed, we in Israel must fight for secularism – but that is an entirely different struggle from the one that is being fought now against the religious. It must be a struggle for the total separation of religion and state, a struggle for the separation of ethnicity and state. It is a struggle for a secular and democratic state, a state of all its citizens.

19
Beyond Judea and Israel

At the beginning of the 1980s, Meir Kahane and the Jewish Defense League led a campaign to create a new state, the State of Judea. According to this fascist rabbi and his followers, the State of Israel, despite its pretensions, was not really a Jewish State; there were too many Arabs with civil rights, and democratic principles barred the strict application of Jewish law, the Torah. Taking the plan for a Jewish State literally, and believing that Jewishness was defined purely in religious terms and not in national or cultural ones, they wanted to establish a theocracy. Huge posters were put up on the walls of Israeli cities, asking: "A Jewish State or a democratic State?" thus repeating an old Matzpen slogan, but the wrong way round.

Few people at the time took seriously this idea of the State of Judea. It disappeared from political discourse with the death of Kahane, assassinated in New York by an Arab after he had been elected to the Knesset. Yet fifteen years later, the idea of a partition between Judea and Israel reappeared, this time in the writings of a man of the left, Yoram Kaniouk. In an op-ed piece published by the daily *Haaretz,* a few days after a political provocation by the Netanyahu government led to the death of almost ninety Israelis and Palestinians, Kaniouk announced that he no longer wanted any part of this state. He wanted to distance himself from the government and all the extremists, settlers and other fundamentalists who supported it, and to create his own democratic and civilized state.

I could not find Kaniouk's text but here, essentially, is what he said: "Take Jerusalem and the hills of the West Bank, keep your settlements, build your nationalist theocracy and let us have Tel Aviv and the coastal strip to keep alive our dream of a secular, democratic and modern Israel, open to the world."

A few years later, following the publication of an article in a newspaper with a large circulation, in which a professor at Haifa University also called for rebuilding the Jewish State overseas, without the nauseating smells and noise of the Middle Easterners, dozens of people sent letters to the editor, expressing their wish to join in that adventure...

The fantasies of Kahane and of Kaniouk had two things in common: first, realization that Israel was profoundly divided by a veritable cultural war between radically different, indeed, contradictory blueprints for society; and second, the refusal even to contemplate coexistence based on pluralism and democratic confrontation. It's either you or us!

To a certain extent, Judea represents the antithesis of the original plan of the founding fathers of the Jewish State. For the latter, Zionism was a product of its time, and was to be the means by which the Jews – of Eastern Europe – could truly enter the modern age. Their models were Germany, France and Great Britain. Ostensibly turning its back on religion, Zionism adopted, for its nation-building plan, the norms, values and institutions of industrialized and democratic Europe, although its colonial aspect would often bring it into conflict with the latter.

For a long time, the idea of progress guided Zionist philosophy: by means of a voluntarism that was dismissed by the majority of Jewish thinkers and leaders at the beginning of the twentieth century, one had to bring the Jews out of the Middle Ages, where they were still trapped, and push them towards the benefits and achievements of modern Western civilization. The socialist, or rather cooperativist, dimension of this plan, which became dominant in the 1930s, was only another aspect of this desire to be progressive, under the influence, this time, of the socialist and especially the populist movements of the Czarist Empire.

However, because the Zionist platform could not or did not want to be secular, its revolution ran out of steam in less than two generations, allowing its antithesis to develop in the swamp of its contradictions. Judea was born of the opposition between a democratic and a Jewish State, between modernity and ethnicity, between the religion of progress and a legitimacy drawn from the past and from holy books. In fact, the social program that has been developed over the last generation within that part of society that is called "the other Israel" clearly harks back to the past: "Revive the glorious past" is the electoral slogan of the Shass Party, which succeeded in galvanizing hundreds of thousands of Jews of Arab culture.

In the media the Third Kingdom of Israel is talked about openly, and in 1998, in the presence of cabinet ministers – including the Secretary for Education – and numerous MPs, not all of them religious, several thousand people seriously debated the concrete problems of rebuilding the Temple in Jerusalem, including practical issues linked to the resumption, after two thousand years, of ritual sacrifices. The moderate wing of that movement for the rebuilding of the Temple left it to God to resolve the thorny issue of the mosques located on the site where the spiritual and political center of Judaism should be rebuilt, the radicals defending a more aggressively voluntarist approach...

The religious world, which increasingly sets the tone for this part of Israeli society, went through a hardening process that saw different branches of Judaism absorbing the most fundamentalist aspects of their rivals: Sephardic Judaism (of the Arab and Mediterranean world), traditionally moderate and tolerant, adopted the intransigent fundamentalism of the Judaism originally from Lithuania, and Western Judaism, generally more resistant to mysticism and superstition, acquired a taste for amulets and rabbinical miracle-makers.[1]

This dual development has been the subject of a correspondence I have had for several years with Abraham Serfaty, who insisted in describing the Shass Party as a moderating element, based on the moderate and tolerant tradition of Sephardic Judaism, while failing to see that during the course of the last two decades its spiritual leaders had, for the most part, succumbed to the dominant power of the fanaticism of the Talmudic schools of Lithuanian origin.[2]

Whether they be Western or Eastern, the two currents of religious Judaism now integrate their theological concepts into a political plan, or rather a religious vision that requires a political practice. That is why one can speak of fundamentalism, that is, of a Judaism with political aims, or political Judaism. To rebuild a Jewish Empire that would be ruled by the precepts of the Torah and led by the doctors of the law requires a double crusade: one against the modern state and its democratic structures, and one against the Arabs in order to guarantee its ethnic homogeneity.

Under the influence of the rabbis, state institutions over the last two decades have lost much of their legitimacy. To the great demonstrations against the judicial system one has to add the discrediting of legislative power, although the religious parties do not hesitate to use it to strengthen religious legislation.[3]

It was in this context that Yitzhak Rabin was assassinated on 4 November 1995. For more than two years, the rabbis of the extreme

1. Rachlevsky, *The Messiah's Donkey,* pp. 261–78.
2. Abraham Serfaty and Mikhaël Elbaz, *L'Insoumis. Juifs marocains et rebelles,* Paris, Desclée de Brouwer, 2001.
3. Hayerushalmi, *The Domineering Yarmulke,* pp. 170–8.

right had undermined the Prime Minister's legitimacy, arguing that certain political decisions made by his government defied Divine will, therefore making him a traitor. Giving hardly any credit to the fact that Rabin and his government had been elected by the majority of the people, and at times resorting to the argument that only a minority of the *Jewish* electorate had voted for Rabin, the right and a large section of public opinion were gradually persuaded that he was a usurper, if not an agent of the enemy. Although one could see posters caricaturing Rabin as an SS officer, he really was being likened to Pétain, or rather to an amalgamation of the Marshal and of King Achab of the First Book of Kings, killed like a dog for having dared to defy the voice of God and His prophets.[4]

Yigal Amir murdered the Israeli Prime Minister because his teachers had convinced him that Divine will demanded the annihilation of a policy that challenged the future of the Kingdom of God on earth. To this day, for hundreds of thousands of Israelis, Yigal Amir is not an assassin but a hero who succeeded in putting an end to a political plan that threatened to become an obstacle to the coming of the Messiah, or at least, to the establishment of a Jewish State in the religious sense of the term. Even those who won't excuse his criminal act insist that, although Rabin did not deserve to die, he should have taken into account the public opinion hostile to his strategy. In failing to do so, he became responsible for a split in Israeli society.

Because this new Jewish Messianism also implies an ultranationalist policy against the Arabs and the rejection of any territorial concessions, a part of the non-religious right has chosen to include fundamentalist currents and some of its theological–political discourse in its own strategy, at the risk of destabilizing the state and clearing the way for a theocracy.

Yet an important segment of the secular right is not ready to take that risk. In 1998 it united with Labor to topple Netanyahu, who was seen as a sorcerer's apprentice for having forged a cultural as well as ideological political bloc with the most fundamentalist currents, thus seriously destabilizing the institutional organization of Israel in place for half a century. But that reaction on the part of the old politico-economic elites of the traditional right only served to reinforce the perception of a split between the elites on the one hand,

4. *Ibid.* pp. 145–7; Shahak and Mezvinsky, *Jewish Fundamentalism in Israel*, pp. 113–49.

irrespective of their party loyalties, and, on the other, a relatively important segment of the people who felt more and more alienated from the State of Israel as it is. It also intensified a desire for a State of Judea, where the periphery, meaning the lower classes of Judeo-Arab origin, and the religious communities, could be at home in their own country, building what they perceived to be the real objective of Zionism. Judea means both a ghetto and a bunker, sealed up against the outside world and armed to the teeth, the third Jewish Kingdom but the third Temple as well, a true theocracy governed by the precepts of the Torah, not very different in principle from the Iran of the Ayatollahs or the Afghanistan of the Taliban.

Exaggeration? Dramatization of a phenomenon that, when all is said and done, is still marginal? Unfortunately not. In the early 1980s, when he called for the establishment of the State of Judea, Rabbi Meir Kahane seemed like a lone madman, but twenty years later almost one-third of the members of the Knesset openly share that vision of Israel's future. That is more than 40 percent of Jewish public opinion. For those who fear the prospect of a theocratic state, militarized to the extreme, and ready to unleash the apocalyptic war of Gog and Magog in order to rebuild the Temple and establish the Kingdom of God on earth, it is something to think about. To think about and to act on.

Unfortunately, those who are frightened by this prospect, and who would prefer a more secular, more democratic Israel, which is more modern and more open to the world, are doing nothing to halt the Messianic train. They content themselves mostly with bemoaning a paradise lost and fantasizing about a new Israel without its Levantines and its religions.

Faced with the Messianic faith that inspires the rightist bloc and propels its most extremist elements to act, the Zionist left has chosen the path of resignation. The clearest sign of this was the reaction of Léa Rabin the day after the victory of Benjamin Netanyahu, only a few months after her husband's murder: devastated and immeasurably saddened, she declared: "It's time to pack your bags and leave." Like the rest of her generation, which fought to found Israel, and also the one with the crimes of the Naqba on its conscience, Léa Rabin saw her dream blown to pieces and its legacy squandered by those with whom she had wanted to share the benefits of Zionism.

The assassination of Yitzhak Rabin was, as so often repeated, the murder of the father, and through him, the symbolic murder of an entire generation and its utopia, entangled in the contradictions between its emancipatory vision and its colonialist methods, between ethnic and democratic state, between secularism and the urgent needs of religious legitimacy. Secular and "sane" Zionism, as it likes to call itself, had arrived at an impasse. It is no coincidence that the phrase most commonly used by Israeli sociologists and media to describe the third generation is the "crisis of motivation."

In the months following the assassination of the Prime Minister, it was fashionable to organize meetings of youth (Jewish) of different origins and ideologies. National reconciliation, everybody agreed, was the order of the day. Although vehemently opposed to this perverse idea of national reconciliation, as an educator and a member of the parents' association of my daughter Talila's high school, I had the occasion to lead several of those meetings. Like my friends who went through the same experience, I came out profoundly demoralized. "Our" youngsters, whose parents considered themselves to be leftists, secular and pro-peace, or at least moderates, were incapable of responding to the questioning of the youth brought up in the extreme right religious schools. They were literally mute. "If you are not religious, why do you want a Jewish State? If you do not believe in the Divine Covenant, how can you justify what we are doing to the Arabs? Who gave you the right to live here? Why not live in Europe where life is easier and where one is more secure? What makes you consider yourself a Jew? Why give Hebron and Ramallah to the Palestinians and not Haifa and Jaffa? What is it about the settlements of the 1920s and 1930s that is more legitimate than those of recent years?" Almost all of these highly relevant questions were greeted with embarrassed silence.

After having for two generations successfully indoctrinated the young with an all-encompassing nationalism, liberal and secular Zionism found itself unable to get a second wind when Israel's situation seemed about to get back to normal. It became difficult, if not impossible, to give the new generation the politico-cultural benchmarks that would define identity and confer a sense of citizenship. Hence the attraction of the religious sects or the fascination with India and its ashrams for a segment of secular youth. Of course, at the turn of the millennium, this phenomenon was not particular to Israel. It is found, in different forms, in all the industrialized countries, but in New York, London or Amsterdam young people were not confronted with the real and present danger of a fundamentalist revolution and a war that threatened to destroy their society.

The crisis of motivation is most evident in the precipitous decline, among secular and liberal youth, of voluntary enlistment in the elite units and the officers' corps. Those who for two generations formed the backbone of the Israeli army, particularly the kibbutzniks, are becoming more and more of a minority, making room for religious youth educated in the Talmudic schools of the extreme right, who by 1998 already accounted for 25 percent of the junior officers. We are long past the time when my aunt Claire proudly showed me Elhanan Blumental, that rare bird: a paratrooper with a yarmulke, the pride of our synagogue. Although, in spite of her statement, Léa Rabin did not leave Israel, some of the urban, secular and liberal youth are going, or at least considering departure. In a world where borders are becoming increasingly open to the well-off and the educated of the Northern countries, why should they live in Israel, when other countries offer, or seem to offer, more attractive possibilities, without the problems of security and without, apparently, a fundamentalist threat?

On the other hand, those who are trying to preserve a certain kind of Israel are caught up in apparently insurmountable contradictions. They refuse to retreat into a new Jewish ghetto and want to be open to the world, but they dread an opening to the Arab world around them and would prefer to seal it off with a sort of iron curtain. They want peace, of course, but they are incapable of getting rid of their colonial mentality, so they regard the Orient in which they live and with which they must come to terms with a mixture of fear and arrogance. They have chosen modernity, secularism and worldliness, but they remain passionately attached to a traditionalist and religious discourse without which the very idea of a Jewish State loses all meaning. Finally, and above all, the clan mentality and its consequences – the consensus and national unity – are deeply ingrained in them.

A return to the mythical years of young Israel still stirs their dreams, even though they know it is a paradise forever lost. Therefore, confronted with the advocates of a new Judea, they capitulate and lament, trying to minimize the risks of fundamentalism by cozying up to it, knowing full well that, little by little, they are digging their own grave.

Between on the one hand an Israel whose paradigm remained the Zionist epic from the 1920s to the 1970s, and the dream of reconstituting national unity around a colonialism with a human face, and on the other the headlong flight towards an archaic, Messianic, nationalist and fundamentalist Judaism, there is nevertheless, a third way, capable of leading to a normalization of Israeli society and peaceful coexistence with the Arab world. As often happens nowadays, it first took hold in intellectual circles and among the young.

I have already mentioned the New Historians who took up the task of re-examining the entire history of Israel and of relocating the Israeli–Arab conflict in its historical reality. As Dominique Vidal showed so well,[5] their importance as a social phenomenon and not merely as an ivory tower abstraction cannot be ignored. From a minority challenge to official historiography, the New Historians have become, in under twenty years, the dominant trend at Israeli universities, and their research into Jewish history as well as the history of Israel and Palestine appears finally to have unmasked the apologetic legends, disguised as science, of the Zionist ideologues. It is also a social phenomenon, because the work of these New Historians allows Israeli society to ponder its existence, its origins and its current manifestations with tools more likely to provide rational explanations of political phenomena. Thus they have succeeded in gradually marginalizing the discourse that explained the Israeli–Arab conflict as a product of the atavistic hatred by the Arabs for the Jews, and have substituted an explanation based on resistance to a colonial enterprise. Even the political class has had to take their work into consideration, and in the course of negotiations on the question of refugees their work has provided common reference points for Palestinians and Israelis.

Not quite as well known as their historian counterparts, the New Sociologists[6] have produced, during the last decade, a serious body of critical work on Israeli social development, particularly on the relations between its ethnic groups, the issue of citizenship and the problem of democracy in a state that is supposed to be institutionally Jewish. Although analyses defining Israel as a colonial state, or as the product of a colonial process, are still not commonplace, the challenge to the concept of a "Jewish and democratic State" has become widely accepted. Here too the importance of scientific criticism has extended

5. Dominique Vidal, *Le Péché originel d'Israël. L'expulsion des palestiniens revisitée par les nouveaux historiens israéliens*, Paris, Éditions de l'Atelier, 1998.
6. To name but a few: Henriette Dahan, Lev Grinberg, Baruch Kimmerling, Yoav Peled, Uri Ram, Yehuda Shenhav, Sami Samoha, Ella Shohat and Shlomo Swirsky.

well beyond the university centers to influence the political domain by setting out the broad lines of a challenge to the regime and its institutions.

In this way, the post-Zionists, as they like to call themselves, have broken simultaneously with Ben Gurion's Israel and with its Labor successors on the left and the right, regarding both its colonial relation with the Palestinians and the sociocultural relations of domination (it should be noted that the socioeconomic realm is not a central concern of the new Israeli intellectuals) as well as the Judaic perspective of its fundamentalist, Messianic and nationalist views. In their critique, these intellectuals reject the Jewish State as a concept as well as a social project.

The New Historians and New Sociologists acknowledge, for the most part, that they are only confirming, with the new tools of scientific research and a more sophisticated and less moralizing language, the positions defended by Matzpen thirty years earlier, whether on the history of Zionism or the analysis of the Jewish State and Israeli society.[7] It is a belated acknowledgement, but no less significant, of a political analysis that simply refused to be trapped in the premises of hegemonic thinking, and above all, bestowed a legitimacy on the discourse of the Other, his testimony as well as his rights.

This generation of critical intellectuals, who can also be found in the media and the arts, rejects in different ways, and with varying degrees of intensity, the premises of Zionism and its fundamental objectives. Nonetheless, most of them prefer the term post-Zionist to that of anti-Zionist, because the only subject that remains taboo in their intellectual audacity is precisely Zionism as such. There are very few works devoted to a critical analysis of Zionism. The majority of these intellectuals prefer to make do with vague explanations about the fact that Zionism is an outdated ideology long overtaken by reality. In their eyes, Israel must and can become a normal state by putting an end to the occupation of the West Bank and the Gaza Strip, by accepting responsibility for its past and undertaking the reforms required for its democratization. Of course, the combination of these measures would mean the end of the Zionist regime, but the lack of any serious and critical thinking about this possibility makes it difficult to evaluate the huge obstacles on a path of radical democratization,

7. See the introduction to Uri Ram, *Israeli Society: Critical perspectives* (in Hebrew), Tel Aviv, Brerot Publishers, 1993.

and therefore to the development of effective strategies. Ending the Zionist regime requires political action, which for the most part holds no attraction for this generation of intellectuals, who are settled in university careers and afforded increasing recognition. The generalized disrepute of institutional politics and the realities of an activist's life, often thankless and rarely gratifying, lead some of the most critical members of the Israeli intelligentsia to abandon the political arena, if not Israel itself.

Nonetheless, there are Israelis actively engaged in trying to fashion a new democratic Israel, committed to universalism. They are young – the majority of them were not yet ten years old at the time of the first Intifada – and they became politically aware when the Oslo process was already a reality. Freed of all forms of nationalism, indeed often even of national identity, and truly secular, they know nothing of the ideological indoctrination or the other forms of political culture that branded previous generations. Their training comes through the Internet; their models are Greenpeace, José Bové and sub-commandante Marcos. Their benchmarks are the demonstrations against multinationals, ecological struggles and peace movements the world over. They discovered solidarity with the Palestinians through struggles against globalization and the values this engendered.

In Israel, as in many other corners of the globe, this generation – meaning a social phenomenon as opposed to merely fringe groups – is politicized through the rejection of a market-based society and its devastating effects on the lives of people and their environment. For these radicalized youth, a social and cultural critique precedes a political one. Some years ago I succeeded in persuading several dozen of them to participate in a demonstration against the construction of a bypass road in the Ramallah region, one of those highway loops designed to link the settlements with Israeli territory and divide Palestinian territory into dozens of Bantustans. Imagine our surprise when they unfurled their banners reading: "Bypass road no, train yes!"

For this new, militant generation, whose country is the world, the idea of a Jewish State is obsolete. They abhor racism in all its manifestations, reject the confines of Jewish identity or Israeli patriotism, and although the majority still perform military service, they do so without the chauvinism that motivated previous generations. For them, solidarity with the Palestinians is evidence of their engagement with a broader solidarity with all who suffer oppression, from the Albanians of Kosovo to Filipino children exploited by Nike, the Indians of Guatemala, the baby seals of the Antarctic...

In their wholesale rejection of market-based globalization, these young people face difficult choices and sometimes contradictory priorities. In 2001, José Bové participated in a Civilian Mission for the Protection of the Palestinians; in the course of a meeting with anti-globalization activists, in which he wanted to discuss solidarity work with the Palestinians, he was surprised by their interest in genetically engineered corn, and their detailed knowledge of the struggles against McDonald's, but also at their apparent scant interest in the Palestinian question. "Some of them had been to Seattle and to Prague and undoubtedly want to go to Genoa, but they had never demonstrated in front of an Israeli roadblock at the gates of Bethlehem..."

José Bové need not worry too much: Israeli reality will soon catch up with them. The ideals of solidarity that motivate this part of Israeli youth, and their profound rejection of all forms of tribalism, will quickly make them into the formative elements of a new peace movement, a movement that, in contrast to its predecessors, will not be motivated by the desire for separation, but by the ideals of justice, cooperation and coexistence.

20
Homecomings

Once again, I was detained in the regimental camp stationed in the Bethlehem region. The Palestinian village of El-Khader had been declared a "closed military zone" as soon as we showed up there.

I had had the same experience in 1993, a few months before the signing of the Oslo accords.

The settlers of Efrata seize one of the hills in El-Khader, and at four o'clock in the morning the residents of the village call us for help. They are ready to stop the bulldozers with their own bodies but they want some Israelis alongside. Although it is still dark, and we are still half asleep, the staff of the Alternative Information Center, joined by a half dozen or so activists from Bat Shalom*, arrive at this beautiful village south of Bethlehem and join up with several dozen villagers who are camping out next to an immense bulldozer. When the driver arrives, accompanied by soldiers and a group of settlers led by one of my former colleagues from Merkaz Harav, we lie down on the ground, in front of the bulldozer. The soldiers arrest us without much violence, but a television crew is already on the scene, and before being led off to the regimental barracks for questioning, we see several dozen activists arrive from Jerusalem, alerted by the TV news. The bulldozer stays put all day.

For the entire week, this little guerrilla war continued: blockage, dispersal, arrest, conditional release, return to the site, blockage, etc. Tired of arresting us every morning, the military zone commander banned some of us from entering the Bethlehem region, and picked us up as soon as we crossed the border between Jerusalem and the occupied territories. But it was too late: after a week of confrontations, "Peace Now!" joined the fight and got the Meretz ministers to intervene. Rabin decides: the settlement can continue to expand but this hill will be spared. Victory?

Then there was Oslo, and the hopes for a freeze on the settlements. Then came the assassination of Rabin and the return of the right: Netanyahu–Barak–Sharon. The settlers reoccupied the Hill of the Olive Tree, as it was called on the settlement maps, the army protected them and the bulldozers carved out a road almost as wide as the Haifa–Tel Aviv freeway, though the Palestinians respected every fine print detail of their commitment not to farm their own lands on this hill, coveted by the vultures of Efrata. We rediscovered our old reflexes, a bit dulled, admittedly, by seven years of the "peace process." Circumventing the roadblocks in order to cross the border, moving to the front line of the demonstration, but relying on the Palestinians to determine the forms or the limits of the action, negotiating with the young colonel who, for once, seemed impressed by the determination of the demonstrators, and then, when the negotiations failed, forcing our way through the roadblock. This time we were accompanied by José Bové of the *Confédération Paysanne*, Jean-Claude Amara of *Droits devant!,* Marcel Francis Kahn of the France–Palestine Association and about fifteen other French activists who had come to express solidarity with the Palestinian farmers, who were trying to clear our way to the occupied hill. There were scuffles, arrests and brief detentions in the regimental barracks. Nothing had changed: the offices were as dirty as they had been eight years before, the buildings even more run down; if the soldiers seemed younger, I was the one who had aged a few years. The only apparent change was the skullcap sitting on the heads of most of the officers...

Is history doomed to repeat itself forever? Police custody is a good place for reflecting. I have experienced it numerous times, and the courtyard, where we were waiting for the authorities to decide our fate (a few hours later we were released unconditionally, but I knew I would later be charged with resisting arrest), brings back many memories. Despite José and Jean-Claude's jokes, I found myself thinking about history. It is not a smooth road towards the good; there are always bumps. We learned that at the end of the 1970s, when the revolution turned out to be a long way off, with the last remaining achievements of the October Revolution crumbling under the offensive by McDonald's and Coca-Cola, and Walter Benjamin had become one of our new classics. But what does it mean for our conflict, here, in Israel–Palestine?

Over twelve years ago, when the idea of this book was conceived, the first Intifada was coming to an end, Israeli society seemed to be moving towards normalization, and the Israeli–Palestinian conflict had come up with a solution that satisfied both parties. After a generation spent wandering in the desert, cracks had appeared in the Zionist consensus, and the airtight wall that separated the discourse and hopes of both peoples seemed to be cracking. The viewpoints of that small minority, marginal in both societies, that had bet on a coexistence based on rights, mutual respect and justice, found resonance in increasingly larger sectors of our respective societies. I thought, naïvely, I admit, that after *The desert* and *Cracks*, the third part of this book would be called *New horizons* and would describe the imminent fall of that wall that divides the inhabitants of Israel into two enemy camps. The vision, of a future based on coexistence, solidarity and cooperation, a noble utopia, which had motivated our struggle during the course of the last three decades, seemed to be taking real shape as a project that could capture the imaginations and energies of tens of thousands of men and women, Israelis and Palestinians.

The continuation of the settlement program, the intensification of nationalist–Messianic ideologies, the persistence of colonial mentalities, seemed to me to be the last gasps of a reality that not only had no future, but one that the Israeli people no longer wanted, or in any case no longer wanted to pay the price for. All the more so because, on the other side of the border, the Palestinian people had extended their hand and proposed a compromise whose generosity was astonishing. Mistake. Big mistake. History is not an unwavering march towards good, guided by reason that clears the way along the rocky path of malevolence, prejudice, errors in judgment or fundamentalism. At best it opens up opportunities, which one does or does not grasp, and which, depending on the choices made at those momentary crossroads, either leads to more progress or to more barbarism.[1]

Oslo was undoubtedly one of those moments, and for reasons described in the previous chapters, Israel's choice was, after a period of hesitation of less than two years, to continue the policy of settlements. With the assassination of Yitzhak Rabin and the destruction of any hope for peace in the Middle East, a new period of generalized reaction opened up. The election of Ariel Sharon in 2001 illustrates the political choice of a society incapable of breaking with its colonial history, its illegal practices and its expansionist dynamic.

> Last week we saw many photos of dead children; children who had gone out to have a good time, unconscious of the problems surrounding their existence in this country. Another child took his own life along with one of theirs, as if to say, with Samson: "Let me die with the Philistines." But neither one nor the other were Philistines. The Philistines are those

1. See Daniel Bensaïd, *Walter Benjamin, sentinelle messianique*, Paris, Plon, 1990, pp. 220–5.

> who still, after forty years, send their children to their death. Children in and out of uniform armed with rifles or Molotov cocktails, children of Israeli commandos or Palestinian guerrillas. All to satisfy the murderous ambitions of the Philistines and their insatiable greed for a land that doesn't belong to them. The Philistines are those who leave mothers like me with our sorrow, from useless wars that our children are forced to fight. War conducted supposedly for the love of country, the love of God or the love of the nation. But the truth is that these wars are made only because of the madness and megalomania of the heads of state. For them, children are an abstract notion; you kill mine and I'll kill three hundred of yours and we're even.[2]

That's how Nurit Peled-Elhanan, daughter of my comrade, General Matti Peled and mother of Smadar – killed in 1997 in an attack in Jerusalem's pedestrian walkway – described the situation in Israel during a demonstration in Jerusalem by the Women in Black on 8 June 2001. Several weeks later, the writer David Grossman, in a poignant interview on Israeli television, asked: "Who are we becoming?" The Israeli army had just deported several cave-dwelling Bedouin families, blocked up their grottoes, and filled up their wells with sand and rocks, all in order to create a contiguous Jewish presence between the settlements in the south of the West Bank and Israeli territory.

All this is taking place as if the hard-won achievements of the last twenty-five years had been erased in several months. It is not merely a retreat to the years of the consensual desert and the denial of the Other, but, worse, a new barbarism where the Other becomes the object of a conscious and planned crusade, whose aim is his disappearance as a nation, even his plain and simple expulsion to the other side of the Jordan. It is truly tragic that Ehud Barak was able to convince the majority of Israelis that the Palestinians do not want peace and that Ariel Sharon can persuade people to think, as they did during the era of Golda Meir and Yitzhak Shamir, that the Arabs are still determined to expel the Jews for good, one day. We are, once again, the victims, and even though in most cases we are doing the killing, we are within our rights, because we know that their intention, sooner or later, is to massacre us all.

As before, in the paranoiac discourse of Golda Meir, the enemy is everywhere. Arab citizens are a fifth column and every protest is labeled terrorism. This is why 13 people were killed in the bloody

2. Quoted on the website of Bat Shalom, July 2001.

repression of the October 2000 demonstrations; why there are new laws designed to exclude certain Arab parties from the democratic process and to limit the rights of the Arab MPs; why there has been a renewal of the policy of expropriation in Israel proper; why funds already allocated have been suspended and projects undertaken by the Rabin government, intended to reduce the inequalities between Jewish and Arab citizens, have been canceled. Does anyone think they'll be able to stop there? The state of virtual war will demand the broadening of repressive measures against Jews who refuse to rejoin the national unity and persist in believing that a peace based on real self-determination and justice is not only possible but necessary to guarantee the security of the Israeli people.

The militarization of Israeli discourse at the dawn of the third millennium, the policy of total repression in the occupied territories and the systematic sabotage of every possibility for peace goes hand in hand with a challenge to the whole process of liberalization that Israel has experienced during the last two decades. But worst of all was the effort to put an end to political and ideological pluralism and to paper over the cracks in the national consensus. A spokesman for the right called it a "healing of the wounds."

If the present trends are not quickly reversed, Israel will once again become the society of national consensus that it was during the first two decades of its existence, with the addition of the strong influence of the fundamentalist parties and all that follows in terms of public freedoms and individual rights.

After the hopes of Oslo came disillusionment and then hatred. That hatred, which had been miraculously contained for more than three decades, is now present, heavy and oppressive. The Israelis had chosen separation, not peace; the Palestinians had chosen compromise, not humiliation. Yet this engendered hatred. We have stepped away from a conflict against the occupation, from a struggle between colonization and national emancipation, to find ourselves confronted with what increasingly seemed like an inter-ethnic war, Palestinians against Israelis, Jews against Arabs.

The cross-border bridges, so carefully built during the 1980s, have collapsed. Virtually nobody is crossing them any more. Everybody is in his or her own place. The dream of Ehud Barak and Yossef Sarid had come true: they stay in their place, and we stay in ours; and make sure you don't get caught, whether by choice or by mistake, on the other side of the border.

Once again I slip through the cloister of a Lutheran church in order to bypass the roadblocks that encircle the Bethlehem area. I need to get to a meeting of the board of directors of the AIC, or rather to a meeting with only some of the members of that body, because for those of them who live in Ramallah or Nablus, Bethlehem has suddenly become thousands of kilometers away, past some fifteen roadblocks, beyond real space. Ahmad is supposed to pick us up at the other side of the school, in the formerly autonomous Palestinian zone. Happily, there are schools and monasteries that straddle the new border imposed by the Israeli occupation, which divide Palestinian territory into about twenty Bantustans, completely cut off from one another. When the closure becomes a real state of siege, even the priests, Lutheran, Orthodox or Catholic, become smugglers; for laborers trying to earn a little money, for the elderly who want to pray at el-Aqsa, for pregnant women who would like to give birth at the hospital, and, from time to time, for Jews or Arabs who refuse to accept the dynamic of inter-ethnic conflict and do not want to renounce the joy of working together.

Once again we had to row upstream, once again out of step. The stakes are painfully simple, as Dr Majed Nassar, director of the clinic of Beit-Shahour and co-president of the AIC, explained to me:

> Now our only objective must be to prevent the transformation of a national and anti-colonial conflict into an ethnic war. If we fail in that job, it will be terrible. Not only in terms of violence, of destruction of innocent victims, but above all for the future of our respective societies. Ethnic wars lead to ethnic societies, closed in on themselves, repressive, sterile and degenerate. There is never a winner in an ethnic war. We are the last handful who reject the ethnicization of the conflict and continue a transnational cooperation. Our only objective is to keep this little crack in the border, that we represent, open, and allow messages of solidarity and cooperation to flow through it.

Terribly simple, because any other solution is simply terrible: a new war of religions between a Jewish State with fewer than ten million inhabitants and a Muslim world with more than a billion people. Ever since the Israeli Prime Minister dared to suggest Jewish sovereignty over nothing less than part of the esplanade of mosques of Jerusalem, I know that this apocalyptic vision of the future is within the realms of possibility. Since the summer of 2000, the words spoken by my mother, to a delegation of the CCFD* visiting Jerusalem, have haunted me: "On two occasions this land vomited us out because we were not morally worthy of it; our intransigence and our contempt for the other risk us being vomited out yet a third time." But for her, practicing Jew that she is, what counts is the perpetuity of the Jewish people, in the Holy Land or in the Diaspora, whereas for me it is the men and women of Israel that I worry about, the friends of Nissan and Talila, my neighbors, the children of survivors of the Nazi Judeocide – don't they deserve better than the Generals Ehud Barak, Ariel Sharon, Fouad Ben Eliezer, Efraim Sneh or Shaul Mofaz? Moreover, doesn't the increasingly total and unconditional identification with Israel by the self-appointed spokespersons for the Jews of the Diaspora risk involving Diaspora Judaism in the catastrophe towards which our leaders are heading? Leaders whose shortsightedness is matched only by their total lack of historical reference? Their philosophy, in sum, is "now," which ignores with pathetic smugness both yesterday and the day after. Their policy is motivated neither by the suffering of their parents, nor by the promise of a radiant future, but simply by a will for power that knows no limits and won't stop until it crashes head-first into the wall of hatred created or supported by decades of arrogance.

"Why don't you leave before it's too late?" some friends, who over the years have chosen a new exile, have asked me, more and more frequently. Léa wonders about the destiny of those German Jews who knew they had to leave in time and the others who waited too long and didn't survive. "How does one know that it's time to go?" she wonders. To those who question me I answer, perhaps too readily, that I am not a deserter, that I have responsibilities to the community I live in and to the values for which I have fought. I do not think I am one of those who would jump ship before the drunken captain destroys his vessel on a reef. But this response is clearly insufficient and therefore wrong, I know. Even if that's my choice, what about Talila? Do I have the right to leave her in a country that seems to be rushing towards catastrophe, and why, as long as it remains possible, do I do nothing that would enable her to choose to settle down elsewhere? Why not join up in Paris with my older son Dror, who never stops repeating that nothing good can come out of a society so saturated with religion? Or with our friends Léa and Yakov, who, after he was called up for the 1973 war, told us that they did not want their children growing up in a country condemned to another Masada, and have since lived the good American life in Queens?

If I don't feel obliged to do everything I can to convince my close relatives to leave Israel it's because part of me refuses to believe that the catastrophe is inevitable or even highly probable, and because I have chosen to bet on common sense. I don't think it's an act of sheer faith, but a reasonable bet.

During the 1960s and 1970s I wandered through the desert of national consensus and National Unity while clearly placing my bet on class interest. It was a bet that was partially won: the consensus was indeed broken after the war of 1973 and National Unity imploded during the war in Lebanon. Of course, it was not "clear class interest" but a survival reflex nurtured by a hefty dose of popular common sense. For me, common sense has both a first and last name: Yakov Marciano. Yakov Marciano is a postman and an active militant of the Likud Party in Jerusalem. He is also a soldier in my reserve battalion. When I announced in 1983 that I had decided to refuse to go with my battalion to Lebanon, Marciano was one of those who used strong language to denounce traitors to the country. Several months later, when I refused to go a second time, Marciano said that he was willing to execute deserters like me, who were responsible for the difficulties our army was encountering in Lebanon. After refusing a third time, I was brought before the commanding general of our brigade, who, seeing the growing number of refuseniks, had decided to try the insubordinates himself. Imagine my surprise when I encountered, among the eight soldiers waiting to be judged, my friend, Yakov Marciano, Likud militant and sworn enemy of *Yesh Gvul*.

> "Welcome, Marciano, to the refuseniks. I knew that deep down you were one of us..."
>
> "No way. My decision not to go has nothing to do with ideology. It's because I don't want to die or get hurt in this sh...y war. So I just simply decided not to go...the military police came to get me at my house, and if I have a choice between the battalion in Lebanon or military prison, this time it's military prison."
>
> "Marciano, come, let me give you a hug. You are the true refusenik and it's thanks to people like you that we are going to win the battle."

The Lebanese–Palestinian resistance, combined with the common sense of thousands of Marcianos, put an end to the war in Lebanon before the price became intolerable. The young Palestinians of Rafah and Nablus, with their rudimentary slingshots, but also with the growing support of thousands of reservists who did not want to be killed or wounded for the settlers of Ofra and Tapouah, succeeded in winning recognition for the PLO and the beginning of negotiations. The Hezbollah guerrillas, combined with the determination of the "Four Mothers,"[3] forced the withdrawal from South Lebanon in 2000.

Betting on common sense is a reasonable gamble. It has paid off. It's betting on Yakov Marciano and Mr Shemesh, my neighbor, who dreams of being able to return to Baghdad and revisit the landscapes of his childhood; on Maya, my other neighbor, a 17-year-old, who wants to serve her country but refuses to wear a uniform that she's ashamed of, and decides to help young people of Ethiopian origin in some lost town in the Negev; on Yehudith Harel, a very popular leader of "Peace Now!" who, during the first Intifada, knew how to take risks that one must still be discreet about – Yehudith had just stormed out of a movement that she had helped found and develop, denouncing the moral betrayal of her former friends who had refused to condemn the assassination by the Israeli army of Dr Thabet Thabet, pioneer of Israeli–Palestinian cooperation. It's betting on Nurit Peled and Izzat Ghazawi, who both lost their nearest and dearest and still struggle for a peace based on equality and justice; on the youth of *Indymedia Israel* and *Indymedia Palestine*, who cross the barriers to exchange experiences and work together for a world that will be more than just a commodity; on Majed Nassar and all the other Palestinian comrades, who are prepared to be human shields when faced by the spread of a devastating fundamentalism; it's betting on the unshakeable faith of my friend Leila Shahid in a true Israeli–Palestinian reconciliation and her uncompromising struggle against the rabble-rousers of communitarian hatred, Jew or Arab, who, from the warm comfort of their Parisian digs, stoke the fires of a conflict that could set the Middle East ablaze in nuclear horror.

The cry of common sense is also the cry of Nurit Peled-Elhanan, when she calls on Israeli mothers to do what they can to halt the mad race to the abyss:

> Today, when there is practically no opposition to the atrocities of the Israeli government, when the peace camp has evaporated into

3. The organization of mothers of soldiers that demanded the withdrawal of the Israeli army from South Lebanon.

> thin air, a cry must be raised, a cry as old as the men and women who have transcended the differences of race, religion or language, the maternal cry: save our children![4]

At the end of his book, Seffi Rachlevsky cites a Talmudic saying: "Man must account for everything his eyes have seen that he has not eaten." And the author of *The Messiah's Donkey* comments:

> The donkey will one day regain its strength by stuffing itself with the grass underfoot, for the Israeli donkey, particularly, has a remarkable appetite. If only he would open his eyes, the donkey, free again, could gallop, gallop, gallop.[5]

4. Website of Bat Shalom.
5. Rachlevsky, *The Messiah's Donkey*, p. 351.

21
Border identities

Although I have chosen to be on the border that separates Jews and Arabs, Israelis and Palestinians, it is unthinkable to adopt the same position on the internal borders of Israeli society – those that separate Israel and Judea, or those that divide the old Israel of the Zionist pioneers, the one that the Western or Westernized middle classes keep dreaming about, from the nationalist–Messianic and fundamentalist plans of those who were excluded in the past and remain excluded now. The future of Jewish existence in the Arab Middle East requires a third way, opposed to fundamentalist, militarist expansionism, but also opposed to a soft, comfortable colonialism that would continue to wage war on the Arab world.

Yet to find this third way, one has to start by espousing resistance. As Daniel Bensaïd says:

> To resist is first of all, quite simply, not to give up, even if the situation is in jeopardy, even if one is in a really tight spot, even if one has been cornered in a temporarily weak or powerless position. To resist means recognizing your weakness, acknowledging an unfavorable balance of power, but without ever acquiescing to it, without bowing to it, accepting it, agreeing with or resigning oneself to it... One can always be beaten, but it's important never to admit defeat, never acknowledge to the victor his victory, never transform the defeat into an oracle of fate or into a shameful capitulation...[1]

To resist by all means any attempts to close up the cracks in the wall that were opened in the last decades and to keep them open, no matter what the cost, in order to prevent the rebuilding of a tribal consensus in which all critical thought is snuffed out and no challenge is tolerated. Like the Mothers of the Plaza de Mayo in Argentina, the Women in Black, despite the insults, the blows and the spitting, demonstrate through their persistent presence every Friday

1. Daniel Bensaïd, *Résistance, essai de taupologie générale,* Paris, Fayard, 2001, pp. 39–40.

in the squares of Israeli cities a rejection of any compromise with the occupation. Just like, some years ago, the French draftees called up for military service and the South African democrats, the Israeli refuseniks, conscripts or reservists, refuse to collaborate with war crimes and with systematic violations of international conventions in the occupied territories; they resist the seductive temptations of tribal camaraderie and the brotherhood of arms. The rabbis who defy Caesar's law and rebuild demolished houses in the name of Jewish ethics are also refuseniks, for they are ready to be outlawed and singled out for scorn in their communities. So too are those intellectuals, artists and journalists who are not afraid to go against the current of the new consensus and who refuse to be the ideologues and spokespersons for old and new myths. Daniel Bensaïd says:

> Essentially and fundamentally untimely, [the resistance] neither thinks like or behaves like its time, in harmony with the spirit of its time, at peace with the present, but out of step and off beat. Being untimely is to take your time going against the grain, rubbing everybody and the entire era the wrong way.[2]

Charting a third way requires a sapper's careful work in undermining the walls that seal the Israeli community within a heavily armed bunker. This bunker gives an illusion of security, while it is actually one of the causes of the growing hostility of the surrounding Arab world, and risks compromising the very existence of the Jewish community in the Middle East forever.

Israel's only future lies in the acceptance of its Middle Eastern reality and its integration into the surrounding Arab world. A voluntary integration requires above all an opening to the other as an equal and partner in building a future where the security and well-being of the one is dependent on the security and well-being of the other. Since common sense dictates that peace is based on relations of reciprocity, equality and mutual respect, a real cultural revolution is needed to move from a state of domination to one of peace. It needs a revolution of attitudes and behavior, a radical reawakening of society and its political, intellectual and spiritual leadership.

Peace, in its fullest sense, and in the context of the Middle East, must repudiate the separatist philosophy at the core of Zionist

2. *Ibid.*

ideology and practice. Zionism springs from the premise that ethnic and cultural homogeneity is the only normal state of affairs, any kind of mixing being an offense against nature. The corollary of that premise is the obsessive rejection of diversity. The decision to settle in a place where, contrary to one of the founding myths, another people has its roots, leads to two and only two alternatives: first, exclusion and expulsion, which branded more than a century of Zionism and which, by definition, made conflict inevitable; and second, integration and inclusion, the way of peace and coexistence. The choice of peace and coexistence is in fact the only choice. In the end, without it, there will be no Jewish existence in the Arab world.

Full recognition of a Palestinian legitimacy in Palestine is clearly one of the minimal but indispensable conditions for the acceptance of Israel by the surrounding Arab world. But that legitimacy implies the illegitimacy of the entire process of pillage and expulsion, and a radical re-examination of self and of the origin of the Jewish national existence in Palestine. Opening up also entails an uncompromising rereading of historical facts, a work of memory. For there cannot be reconciliation without an acknowledgement by Israel, its leaders and its people, of the injustices committed by them and in their name against the Palestinian people. Nor without a plea for forgiveness. It is not merely a matter of a moral debt owed to the victims of more than a century of colonialism and plunder, but also of the need for the Israeli people to understand the roots of their own existence. Peace and reconciliation are incompatible with amnesia; on the contrary, they demand a truthful re-evaluation of one's own history and an honest self-examination. Only a sincere and encompassing plea for forgiveness for the crimes committed can create the conditions of real equality between those who perpetrated the crimes and their victims. It is the essential condition for enabling peace to become the starting point of a true reconciliation.

It is also essential for Israel to realize that it is in the heart of the Arab Orient and not in southern Europe. The presence of a large Arab–Jewish population makes this realization possible and tangible, especially in the light of cultural ties and memories, which, in spite of the state's attempt to eliminate them, have persisted. Likewise, the fact that a Palestinian community has continued to live in the very heart of Israeli society, acquiring some of its traits, while maintaining its adherence to the Arab nation, can help the future integration into the Arab world, by serving as a bridge across the border that separates Israelis and Arabs. Jews of Arab culture and Arabs of Israeli citizenship are border communities, and as such, can play an essential role in dissipating Israel's sense of alienation within its geopolitical and cultural environment.

Is it merely by chance that during these discouraging times, when demoralization looms, I like to spend a few days with my Syrian friends at Majdel Shams, in the occupied Golan Heights? I like the landscape of this volcanic and fertile plateau. I like walking in the verdant, narrow wadis, climbing to the snow-capped peaks of Jebel-el-Sheikh, which the Israelis call Mount Hermon. For me, the Golan Heights is indeed one of the most beautiful places in the world, but even more than its natural beauty, what attracts me to this isolated place in the far northern tip of the country is the men and women who live there. Survivors of a massive expulsion that created more than 130,000 refugees, the residents of four Druze villages in the north of the Golan are at once a community of refuseniks and a border community. The extraordinary determination of this tiny Syrian population of the Golan which, in 1982, started what was really the first Intifada, will, I hope, be the subject of a book I would like to write, not only to pay tribute to the courage and the political intelligence of these 20,000 or so people, but above all, because their experience, the only one of its kind, can serve both as an antidote to depression and as an example to others.[3]

But it is as a border community that I think of my Syrian brothers of the Golan: as a geographic reality wedged between Israel, Syria and Lebanon, and even more, as a cultural reality. Being Syrians, therefore Arabs, to the core, in their patriotism as much as their cultural affinities, they have nonetheless learned how to live in Israel and with the Israelis. Too small to have developed its own society and completely cut off from the Syrian hinterland, the Golan Heights community had to open up to Israel, its economy, its universities and its media. The Hebrew that many of them speak is better than that of the Arab citizens of Israel, and often better than that of the average Israeli. Their knowledge of Israel and its population, its customs and its culture, of its political scene and the complexity of its society is surprising. They don't hesitate to use all the democratic openings available and the best of what Israel has to offer. It is no accident that the staff of the Alternative Information Center has always included

3. See Salman Fakhr-a-Din, *L'Action politique dans le Golan,* Jerusalem, Alternative Information Center, 1999.

one or two comrades from the Golan as translators, editors and, above all, as resources for information on the Arab world.

More so than with the Palestinians, including those who are Israeli citizens, I find that with these friends I have a common language and elements of a shared culture. Perhaps it is owing to the fact that as Syrians, and in spite of their physical isolation, they are less insular and provincial than the Palestinians. Many Israelis fell into the trap of believing that the "druzes"[4] of the Golan Heights had been pacified, in short, Israelized. It is not so. They are profoundly Arab and proudly Syrian, and have never stopped struggling to reintegrate the Golan into their Syrian homeland.

What makes them border people is the fact that they were impervious to the Israeli society that has surrounded them for more than thirty years. They thrived on it. I like to believe that my contact with them has rubbed off on me and I've picked up some of their culture and their way of looking at and living in the world. Be that as it may, I like to be at Majdel Shams or at Bouqatha because I can, for a weekend, feel as if I'm in the Arab world, and I can project, on the basis of the real brotherhood that I experience there, what our future could be like in this region. When the skies are clear, one can see in the distance Damascus, the capital of the Arab world, and I can include it in my imaginary space. My Syrian friends of the Golan, you are surrounded by minefields, by military camps and settlements, and yet you have been able to break through the borders between you, your country and your Syrian brothers, between you and us. I will never be able to express sufficient thanks for this concrete proof that our dream of opening up to each other and to transnationality is not as utopian as it might seem.

While this third way implies breaking through the borders that cut us off from our natural environment and separate human beings by race, nationality and religion, it also demands of us that we build other visible and solid borders within the national collective we inhabit, which would clearly define our system of values, good and evil, and our plan for society. Borders that would delineate "us" from "them" on the ruins of the consensual and tribal "we." Nobody has described this task better than Nurit Peled-Elhanan:

4. Israelis give the name Druzes to the Syrians of the Golan. This does describe their religious affiliation, but they refer to themselves as Syrians.

> When my little girl was killed, a journalist asked me how I could possibly accept condolences from the "other side." I replied without hesitation that I didn't. And when the representatives of the Netanyahu government came to offer their condolences, I left the room and refused to sit down with them. For me, the other side, the enemy, is not the Palestinian people. For me, the struggle is not between the Jews and the Arabs, but between those who want war and those who want peace. My people are those that want peace; my sisters are the mothers in mourning, Israelis and Palestinians, living in Gaza, in Israel and in the refugee camps. My brothers are the fathers who protect their children against the cruel occupation. Although we were born into different histories and languages, there's more that unites us than separates us...The right has abused the slogan "You don't let your brothers down," because those we must never abandon are our brothers and sisters who live in the refugee camps and under the occupation, deprived of food, livelihoods and all other rights...[5]

To resist, to break through the inter-ethnic borders, to break with the consensus and to favor instead a confrontation within the clan based on clear values that brook no compromise – those are the ingredients of an alternative vision for an Israel that seeks at any cost to turn its back on the Orient and impose a neocolonialism based on technological domination, a fundamentalist and chauvinist Judea. Therein lies the third way: democratic, secular and fraternal, open to the other and respectful of differences. It is more than the unveiling of a new ideology, of another policy, indeed another ethic. It is rather, and perhaps above all, a change of identity.

Israeli identity was forged in a process of colonialization and a dual destruction: of both the indigenous Arab population and of Jewish identity, or rather identities, prior to Zionism. It is thus, consciously and willfully, a counter-identity. Being an Israeli means more than sharing the same language and some common cultural references; it is also sharing some common privileges and participating, daily, in that dual destruction process. Being an Israeli means deliberately breaking all continuity with the history of one's grandparents, their culture and the values they embraced, reducing the links to the past to some mythic relationship to a more than 2,000-year history. Being an Israeli is somehow refusing to be either a Jew or an Arab.

5. Website of Bat Shalom.

Israeli identity is the result of consensual will and is perpetuated in unified political practice. In this sense, identity and policy are one and the same. Rejecting this policy, being a dissident, defying the consensus, is to question one's belonging to the collective. In the same way, to defy tribalism is to question Israeli identity itself. How so?

When Mordechai Vanunu, a technician at the nuclear center at Dimona, decided to expose the secrecy surrounding the Israeli nuclear weapons program, he wanted to distance himself from the totality of Israeli policy, to express his absolute dissent. So he decided to convert to Christianity because, for him, the only means of complete differentiation was a break with the tribe. The only way of leaving the clan without running the risk of being rescued by it at the last moment was to join another tribe. An identical decision was made by Haroun Sousan, the hero of *C'est un autre,* by the Iraqi Jewish writer Shimon Balas: "For Sousan," writes Inbal Perelson in an interesting analysis of the literature of Israeli writers of Iraqi origin, " the rejection of Zionism requires a rupture with Judaism, so he decides to embrace Islam. It is not a religious choice, but the expression of a radical break."[6]

Adopting Arab identity may be possible for Israelis whose identity and culture are, at least partially, Arab. But it can hardly be a choice for those whose grandparents are from Western or Eastern Europe. These Israelis can, however, make a similar choice by replacing their identity with an extreme Americanization of their culture and their identity, by becoming citizens of the global village in which McDonald's and Nike are the new totems and CNN/MTV the ideological prop. It is already the choice of a section of Israeli youth.

One hundred years after Zionism's first steps, the central issues of the debates that preoccupied the European Jewish secular world after the French Revolution continue to reverberate: namely, was there a Jewish identity beyond religion, and was assimilation – that is, the loss of a specific identity – the only response to the old-fashioned ways of the rabbis? Translated into present terms, the question that now confronts Israeli society can be formulated as follows: beyond the present alternatives – an Israeli identity forged by Zionism and intrinsically linked to that ideology, or assimilation of the Jewish

6. Inbal Perelson, "Majority and Minority – the utopian dimension," *Mitsad Sheini,* no. 3, May–June 1993, p. 32.

community of Israel by the dominant identity, Arab or globalized – is there not also a third way?

In 1994, when many of us thought that the Oslo accords would lead, if not to the end of the conflict, at least to a form of coexistence that could, in time, open the path to peace and coexistence, I was invited to participate in a round table discussion in Tel Aviv on the topic, "After Oslo, does the left still have a role to play?" I recently found the notes for my presentation:

> Now the left will be able to focus on its main battle, one far more ambitious and difficult than the fight for the rights of the Palestinians and for peace. For that battle is one that we will have to fight alone, without the support of our Palestinian friends. We are talking about fighting for a redefinition of who we are, the redefinition of an Israeli identity and culture in a context that is no longer one of conflict and war, but one of peace and coexistence. We have never previously had such an exciting task... what is an Israeli beyond the Zionist context, beyond a definition in the negative, meaning those who are in conflict with the Palestinians and the Arab world? What identity should we construct, for we want to build one that consciously and clearly replaces the "ugly Israeli," as we call him – arrogant, violent, racist, impolite, but also provincial beyond belief, terrified by everything unfamiliar, and finally, pathetic to the extreme. If I had to name that new culture, that identity to be built for our children, I would use the term a "border identity"...

The border person is one whose identity is forged in an exchange, a permanent interaction with his neighbors. It is an identity that is pluralistic, open and mixed. He lives on the border, but he doesn't like borders, which are for him an obstacle and a barrier to be crossed. "He revealed his Jewish identity," wrote George Steiner about Trotsky, "by his instinctive devotion to internationalism, by his personal and ideological contempt for borders."[7]

The newly reconstructed Israeli identity will be above all a Jewish and Diaspora identity. It must be rerooted in a history and a heritage that Zionism rejects, rediscovering cultural roots and character traits fashioned by two millennia of a complex relation with the surrounding world, often painful, but always charged with

7. George Steiner, *Langage et Silence,* Paris, 10–18, 1967, p. 263.

a sensibility without which culture – Western as well as Arab – would not be what it is. That particular existence imposed on the Diaspora Jew a way of being that is antithetical to what the founding fathers of Israel wanted to impose on the immigrants coming from the four corners of the globe. Steiner continues:

> The Jew drops anchor not in space, but in time, so that he is acutely conscious of real history as an individual experience. Six thousand years of introspection forge a homeland… The uprooting of the Jews, their "cosmopolitan" character, condemned by Hitler, Stalin, Mosley, Maurras and all the hooligans of the right, is no more than a condition imposed by history… But once assumed, this condition, although unpleasant in the extreme, opens up broader perspectives.[8]

For Ben Gurion and his successors, the "return" to the Holy Land, by definition, put an end to exile. But for Orthodox Judaism, by contrast, exile is not a matter of location; it endures even after the establishment of Jewish sovereignty in Israel. It is that Diaspora identity that Israel must reappropriate, tempering its nationalism with a strong dose of that cosmopolitanism so hated not only by the "hooligans of the right" but also by the ideologues of Zionism. It has to moderate its obsession regarding its own security with empathy for the suffering of others, replacing its withdrawal into itself with a systematic opening to the Other.

In the building of this new identity it is essential to restore the ties with whole chapters of Jewish history in the Diaspora: with the convivial spirit that characterized long periods of Jewish life in Morocco; with those revolutionaries of Yiddishland who did not recognize any borders, living "without work, without family and without a fatherland,"[9] but with an identity of their own that most of them would not have exchanged for a property title to an old manor hung with portraits of ancestors rooted in the history of that land.

It is by reappropriating that heritage that the Israeli of tomorrow can fashion that new border identity, where Warsaw and Casablanca,

8. *Ibid.*
9. The title of a book by Gérard de Verbizier [Paris, Calman-Lévy, 1993], about the FTP-MOI brigade of Toulouse. I am grateful to Gérard, a French internationalist of Protestant faith, for the interest he has stimulated in me since 1974 in the MOI, and subsequently in the revolutionaries of Yiddish culture.

Aleppo and Berlin cross-breed, an identity turned towards Damascus and Alexandria, open to the world and receptive to differences. The Zionist enterprise believed that the redemption of Jewish existence would not be possible except by breaking with our Jewish past and turning our back on our Arab environment. On the contrary, it is only by rediscovering its Jewish roots and opening itself up to the Arab dimension of its identity and its environment that Israeli society will be able at last to live normally and plan the future of its children with serenity.

"Ip'ha mistabra" – "You have to start all over again in the opposite direction" – it says in the Talmud.

"Ip'ha mistabra," will say the Talmudist of the twenty-first century.

Glossary

Aliya: literally "going up," "ascent." Refers to the immigration of Jews to Palestine and subsequently Israel

Ashkenazi: name given to Jews originating in Central or Eastern Europe

Bat Shalom: Israeli organization of women for peace, founded at the beginning of the 1990s

CCFD: French Catholic Relief Organization

Chanukah: the holiday that commemorates the "reinauguration" of the Temple after its defilement by the Greco-Syrians in the second century B.C.

DFLP: Democratic Front for the Liberation of Palestine

Fatah: principal movement of the Palestinian resistance

Fedayin: Palestinian guerrilla fighter

FLN: Algerian national liberation movement

FPLP, FDPLP, FP-CG: leftist organizations of the Palestinian resistance

Guirouch: in the Bible refers to repudiation of a spouse, meaning, by extension, banishment, expulsion

Gush Emunim (Bloc of the Faithful): movement of settlers founded in March 1974 by religionists. It fights aggressively for the extension of Israeli sovereignty up to the Jordan and expansion of settlements throughout the occupied territories

Hashomer Hatzair (Young Guard): Zionist socialist youth movement founded in Poland before World War I to train young people for kibbutz life

Hassidism: a mystical movement that developed in Poland around the beginning of the nineteenth century

Herut: right-wing political party founded in 1948 by Menachem Begin; has since become part of the Likud, the principal formation of the Israeli right

Hezbollah: Islamic resistance organization in Lebanon

Hiérosolomitain: resident of Jerusalem

Histadrut: General Confederation of Workers, founded in 1920 as the General Confederation of Hebrew Workers in Eretz Israel, with the goal of "developing a new type of Jewish worker, a product of colonization" (statutes adopted at the founding conference)

Kach: electoral acronym of the Jewish Defense League, an extreme right-wing organization led by Rabbi Meir Kahane; declared illegal because of its racist ideology

Kibbutz (plural: kibbutzim): village based on collectivism in production and consumption. A member of a kibbutz is called a kibbutznik

Knesset: the Israeli Parliament

Kosher: conforms to religious standards for use or consumption

Ladino: Judeo-Spanish dialect spoken by Jews of the Mediterranean basin

Likud: coalition of right-wing parties formed in 1973

Mapai: Party of the Workers of Eretz Israel founded in 1930 by David Ben Gurion. Zionist-socialist party, dominant in the Zionist movement and in the State of Israel until 1977. After a series of mergers with other Zionist-socialist parties in the 1970s, it renamed itself the Labor Party

Mapam: United Workers' Party, formed in 1948 by the unification of the Hashomer Hatzair, the Achdut Ha-Avodah Party and the left wing of the Poale Zion; left-Zionist

Matzpen: movement of the extreme left founded in 1962 by dissidents of the Israeli Communist Party; anti-Zionist

Mellah: since 1438, the Jewish quarter in Morocco

Meretz: party formed in 1984 by the merger of Mapam, the Civil Rights Movement (Ratz) and Shinui

MIR: Movement of the Revolutionary Left: Chilean far-left party

Mizrahi: founded in 1902, the Zionist Religious Party; became known in Israel as the National Religious Party

MOI (*Main d'Oeuvre Immigrée*): organization of immigrant workers, particularly Jews, within the French Communist Party

Moshav (plural: moshavim): village cooperative that combines individual farming with collective ownership of farm and equipment

Mufti: Muslim religious dignitary

Naqba: literally "catastrophe": term designating the expulsion of more than 750,000 Palestinians and the destruction of their towns and their villages in 1948

Palmach: acronym for "shock brigade," elite troops of the Haganah created in 1941; played a critical role in the war of 1948

Payes: side-curls worn by the ultra-Orthodox

Rakah: acronym of the New Communist List; name taken by the Israeli Communist Party after the split of 1965

Ratz: civil rights movement founded by Shulamit Aloni. Merged with Mapam and Shinui to create Meretz in 1984

Sephardic: Jews originating in the Mediterranean basin and the Arab world. Some prefer the term "Mizrahim" (Orientals) or Jewish-Arabs.

Shabbat: seventh day of the week, set aside for rest

Shaddaï: "All powerful": one of the attributes of God; often represented on lockets by the letters "SH"

Shas: Religious Party, founded in 1984. Represents the majority of Sephardic Jews. In 1999 elections, Shas won 17 seats, or 15% of the electorate

Shin Bet: Israel's domestic intelligence service

Shinui: Anti-Religious Party founded in 1999 by right-wing journalist Yossef Lapid. Attracted disenchanted members of the old Shinui who rejected its merging into Meretz in 1998

Shtetl: Yiddish word for a Jewish village or township in Eastern Europe

Talmud: oral law code

Torah: first five books of the Bible

Tsahal: Israeli army

Tsomet: secular party of the extreme right, founded in 1983 by former Chief of Staff Rafael Eitan. Dissolved after electoral rout in 1999

Yeshiva: literally "the place where one sits," a school of Talmudic studies

Important dates

1896	Theodore Herzl writes *The Jewish State*
1897, 29 August	First Zionist Congress at Basel
1906	Second Jewish immigration to Palestine
1916	Sykes–Picot accords on the division of the Middle East into French and British zones of influence
1917	The Balfour Declaration, which promises the establishment of a "Jewish homeland in Palestine"
1922	The beginning of the British Mandate in Palestine
1933	Hitler seizes power
1933–39	Massive immigration from Germany and Central Europe
1936–39	First Palestinian uprising and bloody repression by British authorities
1937	The Peel Commission's partition plan
1941–45	Genocide of European Jews
1943, April	Warsaw ghetto uprising
1947, 29 November	United Nations Resolution 181 on the partition of Palestine
1948, 14 May	Israel declares its independence. Israeli–Arab war and ethnic cleansing of the territories conquered by Israel (Naqba)
1949	Armistice accords between Israel and the Arab states
1952	Nasser and the Free Officers take power in Egypt
1956	Nationalization of the Suez Canal. Israeli–Franco–British war against Egypt. First occupation of the Sinai by Israel
1957	Retreat from the Sinai
1964	Foundation of the PLO by the Arab League
1965	First military operation by Fatah
1967	Israeli–Arab war and the occupation of the West Bank, the Gaza Strip, the Golan Heights and the Sinai
1970	Black September: the Palestinians are crushed by the Jordanian army
1969–71	War of attrition between Israel and Egypt over the Suez Canal
1970–73	Mass immigration from the Soviet Union. The Black Panther movement in Israel
1974	Treaty of "Separation of Forces": Israel gives up a small part of the occupied territories to Syria and Egypt
1976, 30 March	Day of the Land: general strike by the Palestinians of Israel against new land expropriations; the Israeli police kill six Palestinians
1977	Sadat's visit to Jerusalem. Camp David accords

1982	The end of the retreat from Sinai. Israeli invasion of Lebanon. Massacres at Sabra and Shatila. 30,000 Israelis demonstrate against the war in Lebanon
1985	Retreat from most of Lebanese territory
1987–91	Second Palestinian uprising (first Intifada)
1988	Palestine National Council in Algiers: acceptance of the principle of a "historic compromise" with Israel: a Palestinian state in the West Bank and Gaza and recognition of the State of Israel in the pre-1967 borders
1990	Beginning of the second great wave of immigration from the former USSR
1991	Madrid Conference between Israel, the Arab states and the Palestinians
1992	Washington negotiations between Israel and the Palestinians. No results. Beginning of the closure of the occupied territories
1993, 13 September	Signature of the Oslo Declaration of Principles in Washington
1994, 1 July	The Palestine Authority is installed in Gaza and Jericho
1996, 20 January	Election of the Palestine Council legislature and of Yasser Arafat as the President of the Palestine Authority
1994–99	Israeli–Palestinian negotiations and limited redeployments in the West Bank
2000	Final status negotiations at Camp David. Failure of negotiations
2000, 28 September	Beginning of the third Palestinian uprising (second Intifada)
2001, January	Israeli–Arab negotiations at Taba. Substantial agreements are defined but do not lead to a treaty
2001, February	Ariel Sharon is elected by a large majority as head of the Israeli government
2001, October	Ariel Sharon declares Yasser Arafat "off limits" and the Oslo process is buried

Index

Compiled by Sue Carlton